POLITICAL PARTIES AND ELECTIONS
IN AUSTRIA

POLITICAL PARTIES
AND ELECTIONS IN
AUSTRIA

BY
MELANIE A. SULLY

1981

C. HURST & COMPANY
LONDON

First published in the United Kingdom by
C. Hurst & Co. (Publishers) Ltd.,
38 King Street, Covent Garden, London WC2E 8JT

© 1981 by Melanie A. Sully

ISBN 0-905838-44-0

For Rog

Printed in Great Britain

CONTENTS

MAPS

FIGURES

TABLES

PREFACE

In Austria, behind the coffee-house façade and the cream cakes, there exists a political system. Very little has been written in English on Austrian politics, often regarded as exceptionally predictable, rather quaint and a little intriguing. While similar in many ways to its West German counterpart, political life in Austria exhibits some unique features shaped by the country's historical position in Central Europe. In 1918 Austrians found it difficult to accept the transformation of their country from the heartland of a mighty empire to a small and apparently insignificant republic. Austria's experience in the years before 1945 were shared by many states in Europe attempting to follow the rules of a liberal democracy. The instability of the First Republic culminated in civil war in 1934, followed by the corporate state of Dollfuss and Schuschnigg and then seven years of Nazi tyranny. The Second Republic, established in 1945, was confronted with the Allied occupation which dragged on for ten years until neutrality provided a solution. Today the country has confidence in its own present and future, and has acquired a level of affluence which amazes many of its own citizens who remember the difficult circumstances they became used to in the past.

The political parties have been an important element of continuity throughout the Republic's checkered history and have been influential in creating the structure of the state. The two main parties, the Socialists and the conservative People's Party, formed a Great Coalition in 1945 to tackle post-war problems. This coalition was a predominant feature of political life until 1966, and the influence it had during that period on the organisation of the country's affairs still continues to be felt. The two parties have dominated post-war politics and have managed to create a consensus which was lacking in the First Republic.

I should like to acknowledge the financial assistance provided by the Small Grants Scheme of the Nuffield Foundation, which enabled me to carry out research for this study in Austria. My thanks are also due to North Staffordshire Polytechnic which allowed me sabbatical leave to complete the book.

While in Austria, I found a warm reception and assistance from the different political parties and from many institutions. Special thanks are due to Richard Klucsarits of the Karl Renner Institute for his patience and solid support over many years. I am indebted to Dr. Theodor Prager of the *Arbeiterkammer* for his peceptive comments and help. Professor Karl Stadler of Linz University has always kindly extended hospitality and advice, and to him and his colleagues I am most grateful.

The Documentation Archive of the Austrian Resistance made available useful material from its library in Vienna. My thanks also to the Austrian Ministry of the Interior for information and for the use of maps, which were drawn by Roy Hitchings. I wish to thank Tony Burkett of Loughborough University for his encouragement and ideas on this project. Peter Pulzer's careful reading of the manuscript and his studied comments were much appreciated.

My thanks also to Marjorie Foy for typing the manuscript. My deepest thanks finally to dearest Rog whose steadfast support has been of inestimable value. I hope he will continue to believe in the tranquillity of life in Austria.

Department of Humanities   MELANIE A. SULLY
North Staffordshire Polytechnic

ABBREVIATIONS

Austrian Parties and Interest Groups

ACUS   *Arbeitsgemeinschaft fuer Christentum und Sozialismus* (Study Group on Christianity and Socialism).

AK   *Kammer fuer Arbeiter und Angestellte* (Chamber of Labour).

ANR   *Aktion Neue Rechte* (Action for the New Right).

ARBOe   *Auto-Rad und Kraftfahrerbund Oesterreichs* (Automobile and Cyclists' Association of Austria).

BfS   *Bewegung fuer Sozialismus* (Movement for Socialism).

BSA   *Bund sozialistischer Akademiker* (League of Socialist Academics).

DFP   *Demokratische Fortschrittliche Partei* (Democratic Progressive Party).

DNAP   *Demokratisch-Nationale Arbeiterpartei* (Democratic National Workers' Party).

FCG   *Fraktion Christlicher Gewerkschafter* (Fraction of Christian Trade Unionists).

FOeJ   *Freie Oesterreichische Jugend* (Free Austrian Youth).

FP   *Freiheitspartei* (Free Party).

FPOe   *Freiheitliche Partei Oesterreichs* (Freedom Party of Austria).

FSG   *Fraktion Sozialistischer Gewerkschafter* (Fraction of Socialist Trade Unionists).

FSOe   *Freiheitliche Sammlung Oesterreichs* (Freedom Group of Austria).

GE   *Gewerkschaftliche Einheit* (Trade Union Unity).

GRM   *Gruppe Revolutionaere Marxisten* (Group of Revolutionary Marxists).

IOeAG   *Initiative Oesterreichischer Atomkraftwerksgegner* (Initiative of Austrian Opponents of Atomic Power).

JES   *Junge Europaeische Studenten* (Young European Students).

JG   *Junge Generation* (Young Generation).

JVP   *Junge Volkspartei* (Young People's Party).

KB   *Kommunistischer Bund* (Communist League).

KBOe   *Kommunistischer Bund Oesterreichs* (Communist League of Austria).

KHD   *Kaerntner Heimatdienst* (Carinthian Patriotic Corps).

KJOe   *Kommunistische Jugend Oesterreichs* (Communist Youth of Austria).

KPOe   *Kommunistische Partei Oesterreichs* (Communist Party of Austria).

MLOe   *Marxisten Leninisten Oesterreichs* (Marxist Leninists of Austria).

MLPOe   *Marxistische Leninistische Partei Oesterreichs* (Marxist-Leninist Party of Austria).

NDP   *Nationaldemokratische Partei* (National Democratic Party).

OeAAB   *Oesterreichischer Arbeiter-und Angestelltenbund* (Austrian Workers' and Employees' League).

OeAKT   *Oesterreichischer Arbeiterkammertag* (Council of Austrian Chambers of Labour).

OeBB   *Oesterreichischer Bauernbund* (Austrian Farmers' League).

OeCV   *Oesterreichischer Cartellverband* (Association of Austrian Catholic Fraternities).

OeFB   *Oesterreichische Frauenbewegung* (Austrian Women's Movement).

OeGB   *Oesterreichischer Gewerkschaftsbund* (Austrian Trade Union Federation).

OeJB   *Oesterreichische Jugendbewegung* (Austrian Youth Movement).

OeSB   *Oesterreichischer Seniorenbund* (Austrian Union of Senior Citizens).

OeSU   *Oesterreichische Studentenunion* (Union of Austrian Students).

OeVP   *Oesterreichische Volkspartei* (Austrian People's Party).

OeWB   *Oesterreichischer Wirtschaftsbund* (Austrian Business League).

RS   *Revolutionaere Sozialisten* (Revolutionary Socialists).

RFJ   *Ring Freiheitlicher Jugend* (Ring of Free Youth).

RFS   *Ring Freiheitlicher Studenten* (Ring of Free Students).

SDAP   *Sozialdemokratische Arbeiterpartei* (Social Democratic Workers' Party).

SJOe   *Sozialistische Jugend Oesterreichs* (Socialist Youth of Austria).

SPOe   *Sozialistische Partei Oesterreichs* (Socialist Party of Austria).

VdU   *Verband der Unabhaengigen* (League of Independents).

VRA   *Vereinigung Revolutionaere Arbeiter* (Union of Revolutionary Workers).

VSStOe   *Verband Sozialistischer Studenten Oesterreichs* (Association of Austrian Socialist Students).

WdU   *Wahlpartei der Unabhaengigen* (Electoral Party of Independents).

Laender

(These abbreviations are used in tables and maps)
B   Burgenland.
C   Carinthia
LA   Lower Austria
S   Salzburg
St.   Styria
T   Tyrol
UA   Upper Austria
V   Vienna
Vor.   Vorarlberg

Others

CPSU   Communist Party of the Soviet Union.
CSSR   Czechoslovak Socialist Republic.
FDP   *Freie Demokratische Partei Deutschlands* (Free Democratic Party of Germany).
IAEA   International Atomic Energy Agency.
IFES   *Institut fuer Empirische Sozialforschung* (Institute for Empirical Social Research).
NSDAP *Nationalsozialistische Deutsche Arbeiterpartei* (National Socialist German Workers' Party).
SPD   *Sozialdemokratische Partei Deutschlands* (Social Democratic Party of Germany).
UNIDO United Nations Industrial Development Organisation.
VOeEST *Vereinigte Oesterreichische Eisen- und Stahlwerke* (United Austrian Iron and Steel Works).

1

POLITICS AND GOVERNMENT

(a) The Imperial Legacy

The vast, 'ramshackle' Habsburg empire has been the subject of much derision by modern historians. With 51 million inhabitants in 1910, at the last census before its collapse, and a multiplicity of different ethnic groups, it somehow staggered into the second decade of the twentieth century, but the national tensions and economic and military weaknesses became acute during the First World War. The deliquescence of this unlikely system had been apparent long before, and many had prophesied its final hour while others had sought to reform its anachronistic structure. Its eventual collapse in 1918 came as no great surprise but bestowed a series of complications on its bewildered heirs.

The Habsburgs had dominated Central Europe for centuries and their sudden disappearance left a conspicuous void. The emergence of several successor-states that had been striving for independence for years was just one of the solutions which were possible. For 'German Austria', the state that was left over, it was not the most satisfactory arrangement. In this comparatively insignificant country with a tiny population of just over 6 million, many looked back with nostalgia to the grandeur of the imperial past. A Danubian federation, maintaining the positive aspects of the empire and fulfilling nationalist aspirations, was to remain an elaborate dream. Deprived of this alternative, the reluctant republicans sought a new mission in the disrupted world but adaptation to the political realities was to be a painful process.

The First Republic (1918–34) was characterised by a notable lack of faith in its ability to survive. The political and economic viability (*Lebensfaehigkeit*) was increasingly challenged until finally the entire system submitted to the authoritarian corporate state of Dollfuss and then Schuschnigg (1934–8). The search for identity was partly fulfilled, in the early years of the Republic, by schemes which envisaged a union with Germany. The ban imposed on this by the post-war settlements only served to increase the frustration of the 'German-Austrians'. As Otto Bauer (1881–1938), the intellectual leader of the Social Democrats in the inter-war period, observed,

Forcibly torn out of the great economic sphere whose centre Austria had

1

formed, without sufficient strength to effect with its own resources adaptations to the new conditions of life, the young Republic was doomed to lead an independent life that could only be a life of bitter need, of abject dependence upon the foreigner.[1]

Anschluss with a German 'red republic' (the latter briefly seemed possible immediately after the end of the war) was considered by the left as the best way to proceed to Socialism. The realisation that union with Germany was not possible was followed by despair, and Bauer claimed: 'We could not accomplish a social revolution in our small and weak country.'[2] Demands for an *Anschluss* disappeared from the programme of the Social Democrats in 1933 but this did not mean that the Republic's crisis of identity was over. Paramilitary formations from both the left and the right became increasingly involved in violent clashes. These incidents found their logical culmination in civil war, and in February 1934, after the defeat of the Socialists by the Fascists, all pretence to democracy was finally abandoned.

The civil war was the ultimate physical expression of the famous *Lager* (encampment) mentality endemic in Austria's political culture. This had its roots in the imperial era and consisted of three sub-cultures which developed in the late nineteenth century: a Social-Democratic Marxist camp, a Catholic-Conservative, and a pan-German nationalist *Lager*. These were the embryos of the main political parties which were to play such an important part in the political history of the country, and which have survived in a modified form up to the present day. Despite the traumas experienced by the *Lager* under different governments, they demonstrate a high degree of stability (see Figure 1.i). The 'cradle to the grave' activities of the *Lager* discouraged overlapping membership, and tended to institutionalise societal cleavages.

Each *Lager* drew its support from specific social groups and each had a political organisation which acted as the political representative of its interests. Each *Lager* attempted to develop a *Weltanschauung*, foster social and ideological homogeneity among its followers, and establish 'totalitarian' control over the entire lives of its members.[3]

The strength of these *Lager* has often been greater than the state in which they have flourished. This factor weakened the authority of the First Republic and contributed to its demise. Parties in Austria have been instrumental in constructing political norms and, after both wars, assumed control in the absence of a recognisable sovereign state. Since the establishment of the Second Republic in 1945, the *Lager* have refrained from subverting the system and, unlike in the First Republic, they have been able to establish a peaceful

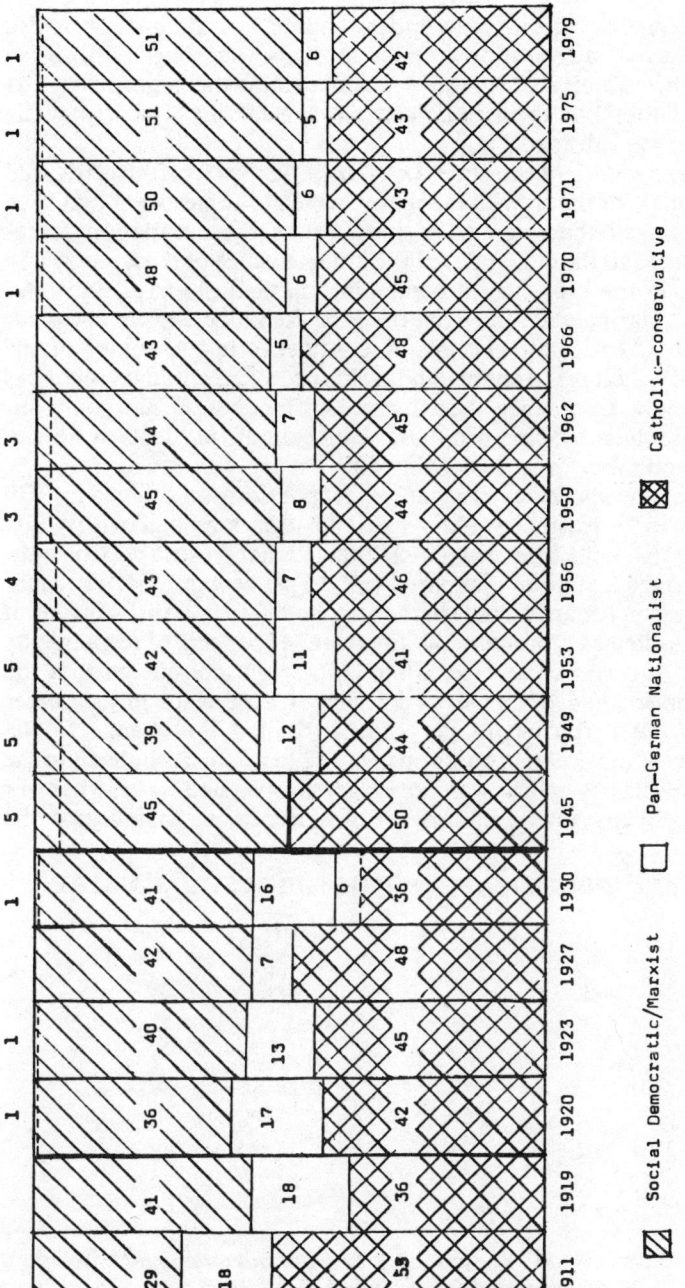

Fig. 1.ii.　DISTRIBUTION OF VOTES BETWEEN THE *LAGER* IN ELECTIONS, 1911–1979

co-existence based on some understanding, a little distrust and a wish to avoid a repetition of past conflicts. The *Lager* still thrive within the state, and to some extent dictate the organisation of political life, but their fanatical 'siege mentality' and 'totalistic claims' have subsided.[4]

The experience of the Nazi *Anschluss* (1938–45) effectively cured hankerings for union with Germany, which to some extent had been present in all the *Lager*. The presence of the occupation forces contributed to the demands for the independence of the country and a belief in the existence of something particularly 'Austrian'. An identity, glaringly absent from the First Republic, slowly emerged, boosted by economic success. A confidence in the ability of the political structures to endure and tackle problems without collapse is greater now than since the empire. An increase in national consciousness has accompanied these changes and is particularly noticeable among the young (see Table 1.i).

This survey discovered that 66 per cent of those questioned in 1970 believed in the existence of an Austrian nation compared with 47 per cent in 1964. Only 8 per cent in 1970 denied that Austria had the right to be termed a 'nation' compared with 15 per cent in 1964. The main single reason for an increase in the attachment to the Austrian nation has been cited as economic stability. Over 44 per cent of respondents believed this to be the case, while 26 per cent considered that the development had occurred as a result of experience in a 'greater Germany'. A further 12 per cent attributed the change to the presence of the occupation troops, and 12 per cent attributed it to the fact that class warfare was no longer propagated.[5] For whatever reason, loyalty to the nation and a belief in the viability of the

Table 1.i. IDENTIFICATION WITH THE AUSTRIAN NATION

	1964 %	1970 %
Total	42	64
Sex		
Men	42	72
Women	40	58
Age		
Under 30	38	74
31–50	44	50
over 50	38	66

Source: H. Konrad (ed.), *Sozialdemokratie und 'Anschluss'*, Europaverlag, Wien, 1978, p.109.

country is greater than during the First Republic. The inclination to seek salvation outside its borders and to look for help from the powerful German neighbour has declined.

Austria today shows greater self-assurance, unity and internal means of support. In .the Second Republic, Austrians have been more absorbed with the problems of the present and the future, and nostalgic yearnings for imperial glories are fading. They continue to seek a mission in Europe and to increase their weight in international affairs, which is restricted by the neutrality clauses. Vienna is the third centre for the United Nations and the headquarters of the International Atomic Energy Agency (IAEA) and the United Nations Industrial Development Organisation (UNIDO). The Chancellor, Dr Bruno Kreisky, likes to be portrayed as a statesman, and is anxious to make neutral Austria an international meeting-place. A Gallup poll discovered that 43 per cent of the population believed that Austria's main role was to act as a neutral zone of peace between the super-powers, and 40 per cent thought that the country should serve as a bridge between East and West.[6] Austria's earlier crisis of identity caused by the abrupt loss of an empire has found some solution in its enthusiastic desire to participate in international organisations and promote understanding in East-West relations.

(b) The Second Republic

In 1945 there seemed little reason to be optimistic about Austria's future, and starvation and chaos once more confronted the population. The liberation of the country by the Allies brought with it the threat of division as the Cold War intensified. The Soviet Union established its position in the east, including Vienna, while the American and British forces moved in from the west. The veteran Social Democrat, Karl Renner, who had been the first Chancellor after the 1914–18 war, showed remarkable astuteness in his negotiations with the Russians. He was instrumental in forming a Provisional Government in April 1945 with the co-operation of members from the opposing conservative camp and the Communists. These 'anti-Fascist' parties, which were then reforming after a long hiatus, took the iniative in organising political life under their respective leaders. Faced with a breakdown in law and order and a lack of a central governing body, the parties pre-empted the political system and were of paramount importance in shaping its future. They resurrected the constitution of the First Republic and proceeded to govern according to its principles. From the beginning, the parties dictated the organisation of political affairs, and this pervasive influence continued. A declaration of independence was issued, and the

Anschluss was regarded as null and void.

Representatives of the Communists were included in the Provisional Government to appease the Soviet Union although Renner ensured that they would be in no position to act independently. His concern to restrict the influence of Communism was not appreciated by the Western allies, particularly the British; they suspected him of being a Soviet stooge and did not recognise the Provisional Government until October 1945, and then on the condition that free elections should follow.

Arrangements were made for the first national post-war elections to be held in November 1945, and the parties that had been busily engaged in the revival of political life began to campaign for official governmental power. The Socialists (SPOe), a conservative, Catholic party named the People's Party (OeVP), and the Communists (KPOe) fought the election and afterwards joined an all-party government under the leadership of the People's Party. The Communists soon withdrew and left the two main parties in coalition, an arrangement which lasted for twenty years. A successor to the pan-German nationalist camp was not allowed to participate in the 1945 election, although it fought the next one. It exists today under the name of the 'Freedom Party' of Austria (FPOe), but cannot be described as a 'liberal' party as that term is understood in Britain or Germany (see Chapter 4). Support for the parties after 1945 showed a continuation of a similar balance of power between the *Lager* as it had existed in the First Republic (see Figure 1.i. and Chapter 6). The Communists remained weak (see Chapter 5), and the politics of the Second Republic was dominated by a Great Coalition between the Socialists and the People's Party (OeVP). Although the OeVP had an absolute majority in 1945, the presence of the occupation forces, the threats of division and Communism and the parlous state of the economy prompted the acceptance of a coalition. The governments of the Second Republic were typified by the following phases:

SPOe—OeVP Great Coalition (including KPOe until 1947)	1945–66
OeVP majority government	1966–70
SPOe minority government	1970–1
SPOe majority government	1971–

Austria had been divided into four zones of occupation in July 1945, and Vienna was split into four sectors with the inner city under four-power control (see map 1.i). Many problems, both political and economic, confronted the new Government, but its very existence,

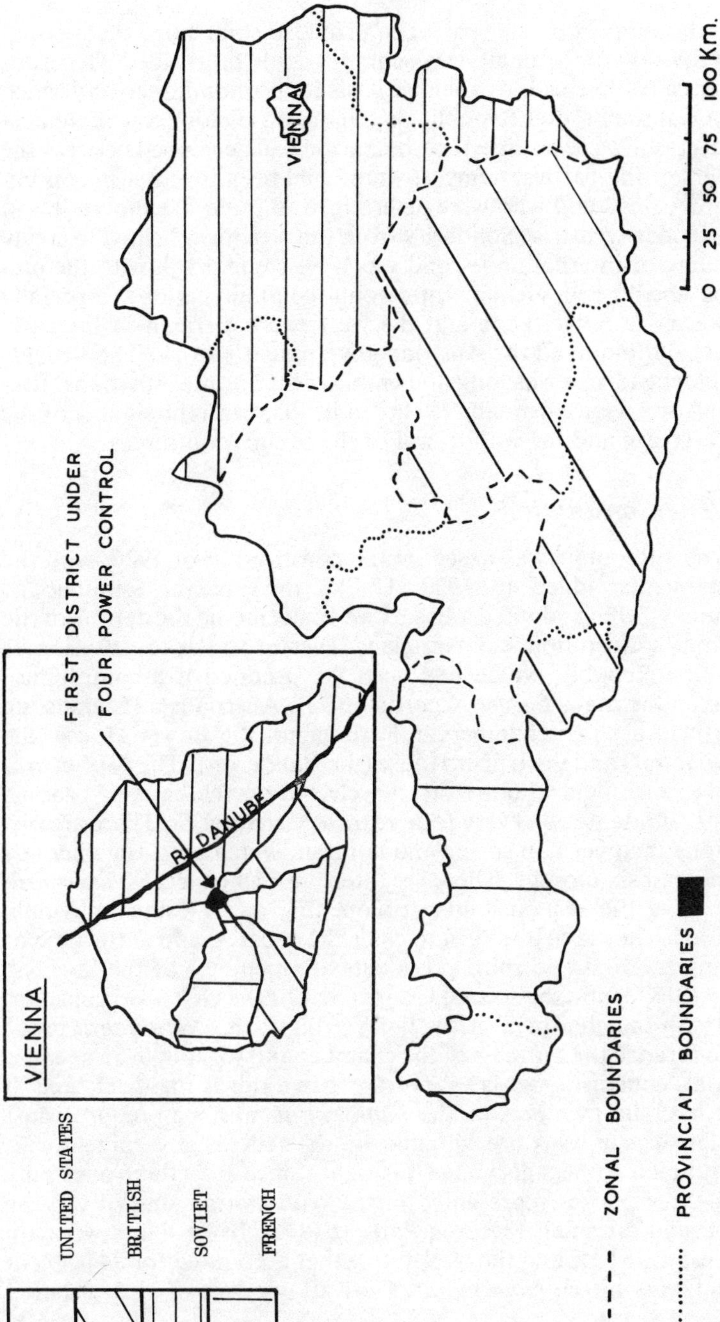

UNITED STATES

BRITISH

SOVIET

FRENCH

VIENNA

R. DANUBE

FIRST DISTRICT UNDER
FOUR POWER CONTROL

VIENNA

- - - - - ZONAL BOUNDARIES

· · · · · · · PROVINCIAL BOUNDARIES ■

0 25 50 75 100 Km.

Map 1.i. AUSTRIA UNDER OCCUPATION

with the support of the provinces, provided some hope that permanent division of the small, weak country could be avoided. Generous American aid helped to provide a basis for economic recovery which launched the Second Republic on a more auspicious course than its predecessor. A new spirit of co-operation had developed between the leaders of the parties, many of whom had been together in concentration camps and who were determined to build a democratic and independent Austria. Solidarity from the provinces helped to create a feeling of internal unity, and was a welcome break with the previous hostility to Vienna. Inter-zonal communications, especially between the Soviet zone and the west, were difficult in the early years, and hindered the Austrian government's work. The struggle for independence was long and embittered, but the Austrians' tireless efforts were eventually rewarded in 1955 with the signing of the State Treaty and the withdrawal of the occupation forces.

(c) The Constitution

The new Republic was based on the constitution of 1920, with the amendments added in 1929. Unlike the Federal Republic of Germany, which adopted a Basic Law to overcome the defects of the Weimar constitution, the Austrians reverted to the constitution of the First Republic which had been the product of a compromise between the main *Lager*. According to it, Austria is a federal state and there are two chambers in Parliament, the Lower House (the *Nationalrat*) and the Upper House (the *Bundesrat*). The *Nationalrat* has 183 members who are directly elected on the basis of proportional representation every four years (see chapter 6). There are two sessions each year, in spring and autumn, which must together last for at least six months. There are three presidents in the *Nationalrat* who have the responsibility for opening and closing individual sessions. They take it in turn to chair the debates, and at the time of writing the first and third presidents are members of the Socialist party (SPOe) and the second is a member of the OeVP. In consultation with the chairmen of the party groups, the *Nationalrat* presidents arrange the business of the chamber and formulate an agenda. Special 'constitutional laws' require a two-thirds majority, and at least half the members of the *Nationalrat* must be present. Most legislative proposals are initiated by the federal government, but individual members also have this right. Since 1959 there have only been three parties represented in the *Nationalrat*—the SPOe, the OeVP and the small Freedom Party (FPOe). In 1979 the two main parties, the SPOe and the OeVP, together accounted for 94 per cent of the seats in the *Nationalrat*. Over 80 per cent of all legislation is on average adopted unanimously, and this basic consensus shows little signs of waning even under a government with an absolute majority.

Table 1.ii. ADOPTION OF PARLIAMENTARY LEGISLATION (%)

Passed	OeVP majority government	SPOe minority government	SPOe majority government
Unanimously	72	89	84
By more than one party	16	11	8
By the government only	12	–	8

Source: H. Fischer, ed., *Das Politische System Oesterreichs*, Europaverlag, Wien, 1977, p.89.

The *Bundesrat* represents the interests of the nine provinces (*Laender*) and the number of deputies depends on their population. According to Article 34 of the constitution,

The *Land* with the largest number of citizens delegates twelve members, every other *Land* as many as the ratio in which its citizens stand to those in the first-mentioned *Land*, with remainders which exceed half the coefficient counting as full. Every *Land* is however entitled to a representation of at least three members.

The fifty-eight members of the *Bundesrat* are indirectly elected by the provincial legislatures (*Landtage*) in accordance with the principle of proportional representation, but

At least one seat must fall to the party having the second largest number of seats in a *Landtag* or, should several parties have the same number of seats, the second highest number of votes at the last election to a *Landtag*.

The chairmanship of the *Bundesrat* rotates between the *Laender* every six months in alphabetical order. This can be particularly important when, as is currently the case, the number of deputies from each party is the same, the chairman having no voting rights. In practice, the *Bundesrat* represents the interests of the parties rather than the *Laender*, and there have been calls for reform to strengthen the federal element in the constitution. The FPOe would like to see an increase in the powers of the *Bundesrat* so that it could veto financial legislation. Its weakness, compared with its equivalent in West Germany, is considered by the FPOe to be farcical. It can, on most issues, object to proposals from the first chamber, but if the latter adopts the original resolution with at least half of its members present, the Bill becomes Law. The Austrian constitution assigns considerable power to the *Nationalrat*, and it can pass legislation on the federal budget and on its own dissolution without the consent of the *Bundesrat*. The *Bundesrat* can propose legislative motions for discussion in the *Nationalrat* by submitting these to the Federal Government.

Table 1.iii. PARTY COMPOSITION OF THE *BUNDESRAT* SINCE 1945

	SPOe	OeVP	(VdU) FPOe	KPOe
1945–9	23	27	–	–
1949–53	20	25	4	1
1953–4	21	25	3	1
1954–5	23	25	2	–
1955–7	24	25	1	–
1957–62	24	26	–	–
1962–4	25	29	–	–
1964–7	26	28	–	–
1967–9	27	27	–	–
1969–70	28	26	–	–
1970–72	29	25	–	–
1972–3	30	28	–	–
1973–	29	29	–	–

Source: E. Weinzierl and K. Skalnik (eds.), *Das Neue Oesterreich: Geschichte der Zweiten Republik*, Verlag Styria, Graz, 1975, p.375.

There have been complaints that parties are too dominant in the political system and that this has contributed to the atrophy of Parliament. When the Great Coalition of the SPOe and OeVP was in existence, the *Bundesrat* played a very modest role, objecting to only sixteen resolutions of the *Nationalrat* in just over twenty years. After the Great Coalition had been replaced in 1966 by a single-party Government of the OeVP, more scope existed for the exercise of parliamentary procedures. Following successes in provincial elections in 1968, the SPOe for the first time had a majority in the *Bundesrat*, which confronted a conservative majority in the *Nationalrat*. This resulted in an increase in objections from the *Bundesrat*, although restrictions on its power meant that no major conflicts occurred, and controversial legislation was merely delayed. The SPOe now has a majority in the *Nationalrat*, and since 1973 has had the same number of seats in the *Bundesrat* as the OeVP. When the Socialist-dominated provinces (Burgenland, Carinthia and Vienna) provide the chairman of the *Bundesrat*, the OeVP has an advantage of one since the chairman sacrifices the right to vote. No major constitutional crisis has developed between the two chambers and, for the most part, the Socialists have a lead of one when members from the remaining six OeVP provinces are in the chair.

Most of the members of Parliament are public service employees or are connected with the major interest groups: the trade unions or the Chambers of Labour, Commerce and Agriculture. In 1979, thirty-four of the fifty-eight deputies in the *Bundesrat* and 102 of the 183 members in the *Nationalrat* came from this background. Almost 64 per cent of members in the second chamber were over fifty compared with 58 per cent in the *Nationalrat*, as is seen in Table 1.iv.

Table 1.iv. AGE OF DEPUTIES IN PARLIAMENT 1979 (%)

	Bundesrat	*Nationalrat*
Under 30	–	0.55
30–40	12.07	11.48
40–50	24.14	29.51
50–60	58.62	49.18
Over 60	5.17	9.29
	Years	*Years*
Youngest member	32	29
Oldest member	70	70

Information supplied by the Archivist of the Austrian Parliament.

About 15 per cent of members of the *Bundesrat* are women, compared with 10 per cent in the *Nationalrat*. There are no women deputies in Parliament from the FPOe, and in the *Nationalrat* there are eleven women deputies in the SPOe and seven in the OeVP. Only 3 per cent of members in the *Bundesrat* are classified as 'workers' (i.e. manual) compared with 7 per cent in the *Nationalrat*. These figures suggest a danger of isolation of members from the population. The status of Parliament was not enhanced during the days of the Great Coalition, when major policy decisions were agreed between the two parties outside the parliamentary arena. The existence of powerful interest groups in Austria contributes to a continued public suspicion that Parliament is ineffective. Much of the work of the *Nationalrat* is carried out by committees. A main committee and a standing sub-committee are elected according to the strength of the parties. If the *Nationalrat* is dissolved, executive power devolves upon the standing sub-committee. An election must follow to enable the new *Nationalrat* to meet within 100 days.

An amendment of 1929 to the 1920 constitution determined that the Federal President should be popularly elected. This takes place every six years and voting is compulsory. The procedure is as follows:

The candidate who polls more than half of all valid votes has been elected. If no such majority results, a second ballot takes place. Votes in this can validly be cast only for one of the two candidates who have polled the most votes in the first ballot; but each of the two groups of voters who put up these two candidates can in the second ballot nominate another individual to replace its original candidate.[7]

Re-election can only take place once, so the President can hold office for a maximum of twelve years. The first direct elections did not take place until 1951, and in 1945 Dr. Karl Renner was appointed President by Parliament. (For the results of Presidential elections, see Appendix A.) The Federal President has mainly ceremonial duties; he is the official head of state and represents the Republic abroad. He appoints the Federal Chancellor, and in rare cases can exercise discretionary powers. The constitution does not invest the President with great powers, and his official acts require the counter-signature of the Chancellor or the relevant Federal minister. Members of the Federal Government are appointed by the President on the recommendation of the Chancellor. The Federal President convenes and prorogues Parliament and is empowered to dissolve the *Nationalrat* which can only be enacted once for the same reason. The constitution allows for the *Nationalrat* to vote its own dissolution by simple law. Both chambers meet together in a Federal Assembly (*Bundesversammlung*) to accept the oath of allegiance to the Republic by the President. The election of the Federal Chancellor usually follows from the strength of the parties in the *Nationalrat*. After a narrow election result, the President can intervene to exercise decisive power, and this happened in 1953, 1959 and 1970. In the life of the Second Republic, the Federal President has never abused this power, and has faithfully interpreted the verdict of the electorate. Since 1945 the President has always been a member or a nominee of the Socialist Party.

FEDERAL PRESIDENTS IN THE SECOND REPUBLIC
Dr Karl Renner (SPOe)	1945–50
Dr Theodor Koerner (SPOe)	1951–7
Dr Adolf Schaerf (SPOe)	1957–65
Franz Jonas (SPOe)	1965–74
Dr Rudolf Kirchschlaeger (Non-party)	1974–

A motion of no-confidence can be passed by the *Nationalrat* in the Federal Government or in an individual minister, which necessitates resignation. According to Article 71 of the constitution,

Should the Federal Government have left office, the Federal President shall entrust members of the outgoing Government or senior officials of the Federal departments with continuation of the administration and one of them with the chairmanship of the provisional Federal Government until the formation of the new Federal Government.

Since it is usually the case for the opposition to be in the minority, control of the government is exercised through the medium of question time. There is no provision for a 'constructive vote of no confidence', as exists in the West German Basic Law. The Federal Chancellor can call on the *Bundesversammlung* to arrange for the removal of the Federal President by a referendum; this requires a two-thirds majority in the *Nationalrat* for the Chancellor to instigate these proceedings, but the strict observance of constitutional etiquette has made this drastic step unnecessary. It serves to check the possible arbitrary rule by a president who could claim excessive powers on the grounds that his authority is derived from the people. It is significant that members of the former Habsburg royal family are barred from standing for the Presidency, thus avoiding the danger of absolutist rule by an aspiring *Ersatzkaiser*.

The Federal Chancellor has the power to dismiss the individual members of his Government. He is entrusted with the direction of the chancellery and the administration of the affairs of state in so far as these are not specifically assigned to the president.

CHANCELLORS SINCE 1945

Leopold Figl (OeVP)	1945–53
Julius Raab (OeVP)	1953–61
Alfons Gorbach (OeVP)	1961–64
Josef Klaus (OeVP)	1964–70
Bruno Kreisky (SPOe)	1970–

The Austrian constitution does not elaborate on the powers of the Chancellor and is not as detailed as the Basic Law of West Germany. It is neither designed as an antidote to a former, disastrous constitution, nor is it based on the assumption of inevitable collapse and catastrophe. Its substantive sections are sixty years old and, although some revisions have been made, it is not a maze of legalistic complexities. It has not, so far, devised institutional arrangements for a *Berufsverbot*, on the West German model (closing of public employment to those known to have or suspected of having extremist political leanings), nor does it show a neurotic concern with those seeking to undermine the democratic system. Cynics argue that a *Berufsverbot* is unnecessary, given the party cartel system. This has outlived the Great Coalition and is important in the consideration of applications for posts in the civil service, which includes posts in education. Informal personal contacts can often be helpful in discovering the key to success; most Austrians are aware of this importance. This accounts for the high membership of many societies and parties which are considered beneficial in promoting career ambitions and material interests.[8]

Political involvement of Austrians is high, over 30 per cent of the electorate are party members, and turn-out in elections is over 90 per cent. However, this cannot entirely be attributed to the enthusiasm of Austrians for political activity, but is an indication of the influence of parties in advancing individual interests. Constitutional arrangements, under these circumstances, are relegated to a passive function in the organisation of political life. The failure of parliamentary government in the First Republic contrasts with its stability since 1945, but both systems were rooted in similar rules of procedure, which suggests that constitutions are not necessarily decisive in determining the capacity of a polity to survive.

Safeguards have been built into the constitution to ensure its smooth operation and the resolution of conflict, most notably in the form of the Constitutional Court. This can pronounce judgement in disputes between the *Laender*, between a *Land* and the Federal Government and between courts and the administrative authorities. It decides on the constitutionality of Federal and *Land* laws, and gives rulings on allegations of irregularities in electoral procedure. The Constitutional Court consists of a president, a vice-president, twelve other members and six substitutes. The president and vice-president, six members and three substitute members are appointed by the Federal President on the recommendation of the Federal Government; he appoints the remaining members on the basis of recommendations from the two Houses of Parliament. In addition to the Constitutional Court, the constitution provides for an Administrative Court to ensure the legality of acts of public administration. Any citizen who believes that his rights have been violated by an administrative act, or that his constitutional rights have been infringed, may appeal to the appropriate one of these two Courts. A central auditing authority scrutinises public accounts and the administration of public funds, and presents an annual report to the *Nationalrat*: its terms of reference include the examination of 'arithmetical correctness, compliance with existing regulations, and the employment of thrift, efficiency and expediency'. In 1977, after six years of discussion, a law establishing an ombudsman was passed. When no other means of appeal is available, a citizen who feels that he has been the victim of maladministration may seek help from this official. There are three ombudsmen, who are elected by the *Nationalrat* for six years. If they consider a case justified, they can recommend that suitable action be taken by the relevant authority: this recommendation must be complied with inside eight weeks, or written justification given for ignoring this advice. The 1977 law is experimental for six years, and in 1983, after an assessment of its value, a decision will be taken on whether the ombudsman should become a permanent institution.

(d) Austria and the Provinces

There are nine autonomous provinces (*Laender*) in the Austrian federal state (see Map 1.ii) which together have a population of 7.4 million. In 1976, 9.5 per cent of the adult population were employed in agriculture and forestry, 32.6 per cent in industry and 32.5 per cent in the service industries, and 23.6 per cent were classified as pensioners.

Burgenland—population 272,119 (85 per cent Roman Catholic); capital, Eisenstadt—population 10,600.[9] This region became part of Austria after the First World War, having formerly been part of Hungary. It is mainly an agricultural and wine-growing province. Since 1964, the provincial governor (*Landeshauptmann*) has been a member of the SPOe.

Carinthia—population 525,728 (78 per cent Roman Catholic); capital, Klagenfurt—population 85,500. This is the southernmost province of Austria and a favourite tourist area in the summer. In the winter, unemployment can be relatively high by Austrian standards. The existence of a Slovene minority group has caused some friction with right-wing pan-German nationalist organisations. It has an SPOe provincial governor but the mayor of Klagenfurt is a member of the OeVP dependent on the support of the FPOe.

Lower Austria—population 1,414,161 (98 per cent Roman Catholic); the provincial government is based in Vienna. This is the province with the largest area, and it is the main supplier of agricultural produce such as wheat, sugar-beet and wine. It also has an important industrial sector with the biggest oil-fields in Austria. Of all the provinces it suffered the worst industrial damage during the Second World War, and afterwards it was under Soviet occupation. The country's first nuclear power plant has been built in Lower Austria at Zwentendorf, near Vienna, but a referendum resulted in a vote against putting it on-stream. The provincial governor is a member of the OeVP.

Upper Austria—population 1,233,444 (86 per cent Roman

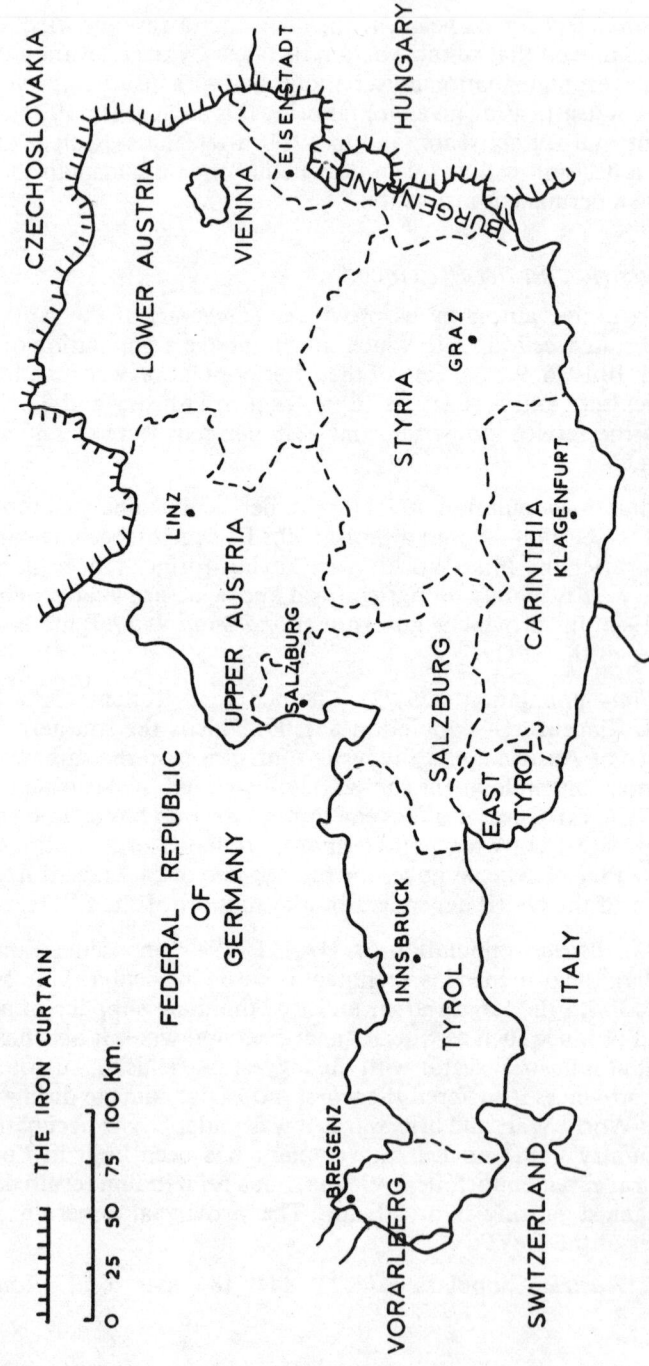

Map 1.ii.   THE LAENDER OF AUSTRIA

Catholic); capital, Linz—population 208,000. This province is well-developed industrially, and is the country's second most important source of oil and natural gas. The industrial conurbation is centred around Linz and is important for the production of iron, steel and chemicals. Much of the industrial development in the province was stimulated by the needs of the Nazi war effort, as with the Hermann Goering Works at Linz. Known today as the nationalised VOeEST —Alpine Steel Works, it has a labour force of around 25,000. The provincial governor is a member of the OeVP, although the city of Linz has a socialist mayor.

Salzburg—population 401,766 (89 per cent Roman Catholic); capital, Salzburg city—population 138,500. The early home of Mozart, and including many spa resorts and ski-ing centres, the entire province flourishes on tourism throughout the year. A strong Germanic influence has contributed to the strength of the FPOe in the area (see Chapter 4), but the provincial governor is a member of the OeVP.

Styria—population 1,192,442 (90 per cent Roman Catholic); capital, Graz—population 249,100. Graz is the second largest city in the country and its mayor is a member of the FPOe, dependent for support on the OeVP. The province likes to describe itself as the 'green heart' of Austria, and about half of it consists of forests. The industrial sector is based in the mountainous regions in the north of Styria, which contain rich deposits of iron ore. There are important cellulose, paper and electrical industries in addition to iron, steel and engineering. Graz is an important cultural centre, and has a thriving university, although students complain that it is a pensioners' city. In the days of the monarchy, it was a favourite place of retirement for state officials. Later it became a flourishing centre for pan-German nationalism. After the Second World War it was part of the British zone of occupation. The provincial governor is a member of the OeVP.

Tyrol—population 540,771 (97 per cent Roman Catholic); capital, Innsbruck—population 122,600. The capital was the centre of the winter Olympics in 1964 and 1976. With impressive mountains and picturesque villages and farmhouses, the Austrian Tyrol is the most important province in terms of earning foreign currency from tourism, and is the least densely populated. A motorway tunnel 10,248 metres long through the Arlberg Massif links it with the province of Vorarlberg. Tyrol's provincial governor is a popular figure and a member of the OeVP.

Vorarlberg—population 271,473 (93 per cent Roman Catholic); capital, Bregenz—population 26,200. The commercial centre of the province is Dornbirn, which has the biggest population (37,900). The Alemannic dialect has a greater affinity with that spoken in neighbouring Switzerland and with Swabian German than with the language used in the rest of Austria. Vorarlberg is the smallest province in terms of population and, apart from Vienna, in area. Separated from the rest of the country by the Arlberg mountain range it has a feeling of remoteness from Austria and certainly from Vienna, which is 659 km from Bregenz. Regional identity, strong in all the provinces, is particularly noticeable in Vorarlberg. Recently a movement called 'pro-Vorarlberg', fuelled by frustration with lack of action from Vienna, has demanded more autonomy for the area. After the First World War, 80 per cent in the province voted in a plebiscite to join Switzerland, and, periodically, yearnings for closer integration with Austria's neighbours come to the surface. Apart from the tourist industry Vorarlberg has huge reserves of hydro-electric power and a textile industry which has recently encountered difficulties resulting from foreign competition. The province has a governor from the OeVP, although Bregenz has a Socialist mayor propped up in a coalition with the FPOe.

Vienna—population 1,614,841 (79 per cent Roman Catholic); the capital of Austria and a separate *Land* as well as a municipality. Over 21 per cent of the entire population live here, although this proportion has been declining. A shift in population from east to west occurred during the Soviet occupation, encouraged by the development of industry in the western provinces as the Americans were more disposed to invest in areas under their influence. Its proximity to the Czechoslovak border has encouraged those thinking of leaving the capital to move to the western provinces. Traditionally a centre of music and with a cosmopolitan culture, it is also a focal point for commerce and trade. It has kept its reputation as 'red Vienna' and has a Socialist mayor, Leopold Gratz, a former Minister of Education. Over 70 per cent of the vote in the traditionally working-class districts of Favoriten, Simmering, Brigittenau, Floridsdorf and Donaustadt went to the SPOe in the 1979 general election. These parts of the city were mostly under the control of the Soviet forces from 1945 to 1955. The Communist vote in the city exceeded 2.0 per cent in 1979 in only two districts—Floridsdorf and Donaustadt. (For elections to all the *Landtage*, see Appendix D.)

   The federalist principle was incorporated into the constitution in 1920 under pressure from the conservative Christian Social Party. In addition to checking the power of the 'red' capital, it served to give expression to particularist feelings which were more forcefully articulated in the First Republic. The Federation (*Bund*) has sole powers over international treaties, currency, external commerce, customs and excise, the military, the police and defence. Federal jurisdiction extends to secondary and higher education, the judiciary, the administration of the postal service, the railways and weights and measures. The provinces can legislate on residuary affairs relating to building laws, agriculture and forestry, the local police, nature conservation and sport. The Federal Government can veto legislative decisions made by the *Laender*, although a province can re-adopt the original resolution if half of the members in its Government (*Landtag*) are present.

The provinces, with few exceptions, have no revenue-raising capacity—which perpetuates their chronic weakness. A close liaison has developed between provincial and federal politicians on regional planning, motorway construction, culture and the arts. Some amendments have been introduced to give the provinces executive powers over inland shipping and the river police. The possibility now exists for provinces to conclude individual agreements with the federal government, but the role of the provinces is limited by the Austrian constitution and underlined by the weakness of the *Bundesrat*.

A survey of 1973 found that 40 per cent of those questioned in Vienna considered that the Federal Government represented their interests more effectively than the *Land* Government. In the rest of eastern Austria only 27.6 per cent showed the same confidence in the Federal Government, while in the western provinces the figure was 27.0 per cent and in the south only 23.7 per cent.[10] Factors such as these have prompted some politicians to argue for decentralisation and more involvement of citizens in local affairs. The 'pro-Vorarlberg' group, formed in 1979, demanded the granting of a special statute for the province which would extend its powers of legislation. It also demanded more influence in education and finance, while conceding that foreign affairs should fall within the competence of the *Bund*. This group was countered by a rival organisation 'citizens of Vorarlberg for Austria', which objected to the separatist claims of 'pro-Vorarlberg'. It considered that the separatists' arguments contained racialist overtones and implied that the people of Vorarlberg worked harder and were more thrifty than the rest of the population. Of the political parties, the FPOe became most closely identified with the 'pro-Vorarlberg' campaign, which was resolutely opposed by the trade unions and the SPOe: this discussion took place just before elections to the *Landtag* of Vorarlberg, and the FPOe was the only party to lose votes in it. Although emotional links with the province cannot be underestimated and a suspicion of the Viennese remains, it is only a minority who would want to see a drastic break from the Republic. While some changes may be made to give the provinces a greater say in the running of local affairs, the financial supremacy of the *Bund* is unlikely to alter dramatically in favour of the provinces. Centralisation in the decision-making process is further reinforced by the important role played by economic interest groups.

(e) Coalition and 'Social Partnership'

From 1945 till 1966, Austria was governed by a Great Coalition of the two major parties, the SPOe and the OeVP. After the departure of the occupation troops in 1955, one major external pressure which had kept the coalition together disappeared. A 'coalition mentality' persisted, partly based on a fear of the opposing party acquiring too much power if allowed a free rein in government. Also, personal contacts, developed in the early years between the leaders of the two parties, had increased mutual understanding of common problems. In the 1960s, discontent with the inability of the coalition to solve important problems grew, and was most apparent in the OeVP. Despite this, when the OeVP won an absolute majority in the 1966 election, it dutifully began negotiations to re-constitute the coalition. The Socialists were even more reluctant to accept the logical consequences of the 1966 result, and tried to find some way of maintaining the *status quo*; but they found they were unable to accept the terms offered by the OeVP, and thus came to the inevitable conclusion that they should go into opposition. Austria's 'permanent' coalition had come to an end, and has not been revived since except in discussions before general elections.

The 'red-black' coalition was based on a delicate balance institutionalised in a series of extra-constitutional coalition pacts. The parties acquired separate spheres of influence in the distribution of civil service and cabinet posts and in the control of the nationalised banks and industries. The ratio (*Proporz*) for each party was determined by the result of the previous general election. Under the terms of the coalition pacts, the parties agreed to send an equal number of delegates to a coalition committee (see Figure 1.ii). Some members of this committee were drawn from the major economic interest groups, and—significantly—did not have to be parliamentary deputies or cabinet ministers. The functioning of the coalition and party discipline relegated the status of the cabinet and parliament to that of a passive instrument. Major decisions were taken by the coalition committee on the basis of unanimity, and then became binding on

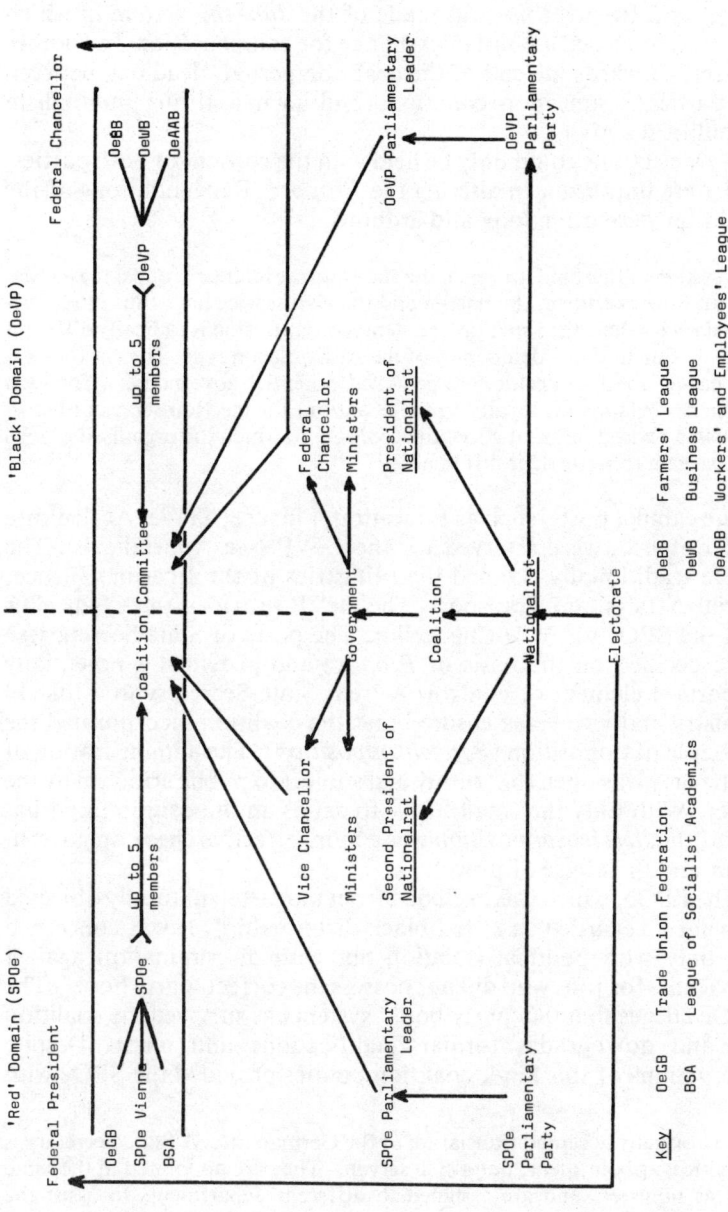

Fig. 1.ii.   **THE POLITICAL ORGANISATION OF THE GREAT COALITION**

Key   OeGB   Trade Union Federation   OeBB   Farmers' League

BSA   League of Socialist Academics   OeWB   Business League

OeABB   Workers' and Employees' League

both partners in Parliament. Bargaining was often involved at this stage, and frequent use was made of the *Junktim* system in which one side conceded a point in exchange for compensation on another matter. Towards the end of the coalition period, deadlock between the parties became more common, resulting in a stifling immobilism of political activity.

New elections could only be held with the consent of both parties, and were important in altering the *Proporz*. Renegotiations of the coalition were often long and arduous.

In a system of this kind, in which the state and the interest groups, the legislative and the executive, the parties and the civil service have thus interpenetrated each other, the function of a democratic election is radically different from its function in a democracy of the Anglo-Saxon type. The electorate is not called upon to decide between rival potential governments, for each partner proclaims his loyalty to the coalition; the election serves rather to furnish a revised index of strength according to which the organised groups can bargain to settle their differences.[11]

Some cabinet posts, such as Education, Finance, Trade, Agriculture and Defence, were reserved for the OeVP (see Appendix B). The SPOe traditionally claimed the Ministries of the Interior, Justice, Social Affairs and Transport. The OeVP provided the Chancellor and the SPOe the Vice-Chancellor. The posts of State Secretaries* were decided on the basis of *Proporz* and provided a potentially important element of control. A 'red' State Secretary in a 'black' ministry and vice versa ensured that the coalition incorporated the principle of opposition (*Bereichsopposition*). The administration of each party was open to scrutiny and subject to public criticism by the other. With only the small FPOe to act as an opposition in parliament, the *Bereichsopposition* was a more effective check on government and the abuse of power.

The FPOe, which was excluded from the cartel, naturally objected to what it regarded as a 'red-black dictatorship'. It was concerned not only with political isolation but with discrimination against applicants for jobs who did not possess the correct 'party book'. The FPOe alleges that the 'party book' system has survived the coalition era and downgrades formal qualifications and merit. Despite reservations of this kind, coalition politics provided the SPOe with

---

*The normally accepted translation of the German title. A State Secretary is a political appointment, not a civil servant. They are appointed in the same way as ministers and are assigned to different departments to assist the minister. Not all ministers have state secretaries. They participate in cabinet sessions but are not entitled to vote.

access to positions of power which had been denied to them in the First Republic. This helped to overcome their hostility to the 'bourgeois' state and contributed to its stability at a time when it was particularly vulnerable.

During the period of the Great Coalition, a 'black' Chancellor was continually balanced by the directly-elected 'red' Federal President. A neat division had been constructed reflecting the wishes of the electorate and contributing to an intense politicisation of the economy and the civil service. Both parties seemed happy with this arrangement and in 1959 accused each other of trying to destroy the coalition. There was a reluctance to entrust one party with sole control of the country.[12] The result of the 1959 election demonstrated this.

After 1959 the coalition was more flexible. The parties agreed to discuss some issues outside of the restrictions of the coalition committee with its mutual veto. The equilibrium maintained by the mechanics of the coalition formally ended in 1966, and it would seem that the electorate are no longer afraid to trust one party with the management of political affairs. Since 1971, the SPOe has enjoyed an absolute majority, and voters show little inclination to check this accumulation of power (see chapter 2). Formerly one of the most suspicious polities in Europe, Austria seems now to show overwhelming faith in the competence of one party. A demonstration that single-party cabinets can provide stability, economic success and security has contributed to this apparent change. The underlying needs and demands of the electorate have not changed, and motives for the endorsement of the coalition or a government with an absolute majority show a basic continuity.

Government-opposition dialogue began a little hesitantly in 1966 as both sides learned a new set of rules. This sharpened subsequently, although relationships between the two main parties remain reasonably amicable. The collapse of the parliamentary system did not follow after 1966, and such internal conflicts as do flare up make the headlines for a few weeks and then quietly subside. The coalition era had left its imprint on political life and established mechanisms for the resolution of conflict through discussion. An important legacy was 'social partnership', which relates to a set of informal arrangements prescribing relationships between the main economic interest groups. This controversial system has been attacked, with some justification, for weakening the authority of Parliament, since economic policy is agreed behind closed doors. However, other important legislation—on social policy, education and penal reform—has not been pre-decided in this way, and has constituted a considerable part of the Socialist government's programme since 1970.

More serious perhaps than secrecy and party patronage, which have been by-products of the coalition days, is the development of an excess of stability. One paradoxical danger of the Second Republic has become its complacent stability and reliance on automatic procedures for the resolution of conflict. A toleration of a certain level of conflict contributes to the democracy of a political system and is an indication of its maturity; but the Austrian Republic, having overcome its coalition fixation, clings to the old regulations dating from the time of the coalition, which conveniently provide a way of accommodating different interests without too much disruption. The object of envy for many outside observers, this system has drawbacks which the Austrians themselves privately recognise. Too much stability can equally cause problems for the functioning of a viable democracy in just the same way as chronic instability. The reluctance to challenge the *status quo* can lead to complacency and the lack of imaginative and thorough reforms.[13]

In the modern world with its crises and recession, Austria feels some pride in maintaining full employment and economic prosperity. It likes to think of itself as the 'island of the blessed', and is anxious to avoid a recrudescence of old hostilities. The country has overcome many of its past difficulties and can be classified as one of the more successful states in the post-war Western world. Its consensus is still, to some extent, rooted in fear, and it has not yet progressed far enough to enable comprehensive, large-scale changes to occur. The Socialist Government may feel confident enough in the future to initiate such changes, but in Austrian society there are strong forces operating against the implementation of radical economic policies. The 'social partners' have a vested interest in stability and are not too perturbed if conflict-avoidance becomes a goal in itself.

Economic and social partnership originated in the late 1940s, and was based on agreements between the unions and employers which sought to check wages and prices. From 1947–51, five wage-price agreements were concluded with the participation of the economic interest groups. In the late 1950s, inflation threatened to hinder economic progress, and the trade union leader, Boehm, proposed to the Chancellor, Raab, that a special committee should be established. In 1957, the Parity Commission for Prices and Wages was conceived as a result of a cabinet resolution which sanctioned the Raab-Boehm agreement. Two representatives from each of the four main interest groups, with the Chancellor and the Ministers of Trade, the Interior and Social Affairs, formed the Commission (see

Figure 1.iii). The Minister of the Interior no longer takes part in discussions of the Commission, and he has been replaced by the Minister of Agriculture.[14] Decisions can only be taken unanimously, which has encouraged the acceptance of compromises. The Commission was originally to review every month proposals for price increases and wage demands, but it has evolved into a more important body in the formulation of all economic policy guidelines. Like the coalition committee, this economic counterpart lacked any constitutional basis, and came under attack for its non-accountability. It has been suggested that the powers of the Parity Commission are so great that it can be regarded as a kind of rival government. Since there is considerable overlapping membership between the Commission and Parliament, this is an over-strong criticism: the two in fact work closely together.

The Parity Commission, called by the American Kurt Steiner the 'paracoalition', outlived the Great Coalition and continues to operate today.[15] While the coalition was in existence, it embodied a balance between the parties: the 'black' Chancellor and Minister of Trade confronted the 'red' Ministers of the Interior and Social Affairs, but under the single-party Government all these posts are 'red', which has destroyed the former precise *Proporz*. Equilibrium has been preserved by the economic interest groups, which wield the most decisive powers. The Parity Commission, now self-evidently a permanent institution, was originally intended as a temporary arrangement to meet economic exigencies. It has expanded to incorporate two sub-committees, one for prices and the other for wages, and a third commission was established for economic and social questions, which consults with experts and can make recommendations. This has given the Parity Commission more scope to concentrate on the co-ordination of overall economic strategy.

Social partnership continues to function, although Rudolf Sallinger, the leader of the business interests in the system, recently expressed dissatisfaction with the existing *modus operandi*. He complained that, under the Socialist Government, business and employers' interests have not been adequately represented because of increased difficulty in access to government departments. A good working relationship has developed between Sallinger and the head of the Austrian Trade Union Federation (OeGB), Anton Benya, which means that this publicly expressed discontent is unlikely to be detrimental to Austria's celebrated social partnership. Personal relationships have been an important ingredient in the successful operation of the Parity Commission; it has no power to enforce its decisions on increases in wages and prices, but it has managed to secure the voluntary assent of both sides of industry. The

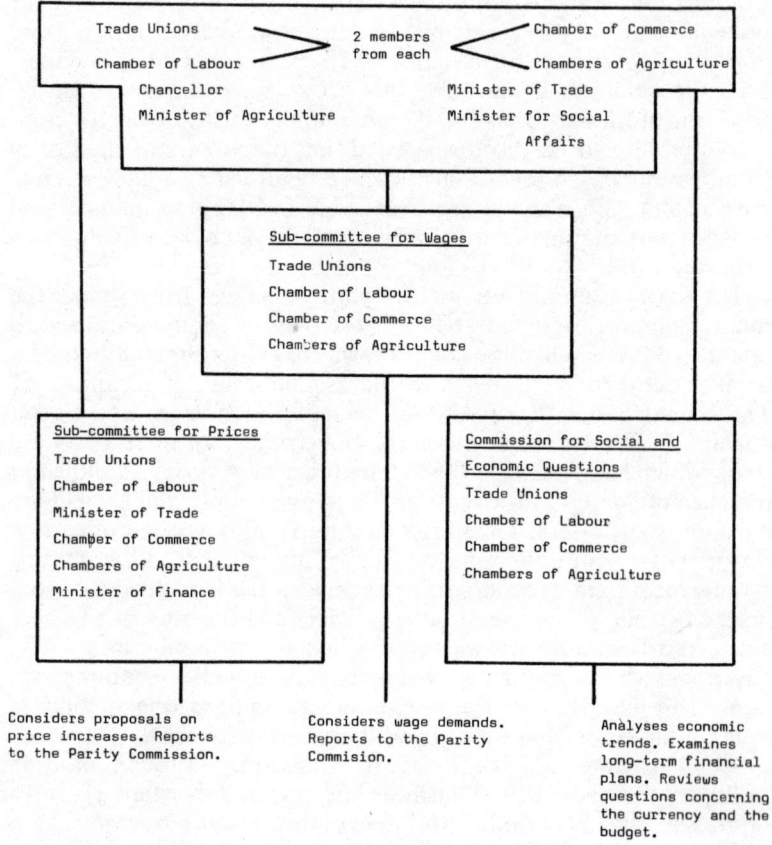

Source: Partizipation und Demokratie, Political Academy, Wien 1974, p. 39.

Fig. 1.iii.   THE PARITY COMMISSION

integration of trade unionists and representatives of labour has given them a sense of responsibility along with their considerable power in the state. They are not inclined to risk the future of this form of collaboration by instigating costly and damaging strikes except as a last resort.

(f) The 'Social Partners'

The economic interest organisations involved in social partnership are the Chamber of Commerce ('black'), the Chambers of Agriculture ('black'), and the Chamber of Labour (AK) ('red'), which have public law status, and the Trade Union Federation (OeGB) ('red'). Membership of the three chambers is compulsory, which is not the case with the trade unions. Other chambers exist for the professions including lawyers, engineers, medical doctors and dentists. As statutory bodies, the three main chambers are empowered to give advice on legislation and have the right of prior consultation. In this capacity they play an important part in the decision-making process, and have direct access to government departments. They are enabled to carry out these tasks efficiently by possessing large research departments engaged in the analysis of data.

The predominance of these institutions has prompted criticism of the growth of a type of corporate state. The strength of the 'para-coalition' cannot be denied, but the system has historical roots which explain this concentration of power and place it in perspective. The parties have traditionally been important at crucial stages in Austrian history. After both world wars they took the initiative in reorganising the state, and subsequently played a dominant part in political activity. This was not regarded as abnormal or undesirable by the legislative and executive élites of the time. The predominance of the main interest groups in the economy was similarly accepted.[16]

At senior level there has always been a close over-lapping membership between the interest groups and the parties. Sallinger, head of the Chamber of Commerce, holds a position of authority in the OeVP, and Benya, the president of the Austrian Trade Union

Table 1.v. PARTY REPRESENTATION IN THE INTEREST GROUPS
(%)

	OeVP	SPOe	FPOe	KPOe
Chamber of Commerce	86	13	–	–
Chambers of Agriculture	84	9	2	–
Chamber of Labour	31	64	3	1
Trade Unions	17	75	–	7

Federation (OeGB), is a prominent Socialist politician. Adolf Czettel, head of the Chamber of Labour, is also a Socialist member of Parliament, and for some years has been a leading trade unionist. This commonly accepted dove-tailing has meant that 'it is by no means easy to determine whether it is the interest groups that speak through the parties or the parties that speak through the interest groups.'[17]

The Chamber of Commerce represents employers in industry, trade, commerce and transport (including the nationalised industries). It comprises nine provincial chambers and a central organisation. Dating from 1848, it is the oldest interest group. It has six sections: commerce; industry; trade; finance, credit and insurance; transport; and tourism. Elections within it take place once every five years on partisan lines. The Chambers of Agriculture exist only at provincial level and represent the interests of those independently employed on the land. (The first was established in Lower Austria in 1922.) A central co-ordinating agency has been set up at Federal level, but without public law status. Elections take place to each of the nine separate provincial Chambers. In addition to these two 'black' Chambers there exists the Federation of Austrian Industrialists, membership of which is voluntary. It does not have any representation on the Parity Commission, although its co-operation is sought on economic and social policy. The Federation operates directly through the medium of the industry section of the Chamber of Commerce—often regarded by the other sections in the Chamber as undue interference.

The Chamber of Labour (AK) was established in 1920 as a body to offset the domination by the Chamber of Commerce. There are nine individual provincial Chambers which are represented at Federal level by an umbrella organisation, the council of the Austrian Chambers of Labour (OeAKT). The Chambers are entrusted with promoting the social, economic, professional and cultural interests of employees, and have a well-qualified staff. Membership fees are deducted automatically and are calculated at a rate of 0.5 per cent of a person's gross earnings. They run special training courses for their members and have excellent facilities for carrying out their educational activities. Agricultural employees are represented in the Chambers of Agriculture. The AK has the same rights as the Chamber of Commerce, and can review and draft legislation and co-operate in its administration. Close links and some duplication of funtions exist between the AK and the OeGB. The AK concentrates on giving legal advice to consumers and employees and leaves wage-bargaining to the OeGB. Elections take place once every five years to the AK (see Table 3.x). Voting occurs in three *curiae*—of workers (manual), employees (non-manual), and transport employees—which together elect 810 Chamber councillors (*Kammerraete*). The Chamber of Labour Act of 1954 regulates the voting procedures. The distribution among the provincial Chambers is as follows:

AK Burgenland, membership 40,000; 40 Chamber councillors.

AK Carinthia, membership 130,000; 70 Chamber councillors.

AK Lower Austria, membership 310,000; 110 Chamber councillors.

AK Upper Austria, membership 330,000; 110 Chamber councillors.

AK Salzburg, membership 120,000; 70 Chamber councillors.

AK Styria, membership 290,000; 110 Chamber councillors.

AK Tyrol, memberhsip 170,000; 70 Chamber councillors.

AK Vorarlberg, membership 100,000; 50 Chamber councillors.

AK Vienna, membership 600,000; 180 Chamber councillors.

Many leading members of the AK also occupy top positions in the fourth main interest group, the Austrian Trade Union Federation (OeGB). This is a highly centralised body, above party, and includes two thirds of the workforce. One of its main tasks is to draw up collective agreements which it can conclude with the Chamber of Commerce. It also plays an important role in organising cultural and educational activities. Different 'fractions' are recognised in the OeGB, the largest of which is the Socialist FSG. The OeGB was formed in 1945 on the principle of industrial unionism, with one exception—the Union of Salaried Clerical, Commercial and Technical Employees. The OeGB consisted of sixteen individual unions until late 1978, when a merger reduced the number to fifteen. Strict financial control reduces the autonomy of these unions, and the OeGB is a wealthy as well as a powerful organisation. The affiliated unions can make their own wage policies but it is the OeGB which has the final say in ratification on all agreements. (A recent detailed study of the OeGB can be found in A. Pelinka, *Gewerkschaften im Parteienstaat*, Duncker and Humblot, Berlin, 1980).

One of the main priorities of the OeGB has been the preservation of full employment. It has met with a sympathetic response from the Socialist government, and in 1979 unemployment was running at 2 per cent. To avoid lay-offs, the government has provided large subsidies to the nationalised industries, which account for one-sixth of the industrial labour force. They include the iron and steel industry, heavy engineering and shipbuilding, large sections of the metallurgical industry, fuel, chemicals and electronics. The number of foreign workers has been reduced to 6 per cent, and the working

Table 1.vi. MEMBERSHIP OF THE UNIONS IN THE OeGB
end of 1978

Union of Salaried Clerical, Commerical and Technical Employees	321,122
Public Service Employees' Union	183,249
Municipal Employees' Union	155,507
Union of Personnel in Arts, Media and Free Professions	15,641
Construction and Wood Workers' Union	197,485
Chemical Workers' Union	65,446
Railwaymen's Union	117,759
Printing and Allied Trades' Union	24,201
Commerce, Transport and Traffic Workers' Union	33,352
Union of Hotel Workers and Domestic Services	43,139
Agricultural and Forestry Workers' Union	22,005
Food, Beverage and Tobacco Workers' Union	45,953
Metal, Mining and Energy Workers' Union	269,610
Textile, Garment and Leather Workers' Union	66,059
Post and Telegraph Services Employees' Union	68,275
OeGB, *total*	1,628,803

week is legally fixed at a maximum of forty hours. Proposals are being discussed for a further reduction of working week and an increase in holidays as a way of maintaining full employment.

With an inflation rate of 3.6 per cent in 1979, economic and social partnership would seem to have provided Austria with the *Lebensfaehigkeit* lacking in the First Republic. In the transition from coalition to single-party governments, the Parity Commission helped to provide an element of continuity. Economic problems do exist and the country has large external and budget deficits. It is clear that Austria cannot remain immune from international trends and is greatly influenced by the West German economy, since the Federal Republic accounts for over 43 per cent of her imports and 29 per cent of her exports. However unpopular measures to restrain domestic demand and keep the Austrian economy buoyant are expected to be negotiated peacefully within the apparatus of 'social partnership'.

(g) Foreign Policy

Over Austria's role in international affairs there is a basic consensus between the two main parties. One of the coalition's major achievements was the restoration of the country's sovereignty, guranteed by the State Treaty of 1955. With the end of the occupation, both parties voted in Parliament for a policy of permanent neutrality. A Federal Constitutional Law of 26 October 1955 stated:

(1) For the purpose of the permanent maintenance of her external independence and for the purpose of the inviolability of her territory, Austria of her own free will declares herewith her permanent neutrality which she is resolved to maintain and defend with all the means at her disposal.

(2) In order to secure these purposes Austria will never in the future accede to any military alliance nor permit the establishment of military bases of foreign states on her territory.[18]

The VdU, the predecessor of the FPOe, did not support this law, regarding it as too restrictive. The choice in 1965, of 26 October as a 'national' holiday provoked further opposition from the FPOe, which believes the Austrian 'nation' to be a figment of the imagination. The withdrawal of the occupation was received enthusiastically by the population, and Chancellor Raab and the Great Coalition gained much of the credit. The occupation itself had been an important element in keeping the coalition partners together in an effort to avoid the 'German example'. In 1955, the SPOe and the OeVP could feel well satisfied with the acknowledgement of a free and independent Austria, even though negotiations had been far from smooth.

Austria claimed that in 1938 she had been a victim of German aggression. The Moscow Declaration of 1943, issued by the governments of the United States, Great Britain and the Soviet Union, sympathised with this view and embodied the idea of a restoration of Austria's independence:

Austria, the first free country to fall a victim to Hitlerite aggression, shall be liberated from German domination.

The powers regard the annexation imposed on Austria by Germany on March 15, 1938 as null and void. They consider themselves as in no way bound by any changes effected in Austria since that date. They declare that they wish to see re-established a free and independent Austria and thereby to open the way for the Austrian people themselves as well as those neighbouring states which will be faced with similar problems, to find that political and economic security which is the only basis of lasting peace.

Austria is reminded, however, that she has a responsibility, which she cannot evade, for participation in the war at the side of Hitlerite Germany, and that in the final settlement account will inevitably be taken of her own contribution to her liberation.[19]

The statement that Austria could not evade all responsibility for participating in a war on Hitler's side, and that 'in the final settlement, account will inevitably be taken of her own contribution to her liberation', gave renewed hope and impetus to the Resistance Movement in Austria. The Austrian question was not quickly settled following the end of the war, but became entangled in issues of the Cold War. One of the main disputes surrounded interpretations of 'German assets', which the Allies could claim under the terms of the Potsdam conference. The Soviet Union had a less definite notion of the idea of 'German assets' than the Western Allies, and was not prepared to make many concessions. One of Austria's most important oil fields was in the Soviet zone, and nationalisation was not successful in removing Soviet control over this vital asset.

Following Stalin's death there was a revision of Soviet foreign policy, and this included the Austrian question. Four-power talks on a State Treaty, which had reached deadlock in 1950, were re-opened. The Foreign Minister, Leopold Figl, pledged that Austria would not join any military alliance, thus partly fulfilling Soviet demands. At the beginning of 1955, the Soviet Union unexpectedly changed its policy of objecting to the signing of a State Treaty, and abandoned its earlier insistence on linking it with the German question. A delegation from the Austrian Government went to Moscow to pursue discussions on the exact status the country would acquire and on German assets. The Chancellor, Julius Raab, was accompanied by the Vice-Chancellor Adolf Schaerf, the Foreign Minister Figl, and the latter's State Secretary Bruno Kreisky. They were forced to make substantial economic concessions, including deliveries of oil and the surrender of the right of oil exploration to the Soviet Union. Payments were completed by the end of 1963 and Austria regained former German assets administered by the Soviet Union for the past ten years. These included the major industrial plants in Lower Austria, oil fields and oil installations, and the assets of the Danube Shipping Company. The State Treaty contained no specific reference to neutrality, and the Western powers were suspicious of the Soviet Union's motives in supporting the idea. While the Treaty endorsed Austria's freedom, independence and territorial integrity, the declaration on neutrality was made separately by the Austrian Parliament in the form of a Constitutional Law. The Austrians were asked by the Soviet Union to proceed with the presentation to Parliament of this law on neutrality, which was to be based on the Swiss model. The State Treaty which restored Austria's sovereignty was signed on 15 May 1955 by Figl and the Foreign Ministers of the four occupying powers, five months before the adoption of this law.

The diplomatic somersault performed by the Soviet Union was not so irrational as it may seem. Austrians had never been ardent supporters of Communism, and the country was lost to the Soviet

Union at the latest by 1950 with the failure of a general strike. One Soviet priority was to prevent the integration of Austria into the political and economic alliances of Western capitalism; neutrality provided a means of halting developments emanating from West Germany, which threatened to absorb Austria. The stategic, military and economic importance of Austria to the Soviets had disappeared by 1955. The withdrawal of the Soviet forces could be cited as evidence of its goodwill and readiness for détente. Very little seemed at stake in Austria compared with East Germany, as is succinctly explained by W. B. Bader:

Eastern Austria was never more than a territorial enclave—moreover, an enclave that could not be organised into an economic and political entity. Austria was also of scant strategic value to the Soviet Union, particularly after 1948. Thus, the Soviet Union—and the Western powers for that matter —could afford to disengage in Austria. East Germany, on the other hand, is a viable political and economic unit and remains an area of the highest strategic concern to the Soviet Union—not only because of East Germany's size and position, but because a united Germany, unlike a unified Austria, could become an acute threat to Soviet security.[20]

The policy pursued by the Austrians has been one of 'active neutrality'. In December 1955, the country became a member of the United Nations, which suggested a less rigid interpretation of neutrality than that practised by Switzerland.[21] In August 1979, Vienna became the third centre of the United Nations Organisation, and in 1972 a former Austrian Foreign Minister, Kurt Waldheim, became Secretary General of the United Nations. During the Hungarian uprising in 1956, the Austrians showed that they were determined not to accept ideological neutrality, and gave all possible assistance to the refugees.[22] Austria became a member of the Council of Europe in 1956, which involved giving assent to the European Convention for the Protection of Human Rights and Fundamental Freedoms.

The ambiguous nature of Austrian neutrality complicated further integration of the country with Western Europe. Membership of the European Economic Community was considered incompatible with neutrality, an assumption which the FPOe has questioned. The FPOe is in favour of sending observers to the European Parliament, but in this it has not received the backing of the Socialist Government. The SPOe was always more inclined to support the European Free Trade Association (EFTA) rather than the EEC; on the other hand, the OeVP sympathised more with the idea of a Christian-Democratic Common Market than with a free trade association including Social Democratic countries.

As a member of EFTA, Austria sought arrangements of various kinds with the EEC, which would ease the discrimination caused by community tariffs and take account of the requirements of neutrality and the State Treaty. Article 4 of the State Treaty prohibited any political or economic union between Austria and Germany, and declared that 'Austria fully recognises its responsibilities in this matter and shall not enter into political or economic union with Germany in any form whatsoever'. Austria needed to ensure freedom of action in trade relations with third countries, usually understood to mean Eastern Europe and the Soviet Union. In the event of armed conflict, Austria had to reserve the right to suspend any agreement with the EEC. Discussions with the EEC met with reservations from member-countries, particularly Italy, and the hostility of the Soviet Union. Free trade agreements with the EEC were finally settled in July 1972, providing for the abolition of customs and trade barriers in commercial and industrial goods. The course of negotiations with the Community had been influenced by different conceptions of Europeanism between and within the two main parties. The economic pressures which forced Austria to seek some concessions were not in dispute, and the underlying consensus was not significantly disturbed. The European question occupied a peripheral position in the relations between the SPOe and OeVP and had only a minor influence on domestic politics.[23]

Strong feelings on the European question have been evident in the two small parties, the FPOe and the KPOe. While the Communists categorically reject the capitalist-oriented EEC, the FPOe supports it as a means of containing Communism and linking Austria more closely with Germany. A survey of 1965 found party preferences expressed as shown in Table 1.vii.

General agreement has existed between the two main parties on

Table 1.vii. ATTITUDES OF THE PARTIES TO EUROPE (%)

Respondents affirming that Austria should:	FPOe	KPOe	OeVP	SPOe
Stay in EFTA	9	42	15	14
Switch to the EEC	37	4	16	9
Aim for membership in both	26	7	22	18
Take a decision depending on terms laid down by the EEC	13	15	20	19
Undecided	15	32	27	40

Source: R. Staeuber, *Der Verband der Unabhaengigen (VdU) und die Freiheitliche Partei Oesterreichs (FPOe)*, OK Organisation Kolb, St. Gallen, 1974 p.204.

the defence of the German-speaking minority in South Tyrol. Austria renewed territorial claims to South Tyrol, which it had lost to Italy after the First World War, but these demands met with no response from the Allies. An agreement between Italy and Austria in 1946 asssured the German-speaking inhabitants of the area equality of rights with the Italian-speaking population. This included the right to education in their native language, dual-language signposts and equality of status for official purposes between the German and Italian languages. The subsequent application of this agreement did not satisfy the Austrian Government: the granting of autonomous legislative and executive regional power, which it allowed for, had not been fulfilled. The Austrians referred the matter to the United Nations and in 1959 the Foreign Minister, Bruno Kreisky, addressed the General Assembly. This provided a framework for the resumption of negotiations between the two countries. The result was a package, finally agreed on in 1969, which envisaged the gradual implementation of contentious points. This was acceptable to both sides, and relations between Italy and Austria have improved.

The FPOe has been the most forceful supporter of 'German' interests in South Tyrol, and an opinion poll of 1967 found that 65 per cent of the party's adherents considered the problem 'very important' compared with 40 per cent in the OeVP, 37 per cent in the SPOe and 21 per cent in the KPOe.[24] The FPOe could not accept the final package deal worked out between Austria and Italy, which it considered inadequate in safeguarding the position of the country's 'German brothers'. The South Tyrol dispute aroused more interest in Western Austria where the OeVP had its main strength; the party could not afford to ignore the treatment of the German-speaking minority over the border. The Socialists also did not want to give an impression of nonchalance, since they were trying to extend their influence in the western provinces. Although the SPOe believed that the final package had been agreed too hastily without sufficient international guarantees, there was no major question of principle at stake to divide it from the OeVP.

As Chancellor, Kreisky has continued to show a keen interest in foreign affairs. He takes a realistic view of détente, welcoming its advantages but steering clear of illusions. He refused to react violently to the Soviet invasion of Afghanistan, and has retained some hope that détente will be resumed. Austria's vulnerable position in Central Europe has caused most politicians to pursue friendly relations with the European Communist countries. Economic, scientific and technical links with the Soviet Union, as well as agreements on deliveries of natural gas, have became more important for Austria. The 'Polish connection' has developed into a promising means of alleviating energy problems. Austria imports 2.4 billion cubic metres of natural gas from the Soviet Union each year and has concluded a contract with Poland on the supply of electricity via Czechoslovakia. Plans exist for large imports of coal from Poland. The essential feature of Kreisky's foreign policy concerns is their economic foundation, and he remains an intransigent opponent of Communism. On the Middle East the Chancellor's statements have frequently provoked the wrath of Israel. In a speech to the United Nations General Assembly in October 1979, he re-affirmed his support for recognition of the Palestine Liberation Organisation. The OeVP has objected to Kreisky's personalised style on foreign affairs and believes it to represent a break with the collaboration established during the coalition era. He has irritated the opposition by neglecting to ask its advice before making major policy statements.

The idea of the Austrian Chancellor as a mediator in international affairs evokes pride in the population—and occasionally cynical amusement from the press. Kreisky is associated by many with a new Austria firmly established on a sound economic basis and respected in diplomatic circles. Foreign affairs fail to arouse much debate in Austria unless the security and stability of the country are threatened. In the election campaign of 1979 Kreisky was photographed as a great statesman beneath a portrait of the Emperor Franz Josef (he is affectionately nicknamed 'Kaiser Bruno'), and it did not seem incongruous that the leader of the Socialists should be depicted in this role. The SPOe has managed to overcome its former aversion to the imperial past, while at the same time settling comfortably into the economic and political system of the Austrian Second Republic.

REFERENCES

1. Otto Bauer, *The Austrian Revolution*, Leonard Parsons, London, 1925, p.125.
2. *Ibid.*, p.161.
3. A. Diamant, 'The Group Basis of Austrian Politics', *Journal of Central European Affairs*, July, 1958, p.137. The theory and analysis of the *Lager* comes from A. Wandruszka, 'Oesterreichs politische Struktur', in H. Benedikt, *Geschichte der Republik Oesterreich*, Verlag fuer Geschichte und Politik, Wien, 1954, pp.289–487.
4. See P. Pulzer, 'Austria', in S. Henig and J. Pinder (ed.), *European Political Parties,* PEP, London, 1969, pp.282–320.
5. R. Staeuber, *Der Verband der Unabhaengigen (VdU) und die Freiheitliche Partei Oesterreichs (FPOe)*, Organisation Kolb, St. Gallen, 1974, p.50.
6. *Ibid.*, p.51.

7.   *The Austrian Federal Constitution*, Manzsche Verlags- und Universitaetsbuchhandlung, Wien, 1972, p.35.
8.   See K. Steiner, *Politics in Austria*, Little, Brown and Co., Boston, 1972, p.288.
9.   Population figures for the individual cities are taken from *Austria*, Federal Press Service, Vienna, 1977.
10. H. Fischer(ed.), *Das politische System Oesterreichs*, Europaverlag, Wien, 1977, p.337.
11. U. Kitzinger, 'The Austrian Election of 1959', *Political studies*, vol. ix, no.2, 1961, p.123. The points of the coalition pacts are stated in O. Kirchheimer, 'The Waning of Opposition in Parliamentary Regimes', *Social Research*, vol.xxiv, Summer 1957, pp.137–8.
12. See U. Kitzinger, *op.cit.*, p.125.
13. See K. Steiner, *op.cit.*, p.424.
14. For a general discussion of the principles and workings of 'social partnership' see T. Lachs, *Wirtschaftspartnerschaft in Oesterreich,* Verlag des OeGB, Wien, 1976.
15. K. Steiner, *op.cit.*, pp.311–18.
16. H.P.Secher, 'Representative Democracy or "Chamber State": The Ambiguous Role of Interest Groups in Austrian Politics', *Western Political Quarterly*, vol. xiii, 1960, p.907.
17. P. Pulzer, *op.cit.*, p.308.
18. *The Austrian Federal Constitution, op. cit.*, p.130.
19. *U.S. Foreign Relations*, 1945, vol. III, Washington D.C., 1968, p.40.
20. W.B.Bader, *Austria between East and West 1945–1955*, Stanford University Press, 1966, p.208.
21. E. Barker, *Austria 1918–1972*, Macmillan, London, 1973, p. 196.
22. K.R. Stadler, *Austria*, Ernest Benn, London, 1971, p.311.
23. See P.J. Katzenstein, 'Trends and Oscillations in Austrian Integration Policy since 1955 : Alternative Explanations', *Journal of Common Market Studies*, December 1975, p.195.
24. R. Staeuber, *op.cit.*, p.225.

2

THE SOCIALIST PARTY

(a) Historical Background

The present Socialist Party of Austria (SPOe) was founded in April 1945, but the origins of the workers' movement in the country date from the nineteenth century when a Social Democratic party was formed. The latter continued its existence until the civil war of 1934, when it suffered a heavy defeat, and it was forced to spend the next eleven years in illegal activity with varying degrees of success. The 'new' party founded in 1945 stressed that it was the heir of this earlier movement, whose development had been brutally curtailed by Austro-Fascism. Among the most striking features of the entire history of Social Democracy in Austria are its unity and its discipline. Its strength is striking too, since today the SPOe dominates the political life of the country, and in three successive elections— those of 1971, 1975 and 1979—has won over 50 per cent of the vote. Its members view the next election, due in 1983, with undisguised optimism.

In the Austrian-Hungarian monarchy the labour movement was slow to develop, as a result of government oppression, retarded industrialisation and fractional rivalries. An early leader, Heinrich Oberwinder, was associated with a group known as the Moderates, which had as its aim the introduction of universal suffrage, social security measures and increased protection for workers. This group was prepared to work within the existing system, and if necessary to co-operate with the liberal bourgeoisie. The Moderates were opposed by the Radicals, who were closer to the revolutionary ideas of Marx and Engels, and were more prepared to support revolutionary activities to achieve their aims.

Victor Adler, a young middle-class doctor of Jewish origin, appealed to both sides to form a united mass party. A 'Unity' conference in Hainfeld, Lower Austria, in 1888−9 was the culmination of his efforts, and the Social Democratic Workers' Party (SDAP) then officially came into existence. Agreement had been reached by means of compromises, which were reflected in the content of the party's programme. Of particular significance was the new party's attitude to Parliament, which was simultaneously condemned, on the one hand, as an instrument of class domination and, on the other, regarded in a postive light as one of the most important

38

forums for agitation and organisational activity. From this period originated two distinctive features of Austro-Marxism which, to some extent, are still in evidence: first a belief that unity was sacred and to be maintained at any price, and secondly, ambiguous references to vital contemporary questions which in the nineteenth century pertained to the nature of the state and the role of parliamentary work.

In practice the Austro-Marxists pursued reformist aims while keeping their formal commitment to a radical programme. The SDAP became steadily integrated into the system, and before the First World War its intellectuals had attempted to devise schemes for the preservation of the decaying Habsburg structure. A publication of the SPOe, *Das grosse Erbe*, proudly summarised the lack of revolutionary zeal of its early theoreticians: 'They did not want the house in which they lived to be destroyed, but wanted it made more habitable for all its occupants.' The Austrian Socialists have always stressed their sense of responsibility and their desire to avoid any dangerous experiments which could result in a reversal of the progress they considered they were making in raising living standards. At the turn of the century, the movement included 540,000 trade unionists and 150,000 party members,[1] and felt strong enough to press for modest social and political reforms.

The outbreak of the First World War was followed by years of uncertainty for the party, and many of its members were uneasy about the enthusiam for the war that had been evident in the party's press. A left opposition group was formed which agitated against the continuation of the war, but was careful not to put the unity of the party in jeopardy. The Social Democrats survived this crisis with their organisation intact, and emerged in the first election of the new Republic in February 1919 as the largest party, with over 40 per cent of the vote. This led to a coalition government with the Christian Social Party which lasted only until 1920. During this time the Social Democrats were able to push through considerable social welfare legislation, but refrained from an open onslaught on the bastions of capitalism. Otto Bauer, the intellectual leader of the party in the inter-war period, considered this justifiable in the light of Austria's weak position in Central Europe. Throughout the 1920s, the SDAP seemed to be paralysed by its painful awareness of the difficulties of successfully implementing a Socialist revolution. Any despair that could have crept in as a result of this analysis was avoided by an unshakeable belief in the invincibility of the movement and the ultimate victory of Socialism.

After the end of the coalition government in 1920, the SDAP was confined to the ranks of the Opposition at national level but remained unassailable in the capital, 'Red Vienna', where it had a two-thirds majority. There the party worked energetically to construct flats, hospitals, parks, sports centres and a modern educational system. Vienna became a symbol of progress and represented the first step towards a socialist society. In its darkest hour, the city was to provide the party with a glimmer of hope:

When Fascism was already on the march throughout Europe and threatening the world with the prospect or war, when the revolution in Russia had degenerated into a bloody tyranny, it was 'Red Vienna' that showed a third and humane way. It was a hope for millions.[2]

One essential aspect of Austro-Marxism was its stress on the need to create a better and a more humane society. Its vision was to transform the lives of workers by providing them with a sense of cultural and intellectual awareness. The party's reformism was one way of helping to fulfil this noble ideal. Also inherent in Austro-Marxism was a need to contemplate a revolutionary implementation of its aims which never developed much further than a theoretical debate. The Social Democrats have tended to regard these two elements as complementary, yet the result of their interaction would seem to have been to produce an obscure and often contradictory position.

The Linz programme, adopted in 1926, illustrates this weakness of Austro-Marxism. One of its sections appealed to the different groups in society, in an effort to win further electoral support. The SDAP believed that it would soon acquire over 50 per cent of the votes and thus possess the necessary democratic legitimisation for the implementation of Socialism. Another section continued to countenance contingency plans in the event of a reactionary attempt to unseat the Socialists. The weapon to be used *if* this occurred was a 'dictatorship', a nebulous and ill-chosen word. The inclusion of this concept conspicuously contradicted the party's professed desire for democracy. It gave credence to the propaganda of the bourgeoisie that the SDAP was a Bolshevist party bent on a revolutionary overthrow of the existing system. It further served to mislead the party's own members by nurturing a belief that it was prepared for militant action. This proved to be an illusion, and at every crisis in the turbulent years of the dying Republic the party desperately sought a peaceful solution in vain. Its eventual, half-hearted participation in the civil war of 1934 came too late to repel Fascism. The confidence in the inevitability of Socialism was rudely shattered by this defeat and by the elimination from open political life of a party which, in 1930, had won more than 40 per cent of the vote.

A reappraisal of the party's strategy took place in the ensuing years of underground work. Of prime concern was the preservation, even if in a diminished form, of its organisation and above all its unity. Links persisted with Otto Bauer and the 'old' party, both at a financial and an emotional level, despite criticisms of the disastrous policies which had led to defeat. The decision by a minority to call themselves 'Revolutionary Socialists' (RS) signified some dissatisfaction with the former leadership and denoted a realisation that, outlawed and in opposition to a Fascist state, an underground party could be nothing else but 'revolutionary'. With the Nazi seizure of the country, many of the RS were arrested or managed to escape abroad. Organisational activities during the war were isolated and unco-ordinated. When the war ended no one was really sure what sort of party would emerge as the successor to the SDAP and the RS. There was also uncertainty about how strong a revived Social Democratic Party would be in the new constellation of political forces. Some feared that the Communists had gained ground during the years of illegality, but the Social Democrats were quickly able to show a remarkable stability in their support.

(b) The Second Republic

The party, which was established in 1945, attempted to embrace both of its predecessors and adopted the clumsy name of 'Socialist Party of Austria (Social Democrats and Revolutionary Socialists)'. It was not long before the words in parentheses were dropped and the more manageable 'Socialist Party of Austria' (SPOe) came to be generally used. The influence of the Revolutionary Socialists on the new party was small, and the tendency was to concentrate on the achievements of the 'old' or legal party that had existed before 1934. Many of those who had been active in the illegal RS chose not to return to Austria, and others who had left were not welcomed back by the new party. 'In the first message, sent from liberated Vienna by the leaders of the reborn Austrian Socialist Party, to their comrades living abroad as refugees (most of them Jews) it was bluntly stated that the return of Jews to Austria in great numbers would be viewed with a certain apprehension.'[3]

Bauer had died in 1938, and the leadership of the SPOe therefore fell in 1945 to those who had managed to live in Austria during the Nazi regime among them Karl Renner (1870–1950), one of Bauer's former opponents. The new men were largely influenced by the right wing of the SDAP and the ideas of Renner. They were less interested in theorising and more concerned with the administration of the new Republic. As the Cold War developed, they became even less tolerant of left-wing ideas and of 'dangerous' flirtations with Communism. One of the Renner's principle altercations with Bauer had centred around Bauer's uncompromising oppositional policy. After the War this was abandoned and the party became a willing convert to coalition politics.

The reconstruction of the SPOe proceeded under the guidance of Renner and Adolf Schaerf, who was to be the party's chairman until 1957. The first major trial for the new organisation came with the election in November 1945, which demonstrated that, far from losing ground, the Socialists had improved on their pre-war position. The only region where the SPOe failed to make any progress was in Vienna.

Table 2.i ELECTORAL POSITION OF THE SOCIAL DEMOCRATS/ SOCIALISTS (%)

	1930	1945
Vienna	59	57
Lower Austria	36	40
Upper Austria	28	38
Salzburg	30	39
Tyrol	22	27
Vorarlberg	21	28
Styria	34	42
Carinthia	39	49
Burgenland	38	45
Austria	41	45

Source: Die Zukunft, September 1948.

The gravity of the economic situation, the four-power occupation and a desire to avoid the mistakes of the past facilitated greater understanding between the SPOe and its political opponents. The coalition that was formed after the 1945 election was based on this and a new, positive attitude of the Socialists towards the state. The party saw that its foremost duties were to co-operate in the national restoration programme and to work for a free and independent Austria. In 1947 it drew up an Action Programme which outlined its main tasks as follows. A planned economy and an extension of nationalisation were included to promote stability and help modernise industry. To achieve its aims, the SPOe appealed to all sections of the working population, in agricultural as well as urban areas. Under the leadership of Schaerf, the party was determined to extend its influence beyond Vienna to the Catholic and rural provinces. It was clear that the capital was already becoming less important for the party. Whereas in 1932 Vienna had accounted for

61.76 per cent of the total membership, in 1946 this had declined to 39.52 per cent. In the 1947 programme the SPOe described itself categorically as a democratic party and, in contrast to the 1926 Linz programme, rejected dictatorship in any form.[4]

Gradually the SPOe revived the old associations of the pre-war party, one notable exception being the SDAP's disciplined paramilitary organisation, the *Schutzbund* (Republican Defence Corps), which had been involved in frequent clashes with the fascist groups of the period. Of concern to the SPOe was to be the high average age of party members; its youth organisation was slow to get on its feet again. Figures for Vienna show that the proportion of members under thirty had declined from 30.1 per cent in 1929 to 14.5 per cent in 1947. Frequent complaints were made in the SPOe's theoretical journal *Die Zukunft* that the young members whom the party had managed to enrol were politically apathetic. Throughout the years of coalition, both the adult party and its youth section avoided a grand ideological debate which could have resurrected old conflicts, and concentrated instead on winning power in the existing state.

(c) Electoral Support

The SPOe has been in power since 1970, and since 1971 it has possessed an absolute majority. Throughout the years of the Second Republic a clear trend favouring the Socialists has been discernible (see Figure 2.i) The slump in its support in the election of 1949 can be attributed partly to the appearance on the scene of a third party which had not been allowed to contest the first post-war election. In 1953 and 1959, the SPOe actually gained more votes than the People's Party, although this was not reflected in the distribution of seats in the *Nationalrat*. The exception to this trend is the election of 1966, which found the SPOe in the midst of an internal crisis and burdened with support from the Communists; to some extent that campaign was lost by the SPOe rather than representing an electoral victory for the OeVP. The SPOe quickly recovered, and increased its share of the vote at every election in the 1970s.

The election of 6 May 1979 gave the Socialists the greatest victory in their history. They won 51.03 per cent of the vote and gained two extra seats in the *Nationalrat*, giving them 95 seats out of a total of 183. Such a result had not been expected by the political pundits, nor even dreamed of by many party workers. Surveys published by the Institute for Empirical Social Research (IFES) show that when the Socialist Government decided on an election in January 1979 only 47.0 per cent would have voted for the SPOe. Six weeks before the election, 50.0 per cent declared that they would vote for the

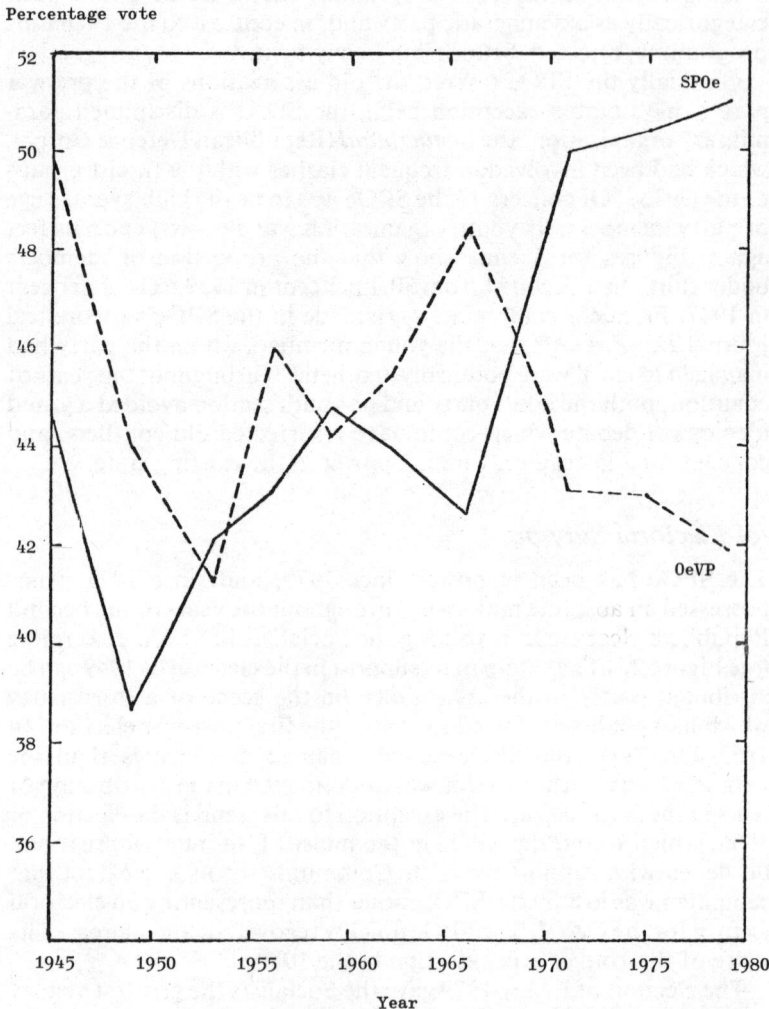

Percentage vote

Fig. 2.i.   ELECTORAL SUPPORT FOR THE TWO MAIN
PARTIES SINCE 1945

Table 2.ii. CHANGES IN ELECTORAL SUPPORT (%)

Changes between	OeVP	SPOe
1966 and 1970	− 3.66	+ 5.86
1970 and 1971	− 1.58	+ 1.62
1971 and 1975	− 0.16	+ 0.38
1975 and 1979	− 1.05	+ 0.61

Government, thus assuring it of a continuation in office without the need to form a coalition. Six months after the election a poll indicated that the SPOe would win 53 per cent of the votes if another election were to be held.

The Chancellor, Bruno Kreisky, consistently enjoyed immense popularity and was preferred by 57 per cent of voters, compared with only 23 per cent who favoured the OeVP leader, Dr. Josef Taus. An IFES survey, carried out immediately after the election, revealed that 23 per cent attributed the SPOe's victory to its policies while 60 per cent put it down to the personality of Kreisky.

Most voters accepted the SPOe's claim that, under the Socialists, they 'had never had it so good'. The 'Austrian Way' was an effective slogan of the SPOe, which was regarded by its managers as being sufficiently vague and yet at the same time capable of evoking a positive response from all sections of the community. This slogan was associated with full employment, social welfare, progressive reforms and stability. The SPOe reinforced its identification with Austria by adopting as its election colours the red-white-red of the country's flag.[5]

The themes of the party's campaigns in the 1970s have been modernity, security and a promise to provide a good future. 'No experiments' and 'safety first' would aptly describe the tone of the SPOe's message. This emphasis, together with the party's concern for the family welfare, has contributed to its popularity with women, who make up over 54 per cent of the electorate. The party is careful not to frighten the owners of small and medium-sized firms, and concentrates on guaranteeing the viability of such enterprises. It is anxious too to reassure the agricultural population that Socialists pose no threat to their existence or their property. On the contrary, the SPOe asserts that these sections of the community can benefit from the creation of the just, humane society which is its chief priority. Ideology was used by the SPOe in a negative way to detract from the campaign of the two opposition parties which, according to the SPOe, would have implemented conservative and retrogressive policies if allowed to assume control. This prospect seems to have been effective in convincing young voters particularly that the SPOe was the better party to vote for. Research on the election shows that the Socialists commanded an absolute majority (53 per cent) of those voting for the first time. They had not been able to achieve this in the election of 1975.

The SPOe continues to be successful among 'floating voters', especially salaried employees and civil servants (see Table 2.vii). It is estimated that between 5 and 6 per cent of the electorate are 'liberal' voters, who have been providing the SPOe with its absolute majority in recent years. These voters have no easily identifiable political home in Austria, and thus can be expected to switch readily from one party to another. They tend to be 'Kreisky' voters, and have come to support the party because of the non-doctrinaire image of the Chancellor. The percentage of voters who changed party allegiance in 1979 was relatively low (3.81 per cent compared with 9.85 per cent in 1970, which was high by Austrian standards). The main shift in votes occurred between the two biggest parties and from the OeVP to the FPOe (see Table 2.iii).

Since 1971, the *Genosse Trend* has been particularly noticeable in small agricultural communities formerly regarded as safe OeVP constituencies. These are predominantly Catholic areas, which indicates that the Socialists have been successful in living down their traditional anti-clerical image. Structural changes in rural communities have meant that an increasing number of small farmers have sought additional employment in industrial areas. Possibly their contact with workers from a predominantly Socialist milieu has brought about a radicalisation in political consciousness.

The gains for the SPOe in the election of 1979 came in fairly similar proportions from all parts of Austria, with the exception of Vorarlberg where its vote fell by 2.5 per cent. In this province, there is a feeling, as we have already noted, that the government in Vienna is too far away fully to understand local issues. There is also a special

Table 2.iii. ELECTORAL MOBILITY IN 1979 (IN THOUSANDS)

Voters transferring to the	Voters transferring from the				
	SPOe	*OeVP*	*FPOe*	*KPOe*	*Total*
SPOe	–	78	10	4	92
OeVP	55	–	2	–	57
FPOe	9	22	–	–	31
KPOe	–	–	–	–	0
Total	64	100	12	4	180

Source: K. Blecha, *Die Nationalratswahl 1979*, Wien, 1979, p.34.

Table 2.iv. THE TREND TO THE SPOe (%)

Type of Community	SPOe 1971–5	SPOe 1975–9
Small	+ 0.9	+ 1.3
Medium-sized	+ 0.4	+ 0.9
Agricultural	+ 1.3	+ 1.8
Industrial	+ 0.6	+ 0.4
Mixed	+ 0.2	+ 0.7
Strong SPOe majority	+ 0.6	+ 0.7
Strong OeVP majority	+ 0.9	+ 1.4
No specific majority	+ 0.2	+ 0.4

Source: K. Blecha, *op. cit.*, p.35.

concern in this region that the Government should show more determination than it has done in opposing the nuclear power programme in Austria. Elsewhere the SPOe could feel satisfied with its performance—particularly in the provinces where it had been weak before the war. From the OeVP it gained one seat directly in Upper Austria and another under the second stage of the distribution of votes, and missed by the narrow margin of 403 votes a third seat in Vienna.

The SPOe now has over 50 per cent of the vote in five *Laender*, and in two others (Salzburg and Lower Austria) its share is slightly higher than that of the OeVP. Socialist gains mean that the OeVP has over 50 per cent of the vote in only two provinces (Tyrol and Vorarlberg). The overall strength of the SPOe contrasts with the party's previous reliance on Vienna (see Table 2.vi). The capital provided the party with 25.3 per cent of its total votes in 1979 compared with 35.4 per cent in 1945 and 46.4 per cent in 1930.

Table 2.v. THE SPOe IN THE ELECTION OF 1979 (%)

	1975	1979	Gain or loss
Burgenland	51.76	52.95	+ 1.19
Lower Austria	47.98	48.41	+ 0.43
Vienna	59.84	60.61	+ 0.77
Carinthia	54.75	56.23	+ 1.48
Upper Austria	48.75	50.25	+ 1.50
Salzburg	44.41	44.93	+ 0.52
Styria	50.27	51.37	+ 1.10
Tyrol	37.20	37.68	+ 0.48
Vorarlberg	35.92	33.42	– 2.50
Austria	50.42	51.03	+ 0.61

This trend has been apparent in *Landtag* elections. The party provides the provincial governor in Carinthia and, since 1964, in Burgenland, as well as the Mayor of Vienna. However, in the Viennese municipal election in October 1978, around 100,000 Socialist voters abstained and the SPOe lost four seats and 3 per cent of the votes to the OeVP. This was a severe blow to morale and can be interpreted as an indication of discontent particularly with the party's policies on transport and environmental affairs. The OeVP in Vienna has been attempting to mobilise voters on these issues and is trying to become identified with the 'alternative-green' movement. The results in the general election suggest that these voters will either abstain as a protest or turn out for the SPOe. Despite some signs of criticism, the lead of the SPOe is indisputable and Vienna is still consistently its strongest area of support (see Fig 2.ii).

The Socialists are entrenched in the Chamber of Labour, and at the Chamber's elections held in 1979 they won 64.3 per cent of the votes and an extra three seats, which gave them 534 out of a possible 810. The Socialist fraction was able to improve its position in all the provinces with the exception of Tyrol (−0.4 per cent), Lower Austria (−0.6 per cent) and Vorarlberg, where its losses were relatively high (−7.5 per cent). Vorarlberg is the only province where the Chamber of Labour does not have a Socialist for its president. It seems that the Socialist juggernaut is unable to penetrate the Arlberg, and the local OeVP is stoutly resisting the national trend. The OeVP is well organised in this province, but in any case it is not unusual for developments in Vorarlberg to contradict theories valid for the rest of Austria.

During the Second Republic, the SPOe has been successful in every election held for the office of Federal President. Most of its candidates have been prominent party members with the exception of the present incumbent, Dr. Kirchschlaeger. He was nominated as the SPOe's candidate in 1974 as part of Kreïsky's policy of recruiting non-Socialists to important posts. Kirchschlaeger, a practising Catholic, was considered a good choice for the party, demonstrating its desire to build bridges with Catholics, liberals and all who felt that they could, in some way, support a Social Democratic programme. Kirchschlaeger won with 51.7 per cent of the votes, and was easily re-elected in 1980. His period in office has been uncontroversial; the main criticism, levelled at him is that he lacks dynamism. Since there are considerable restrictions on the powers which the President can exercise, this does not seem to be a significant weakness. President Kirchschlaeger has not had to deal with any major constitutional crisis and has been content to keep a low profile. In campaigning for re-election in 1980, he openly stated his objections, as a Catholic,

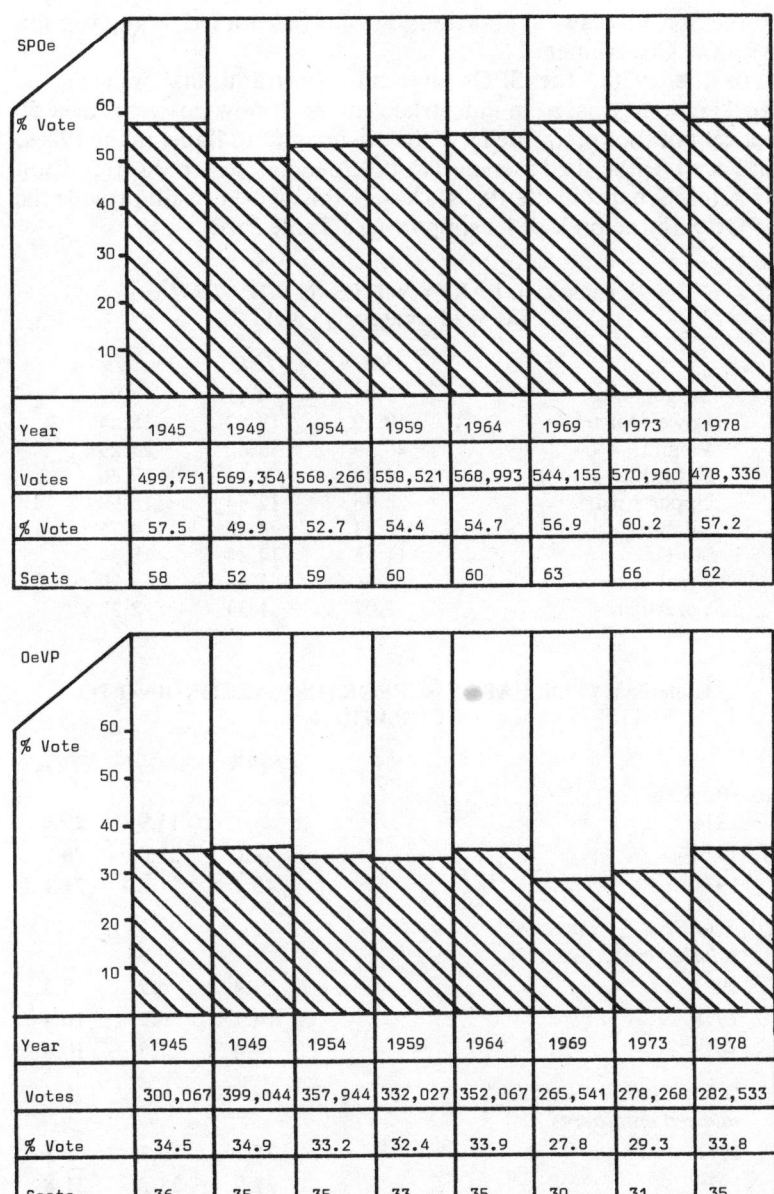

Year	1945	1949	1954	1959	1964	1969	1973	1978
Votes	499,751	569,354	568,266	558,521	568,993	544,155	570,960	478,336
% Vote	57.5	49.9	52.7	54.4	54.7	56.9	60.2	57.2
Seats	58	52	59	60	60	63	66	62

Year	1945	1949	1954	1959	1964	1969	1973	1978
Votes	300,067	399,044	357,944	332,027	352,067	265,541	278,268	282,533
% Vote	34.5	34.9	33.2	32.4	33.9	27.8	29.3	33.8
Seats	36	35	35	33	35	30	31	35

Fig. 2.ii.   PARTY SUPPORT IN THE VIENNESE MUNICIPAL
COUNCIL ELECTIONS

to the Socialist law on abortion, but this has not led to any friction with the Government.

In the 1970s, the SPOe overcame its traditional image of a workers' party based in industrial centres. It now possesses over 50 per cent of the vote, which was the dream of Otto Bauer in the 1920s, and can be described as a 'party of the people', which was the vision of Adolf Schaerf in the 1950s. Despite this, workers still provide the SPOe with the bulk of its support (see Table 2.vii).

Table 2.vi. PARTY VOTES IN *LAENDER*
(as % of total party vote)

	1930	1945	1979
Burgenland	3.35	4.11	3.97
Lower Austria	19.19	19.82	18.44
Vienna	46.39	35.42	25.29
Carinthia	4.48	6.10	7.66
Upper Austria	8.96	12.54	15.99
Salzburg	2.43	3.48	4.75
Styria	11.55	14.34	16.34
Tyrol	2.56	2.85	5.29
Vorarlberg	1.07	1.34	2.27

Table 2.vii % OF PARTY SUPPORTERS ACCORDING TO
OCCUPATION

	SPOe	OeVP	FPOe
(a) Workers			
1971	53.1	15.9	29.0
1976	52.0	21.0	28.7
1978	48.1	21.2	21.1
(b) Top Civil Servants and salaried employees			
1971	3.4	4.7	8.3
1976	4.1	6.2	10.4
1978	4.4	7.4	10.6
(c) Other Civil Servants and salaried employees			
1971	35.7	29.3	33.3
1976	37.9	28.2	31.8
1978	41.2	35.3	44.1
(d) Farmers			
1971	3.4	34.2	11.4

	SPOe	OeVP	FPOe
1976	2.6	32.8	14.6
1978	3.1	23.8	9.4

(e) Self-employed

1971	4.1	15.9	18.7
1976	3.3	11.9	14.5
1978	3.2	12.3	14.4

Source: Die Zukunft, June 1979, p.12.

The self-employed and farmers, groups from which the OeVP has traditionally drawn its support, are declining in number, while ranks of civil servants and salaried employees are swelling—to provide an important source of support for the SPOe in addition to the workers. The electoral success of the SPOe is likely to continue into the 1980s on the basis of these trends.

(d) Organisation

The organisation of the SPOe is impressive and it has been particularly successful in maintaining a mass membership. Membership of the party, which is direct and individual, was 716,340 in 1979, 9.6 per cent of the total population. Women compose only one-third of the SPOe's membership, a proportion which has not increased significantly in the last fifty years (see Table 2.viii).

The party has a high ratio of members to voters, and in 1979, 29.68 per cent of Socialist voters were also party members. In Vienna, 40.37 per cent of the party's voters are also members compared with 9.85 per cent in Vorarlberg. Just over 10 per cent of the membership are organised as unpaid party workers (*Vertrauenspersonen*). This dedicated cadre forms an important link between the ordinary member and the party's leading politicians. It is the *Vertrauenspersonen* who regularly collect the dues from members; in this way a personal contact is maintained and members' grievances receive a sympathetic hearing. A proposal to substitute this traditional means of collecting membership fees by direct payment through a bank has found little support. The *Vertrauenspersonen* are vital for the party in mobilising its voters on election day. They receive a special programme of political education, and are required by the SPOe to behave as exemplary Social Democrats.

The relative decline in the importance of Vienna for the party has been reflected in the membership (see Table 2.ix).

Table 2.viii. PARTY MEMBERSHIP

	Men		Women		Total
	No.	*% of total*	*No.*	*% of total*	*membership*
1929	488,398	68.02	229,658	31.98	718,056
1945	230,794	64.50	127,024	35.50	357,818
1950	397,446	65.45	209,837	34.55	607,283
1955	447,721	64.78	243,429	35.22	691,150
1960	471,659	64.85	255,606	35.15	727,265
1965	462,517	65.33	245,455	34.67	707,972
1970	472,495	65.68	246,894	34.32	719,389
1974	454,634	66.11	233,016	33.89	687,650
1979	473,363	66.08	242,977	33.92	716,340

Table 2.ix. PARTY MEMBERSHIP IN *LAENDER*
(as % of total membership)

	1929	1945	1979
Burgenland	1.79	3.50	4.10
Carinthia	3.00	6.39	6.99
Lower Austria	17.31	21.05	19.35
Upper Austria	7.11	6.54	14.23
Salzburg	1.94	2.89	3.74
Styria	8.87	13.80	14.27
Tyrol	1.31	1.60	2.17
Vorarlberg	0.44	0.67	0.75
Vienna	58.22	43.56	34.40

The party's tireless efforts to enrol more members have been rewarded in the provinces and especially in Upper Austria, which is becoming increasingly important for the SPOe. But although it is winning new members, this does not signify a young party. Over a quarter of the SPOe's members are over 60, nearly 60 per cent are over 40 and over 18 per cent are classified as pensioners.[6] According to the latest official figures, 29.92 per cent of its membership is composed of workers whereas 31.43 per cent are described as salaried employees (*Angestellte*). This represents a significant change in the class nature of a party, which in 1972 could claim that 37.3 per cent of its members were industrial workers. The increasing importance of salaried employees for the SPOe is apparent in its members of the *Nationalrat*. In the parliament of 1956, 60.8 per cent of Socialist deputies were classified as workers and 17.6 per cent as salaried employees. Twenty years later the latter was the largest single group, comprising 37.6 per cent of all SPOe deputies while only 25.8 per cent were workers.[7]

The membership of the party is divided into 3,205 local units, which are grouped into 113 district organisations. These in turn are combined to form nine *Land* organisations of the party, corresponding to the *Laender* of Austria. Representatives from all the *Laender* and the SPOe's district and small local organisations are present at the party conference, which in theory is the supreme decision-making organ of the SPOe.

A party conference is scheduled to take place every two years, but an extraordinary meeting can be called to discuss specific questions such as election strategy or programme changes. The ordinary party conference provides a useful forum for discussion, but contentious issues are not normally aired in public if they are likely to harm party unity. Over 500 members attend conference, which reduces its efficacy as an organ of supreme authority. The composition of the party conference in November 1979 was as shown in the accompanying list.

Reports on the work of the party are presented to conference by the central secretaries. Progress reports from the *Laender* and the parliamentary party are debated. The highlight of the conference is the speech of the party chairman, which in 1979 was given by Kreisky on the theme of 'Social Democracy in Europe'. The conference elects the party chairman, and in 1979 Kreisky was overwhelmingly re-elected with 489 out of 490 votes.

The party executive, which takes the main political decisions of the party, is elected by conference. Conference decisons are implemented by the party executive which is also entrusted with the management of finance and supervision of the party's press. The party executive proposes from its ranks the party chairman and vice-chairmen, who together compose the party presidium. Confirmation by conference is required, but this is a formality. The presidium implements the decisions of the party executive and is

Party Executive	58
Control Commission	19
Women's Committee	17
Burgenland	17
Carinthia	27
Lower Austria	65
Upper Austria	51
Salzburg	17
Styria	50
Tyrol	15
Vorarlberg	7
Vienna	107
Socialist trade unionists	50
Parliamentary Deputies	7
Members of the party's press	3
Education Committee	7
Children's Friends	6
Socialist Youth	6
Young Generation	7
Free Business League	4
League of Working Farmers	3
Co-operative Society	3
Socialist academics	4
Socialist teachers	2
Sports' Association	7
Freedom Fighters	1
Pensioners' Association	10
Total	570

concerned with the daily administration of the SPOe's affairs. The 1979 conference confirmed the existing presidium and endorsed the inclusion of three additional members, making eight altogether. This alteration gave more representation to the provinces by including a member from Carinthia and another from Burgenland.

The SPOe's statute allows for an assembly referred to as the 'small party conference' or party council. This can be invoked by the party executive for special duties such as the nomination of candidates for the *Nationalrat* elections. The party executive, acting on recommendations from the *Land* organisations, proposes candidates for the party list. The party council's freedom of choice is restricted by the presentation of these rcommendations. The Socialists' nominee for the Federal Presidency is decided by the party council, but again this is based on suggestions from the party executive.

An essential feature of the party's structure is its numerous organisations encompassing many recreational interests and functions. In the First Republic, these organisations were ideological in orientation, but since the war they have become less politicised. They survive as an important means of political mobilisation and socialisation, but are not intended to oppose 'bourgeois' society by the construction of a rival Socialist world. Ths SPOe's successful integration in the system has made this task obsolete.

One of the most popular organisations was originally founded in 1925 as the Workers' Sports Association. Since 1972, it has dispensed with the word 'Worker', believing this to be an inappropriate adjective when its membership among salaried employees is on the increase. Today it has around 824,000 members and is the largest sports organisation in Austria, catering for over forty different sports. The 'Workers' Temperance League' changed its name in 1975 to the *Aktion fuer O.O* (i.e. zero.zero) *Promille*. It campaigns, *inter alia*, for a reduction of the permitted level of alcohol in the blood for drivers to zero.

The party communicates its message through a daily newspaper, *Die Arbeiter-Zeitung*, which was founded in the nineteenth century. In the 1960s it was decided here too to delete the word 'worker' (*Arbeiter*) from the title, and the paper was renamed *Die AZ*. It is currently in serious financial difficulties and it may prove impossible for it to be maintained in its present form. The Workers' Cycling League (ARBOe) of the pre-war era has also quietly abandoned the word 'workers' and substituted it with 'automobile', which has enabled it to retain the old initials.

The parents' association, 'the Children's Friends', has not changed its name since its foundation in 1908, and today has a large membership of almost 300,000. It organises the 'Red Falcons', a group for young children, and arranges special holidays for them. The 'Socialist Youth of Austria' (SJOe) is affiliated to the party and officially includes those in the 14–20 age group. It is critical of the SPOe's performance in government, and would like to see structural social changes leading to the overthrow of the capitalist system. It regrets the lack of Socialist goals in the Government's economic policy, which it considers to have posed no threat to the existing order. The SJOe regularly organises seminars to promote political consciousness among the youth. In recent years the movement has given particular attention to the ideas of Otto Bauer, which some consider to be of relevance to the problems of contemporary society. The SJOe is committed to fundamental changes in educational policy, and would like to see the extension of a type of comprehensive school (at present such schools are still in the experimental stage and not common) and schools which would provide instruction in the afternoon as well as the morning (*Ganztagsschule*).

The 'Young Generation' (JG) is a constituent part of the SPOe and includes members under the age of thirty-eight. It consists of many party functionaries and parliamentary deputies, and receives a more sympathetic hearing from the SPOe's leading politicians than the Socialist Youth. The 'Association of Socialist Students' (VSStOe) has not had a very happy history in the adult party. Relations between it and the SPOe have been temporarily suspended until a new generation, more amenable to the party leadership, appears. The Socialist students, through having co-operated with other left-wing groups, have been suspected of 'Trotskyist' leanings. In Salzburg relations between the SPOe and the VSStOe were broken off altogether and many students have drifted to Communist organisations. No VSStOe delegates were present at the 1979 party conference.

Among other important organisations of the party is the Pensioners' Association, with a healthy membership of 364,625. The 'League of Socialist Academics' (BSA) was established after the Second World War, and its membership, 15,427 at a recent count, is steadily expanding. This important party association includes those with university degrees and diplomas; journalists, medical doctors, lawyers and engineers are 'academics' under this classification which is more loosely interpreted than, say, in Britain. Many members of the BSA hold prominent positions in Parliament, in the nationalised industries and in the nationalised banks. Membership of this organisation can be helpful for those seeking careers in public office, and of course can be especially so when the SPOe is the party of government. Other organisations exist of a less political nature: the 'workers' stamp collecting association', music societies, the

Samaritans (who in Austria, besides helping potential suicides, are engaged in social work and arrange aid for developing countries and those hit by natural disasters) and the association of allotment gardeners and small livestock breeders.

Many of the SPOe's organisations were established in the pre-war period with the intention of providing alternatives to the ubiquitous associations of the Catholic Church. Evidence of the change in character of the SPOe is the existence of its Study Group on Christianity and Socialism (ACUS). The latter's aim is to establish a dialogue between the two by examining the role Christians can play in the Socialist movement. Until February 1977, ACUS had been active only in Vienna and Upper Austria, but since then it has built up a national organisation. It is the successor of the League of Religious Socialists, founded in 1926, which provided a home for Christian industrial workers. In the First Republic this group was always overshadowed by the more influential 'Free Thinkers', which could claim a membership of over 65,000 in the 1930s.[8] The 'Free Thinkers' were dissolved by the Government of Dollfuss in 1933 and not revived by the new party after the war. A small group of Socialist free thinkers exists today, but it does not have the official blessing of the party. The SPOe prefers to seek a *modus vivendi* with the Church, which for its part has shown a desire to co-operate. The chairman of ACUS, Dr. Herbert Salcher, a practising Catholic, was brought into the cabinet in 1979 as Minister of Health and the Environment. Salcher, who comes from the Tyrol, is the only representative in the cabinet from the Western Alpine provinces, and his appointment is an indication of Kreisky's concern to win support in strong Catholic areas.

A vital association affiliated to the party is the 'fraction' of Socialists (FSG) in the Austrian Trade Union Federation (OeGB). The FSG is by far the largest of the *Fraktionen* in the OeGB, and there are strong links between this group and the SPOe, although the trade union and Socialist movements are not synonymous as was the case before the war. The OeGB now being supra-partisan, it cannot directly finance the SPOe's activities, but money flows from the OeGB to the Socialist fraction. Every year 1 per cent of the OeGB's income is distributed to the *Fraktionen*, and the FSG regularly receives about 64 per cent of this amount.

All members of the FSG must also belong to the Socialist party and, according to paragraph 14 of the party's statute, SPOe members should, where appropriate, join the FSG. It is estimated that out of 700,000 party members, 500,000 are also in the FSG. Considerable overlapping of membership is apparent at élite level, and the president of the OeGB, Anton Benya, is a member of the

SPOe's party executive. He also represents the party in Parliament as First President in the *Nationalrat*. Of the twenty-two members in Kreisky's cabinet in 1980, five were active members of the FSG: Karl Sekanina, Minister of Construction; Dr Josef Staribacher, Minister of Trade; Dr Gerhard Weissenberg, Minister for Social Affairs; Karl Lausecker, Minister of Transport, and Franziska Fast, State Secretary in the Ministry for Social Affairs. The FSG has traditionally provided the Minister for Social Affairs since 1945*, apart from the period of the OeVP Government of 1966–70. Karl Sekanina and Josef Staribacher are members of the SPOe party executive. Staribacher is also chairman of the Food, Beverage and Tobacco Workers' Union. Sekanina occupies additional powerful positions as vice-president of the OeGB and chairman of the second largest union—the Metal, Mining and Energy Workers' Union. He is widely tipped to succeed Benya as president of the OeGB, and many fear that this could lead to an accumulation of power in the hands of one man—dangerous in principle and dangerous in view of Sekanina's being regarded as unscrupulous and over-ambitious.

Of the ninety-five members of the SPOe in the *Nationalrat*, thirty-one are officials of the FSG, many of whom hold important posts. These include Alfred Dallinger, vice-president of the OeGB and chairman of the Union of Salaried Clerical, Commercial and Technical Employees (*Privatangestellte*), the largest union in the OeGB with over 320,000 members. He is also a member of the SPOe's party executive. The chairman of the Railwaymen's Union and the chairman of the Union of Chemical Workers' are both Socialist deputies. In the *Bundesrat* four officials of the FSG represent the party out of a total of twenty-nine, including the chairman of the Textile Workers' Union. There are fifteen individual unions in the OeGB, and thirteen of these have Socialist chairmen: of the remaining two, the Public Service Employees' Union is chaired by a member of the Christian trade unionists, (FCG—see below, pp.85 and 87), and the chairman of the Arts, Media and Professional Employees' Union is non-partisan. Socialist trade unionists dominate the OeGB executive and currently constitute thirty-nine of its fifty-four members.

Despite this close relationship between the party and the Socialists in the trade unions, the OeGB values its autonomy. The main pre-

---

*This was continued in 1980 after the death of Weissenberg and the appointment of Alfred Dallinger, leader of the largest union in the OeGB, as Minister for Social Affairs. He is regarded as a left-wing trade unionist and as a rival to Sekanina for the presidency of the OeGB after Benya's retirement.

occupation of the OeGB is with the maintenance of full employment, wages and social affairs and generally it avoids interfering in intra-party feuds. The OeGB is an important force in the system of 'social partnership' and is influential in the government's entire decision-making process. This integration has meant that the unions prefer to co-operate with the government of the day rather than risk confrontation. The overlapping of membership through the FSG has meant that the OeGB can work harmoniously with the Socialist Government. Benya has put some pressure on the government to proceed with the nuclear power programme, which was halted by a referendum. Although in an authoritative position as president of the OeGB, Benya has recognised the limits of his influence in the party. His predecessor, Franz Olah, attempted to use his trade union power to further his ambitions in the party but was unsuccessful.

Olah became president of the OeGB in 1959, a post which he exchanged for that of Minister of the Interior in 1963. Backed by strong support from his powerful Construction and Wood Workers' Union, he pursued the leadership of the SPOe, and quickly made enemies by trying to discredit members of the party and accusing his predecessors in the Ministry of the Interior of abuses of power while in office.[9] It seemed that Olah was prepared to crush his rivals by such methods. Many in the party became worried at his total disregard for etiquette and began to press for his removal. It was later revealed that he had misused OeGB funds while its president to lend financial support to the FPOe as a way of disrupting the Great Coalition. Pittermann, then chairman of the party, seemed unable to control Olah's activities, which were causing public embarrassment for the SPOe. A major crisis developed in the party which was on the verge of a split between those who supported and those who opposed Olah. He was obliged to resign as Minister of the Interior and was finally expelled in 1965 from the party. He lives today in retirement near Vienna.

After his expulsion Olah formed his own party, the Democratic Progressive Party (DFP), which stood in the elections of 1966 and 1970. It campaigned on a Christian and strongly anti-Communist platform, and in 1966 won nearly 150,000 votes; in 1970 it won only 17,405 votes. On both occasions it failed to win a parliamentary seat. The electoral threat to the SPOe quickly dispersed after Kreisky became leader, but the Olah case had severe repercussions in the party, and the experience left it badly shaken for some years. Olah had attempted to establish a position of absolute power in the movement, which implied the sacrifice of its inveterate unity; so many in the party were opposed to him that a split would have followed had he taken over. Olah was not the type to make compromises and would have done little to pacify those who disagreed with him. His failure was a confirmation of the SPOe's supreme will to maintain this unity and a clear warning to future careerists contemplating similar methods. Olah was a politician of considerable ability, and many of his ideas for reforming the party—including the adoption of a less doctrinaire course, a break from the coalition mentality and a rapprochement with the Catholic Church—were later put into practice.

Despite its high membership and the activity of many of its organisations, the SPOe is aware of the existence of large numbers of passive members and the dangers of bureaucracy. The party conference in 1976 introduced some changes in its statutes aimed at democratising its structure. These changes allow for secret election of the *Vertrauenspersonen* and the right of ordinary members to question the party executive directly and to receive a reply within eight weeks. Deputies of the SPOe and members of the Government, both at *Land* and federal level, are required to report to their constituents on the work of the party at least once a year. Some attempt was made to restrict the notorious 'accumulation of offices' (*Aemterkumulierung*). According to the new regulations, the *Vertrauenspersonen* are limited to one paid post, although exceptions are possible. Leading politicians of the party must submit in writing every year the number of offices they hold and be prepared to resign some if necessary.

The SPOe describes itself as an 'open party', and these reforms were designed to increase contact with non-members as well as members by encouraging discussion and making more information available. The success of these reforms in increasing inner-party democracy has had a mixed reaction. The left in the SPOe consider them of limited value when all major decisions are taken by Kreisky and Benya, but many other party workers regard them as a significant improvement, and feel that as a result they can play a greater role in the party's decision-making process. Both groups would agree that these reforms are not definitive, and in addition to strengthening its organisation, the party must also possess a clear set of principles for the 1980s.

(e) Ideology

In the 1950s the task of rebuilding the organisation, winning electoral support and fighting for the restoration of Austria's independence absorbed the energies of the party's leaders. The programmatic basis of the party consisted officially of the Linz precepts of 1926. These were in obvious contradiction to the thinking and activity of the new party. After the end of the Occupation, the SPOe felt able to draw up new guidelines more suitable for the post-war era. This debate culminated in the adoption of the *New Programme* in 1958 at a special party conference in Vienna.

The 'new programme' stressed that the SPOe was a party of *all* working people including the self-employed, agricultural workers and academics. It recognised that changes had occured since Marx and that workers had 'more to lose than their chains', but asserted that 'they still have a world to win'. The party avoided the mistakes in the Linz programme, and rejected a dictatorship of any kind. The new philosophy was defined as 'unrestricted political, economic and social democracy; Socialism is democracy fulfilled'. The future Socialist society was to be based on economic planning and democratic control of the means of production. The party accepted a mixed economy in which both the public and private sectors would happily co-exist. It expressed its wish to establish 'a fairer distribution of property and a more efficient economic system, in which the community acquires full control over the essential factors of production'. Private initiative and competition were to be left unmolested so long as the 'public interest' was not endangered. Nationalisation of large companies was to be contemplated on the basis of full compensation, and only if they presented a 'threat to the economic and political interests of the community'. The party had to a large degree moderated its hostility to private property, and further added:

Small and medium-sized firms and the property of working craftsmen will not be nationalised under any circumstances. In view of the dominance of these in the structure of the Austrian economy large sectors will, even in the future, remain reserved for private enterprise.

The programme of 1958 declared that it aimed to advance the interests of both the community and the individual. Freedom for the individual was to be enhanced by the abolition of both the power of private capitalism and the obsession of this system with the profit motive. Liberty, justice and security were to replace the ruthless struggle for personal gain.

The programme of 1958 included many demands which the Socialist Government has implemented since 1970, such as modernisation of the legal system, more equality for women, increased social security and educational reforms. Under pressure from the left wing, the *New Programme* concluded: 'The party fights for a new classless society and thus for a new Socialist humanism.' The retention of this spirit and references to the need for a victory over capitalism and exploitation meant that, despite some revisions of the old programme, the party did not totally abandon Socialism. It seemed that the Austrian Socialists still sought a third way between different systems:

In this divided world, democratic Socialism stands between capitalism and dictatorship. It must achieve its aims while fighting them both: for it can come to terms with neither Communism nor capitalism.[10]

Such a programme was acceptable to the different tendencies in the party. On the left, Josef Hindels regarded it as a Socialist document impregnated with Austro-Marxism, while his right-wing opponents were satisfied that it marked a break with the party's Marxist past.

The SPOe was trying hard to eradicate the negative features of its Marxist image both in theory and practice. Its responsible behaviour, shown by participating in the prevailing economic system and the coalition, gave every indication of its sincerity. Yet the SPOe was to remain vulnerable to charges that it was a Marxist party in disguise—a notion which gained credence from the Communist support it received in the election of 1966. The party's decisive defeat at the polls was attributed to Olah's intervention and Pittermann's pusillanimity in dealing with the Communists.

At a party conference soon after the débâcle, Bruno Kreisky was elected leader by 347 out of 497 votes. Kreisky's success was due to his support in the provinces; most of the 30 per cent of the party hostile to him were centred in Vienna. Kreisky, who came from a wealthy Jewish family, had spent the war years in Sweden where he became influenced by the Scandinavian model of Social Democracy. He began to remould the party on these lines by initiating a flood of reform programmes, which were to serve as a platform at the next election in 1970. Indeed the party's election victories are a confirmation that he has found the right formula. Part of the new package was an unequivocal rejection of Communism and dictatorship which the party executive made explicit in a statement issued in 1969 at Eisenstadt, near the Hungarian border. Kreisky continually stressed that his vision of future society was anchored in a belief that democracy in all aspects of life should be extended. Any attempt to reach a compromise with Communism was regarded as an Austro-Marxist 'illusion'.

From 1967 till 1969 the party was feverishly engaged in formulating policy statements, and enlisted the help of over 1,000 experts in the process. Before the 1970 election was due, the Socialists were able to present concrete alternatives to the OeVP Government on a wide-ranging number of topics including economics, education, housing, defence, culture and transport. All bore the distinctive mark of Kreisky's brand of Social Democracy and stressed the human and moral aspect of politics. The SPOe's enthusiastic acceptance of democratisation and modernisation was attacked by the Communists as reformist and by the conservatives as 'demagogic'.[11] The latter had good reason to be worried, for the SPOe was in the midst of projecting a new image to the public—that of a better 'people's party'.

The discussion on the basic ideological orientation of the party continued after it had captured power from the OeVP. To some extent, the debate increased in intensity, because it was of prime concern to many Socialists to know whether their government was merely proving itself more successful than its predecessors at managing the system, or whether eventually fundamental changes could be expected.[12] One of the most important achievements of Kreisky's reign has been the maintenance of full employment. The Chancellor clearly believes that mass unemployment, as he witnessed it in the 1930s, is a degrading and demoralising experience. Apart from the damage to individual self-respect, Kreisky is acutely aware of the dangers which unemployment can pose to the democratic system. It has been a top priority, although an expensive one, to retain workers in jobs even when 'rationalisation' would have dictated their dismissal.

Under the Socialists the working week has been reduced to forty hours, and all workers are entitled to a minimum of four weeks' holiday. The communications network and the health, penal and educational systems have been modernised to provide better services. Changes in educational policy and the liberalisation of the laws on abortion provoked the greatest opposition from the OeVP. In the legislative period of 1975–9, 80 per cent of all laws were passed unanimously, and only 9 per cent were passed by the votes of the SPOe alone. For the most part, Austria's first Social Democratic Government has operated in an atmosphere characterised by consensus and stability. The reforms of the government were a source of satisfaction for many in the party, and were vindicated by subsequent election victories. But for some these reforms have not answered questions concerning the ultimate purpose of power and the formation of a new social order. It was to discuss problems of this type and to review the relevance of the 1958 programme that in 1976 a working party was established. A comprehensive discussion took place in the party at all levels, under the guidance of intellectuals and international experts. The result was a draft programme which was a combination of the left-wing ideas of academics and the pragmatic policies of the party's politicians. Of prime concern for the left was the 'deepening crisis in capitalism' and the growth in bureaucracy. It wanted to insert a clause in the new programme which criticised the system of 'social partnership', but this was not accepted.

The new programme of the SPOe, superseding that of 1958, was debated and adopted at a party conference in May 1978. In it freedom, equality, justice and solidarity are cited as the guiding principles for the party. The programme retained the reference to the need to create a classless society, and it discussed what the party described as the crises and contradictions of a capitalist system based on the profit motive. The conference, confronted with world recession, displayed more pessimism than twenty years earlier, and acknowledged that the future would bring a slower rate of economic growth and limitations to the development of the welfare state. It showed a concern to control the destructive tendencies inherent in the capitalist system and to preserve the environment.

The new programme recognised the permanent neutrality of Austria, but considered that this did not bar it from playing an active role in international politics. It advocated an increase in development aid and co-operation between industrialised and developing countries. Encouragement was given to the liberation movements in the Third World in their fight against colonialism (*sic*). The idea of a confederation of sovereign, democratic countries in Europe was supported, and the party indicated a desire to see further participation of the country in international organisations. On the Middle East conflict, the programme stated the need to find a peaceful solution based on the right to freedom and territorial integrity. It added that this could only be achieved when a national homeland was secured for the Palestinian people. Kreisky has frequently made controversial remarks on that area of the world, and supports recognition of the PLO as the legitimate representative of the Palestinians. The Chancellor is one of the fourteen vice-presidents of the Socialist International, and values the contribution of this organisation in achieving peace and overcoming poverty by creating a feeling of solidarity between countries. The new programme stated: 'The Socialists want to substitute international solidarity and co-operation for the exploitation of poor countries by the rich and the domination of some states by others.'

Essentially, the 1978 programme tended to reflect the philosophy of Bruno Kreisky as developed in discussions with Olof Palme and Willy Brandt. It described Social Democracy as the greatest 'freedom movement' in Austria, and condemned Communism for suppressing individual liberty. The programme considered the struggle of the labour movement to be divided into three separate historic phases. In the first came the fight for political democracy and the Republic, which was followed in the second by the establishment of the welfare state. The task in the third phase will be to carry on this struggle and to achieve Social Democracy on the foundations built in the first two phases. This third phase of Social Democracy will be:

a society of freedom and equality, of justice and solidarity in which comprehensive social security becomes a living reality. It is based on the right to work and a concern for the welfare of the people in all aspects of life. It includes the right to a humane environment, to extensive education and training of one's own choice. It allows for co-determination and participation in the management of affairs.[13]

The programme acknowledged that open access to information, free from economic or political bias, was a precondition for an increase in participation. The ability of individuals freely to determine their own future in this way was given more emphasis in the programme than was any reform of property relationships. The Austrian Social Democrats are aware that democratic control is more effective than an extension in state ownership in changing the power structure. This concept of Social Democracy, founded on co-determination, is to be applied throughout society in factories, schools and all public institutions. It is imagined that it will be a process that can never be completed, and Kreisky has described this as being dialectical in nature since it can only lead to new contradictions. As Kreisky himself explained:

'Social Democracy was in the past read as Socialist democracy—social and democratic. We now interpret it as democratisation of all realms of society, of culture, of leisure, co-determination. . . . I cannot give you an exact blueprint and timetable. Every area will develop its own form of democracy. It will be an ongoing process towards A.D. 2000.'[14]

In achieving these long-term goals, the new programme welcomed co-operation from those, not necessarily Socialists, who shared the same ideals. The party, which had formally modified its pre-war anti-clericalism in the programme of 1958, extended its friendship to Christians in a warmer and more positive way:

We Socialists recognise the change within the Christian Churches. This is not only evident from official statements, but above all from the social involvement of Christians. We welcome this development with deepest sincerity. Many involved Christians are active in our Socialist movement. Every Christian can become a colleague in the fight for a more just social order and an ally in the struggle to implement our common ideals.[15]

This non-dogmatic ethos and stress on the freedom of the individual was to make the programme attractive to 'liberals' and

Catholics. In addition, the programme contained a Marxist analysis of industrial society, referring to the need to abolish class contradictions and alienation. It was the traditional attempt to synthesise different philosophies, the unending quest to find the third way. The substance of the programme was based on a conviction of the need to transform society. It offered a vision and presented a challenge, and it proved that the Austrian Socialists could still envisage a future based on something more inspiring than mere pragmatism.

The SPOe had again formulated a set of theoretical principles which were overtly to the left of the practical politics of the party. The small left wing in the SPOe is critical in its assessment of a decade of Social Democratic government. It has recently voiced its disappointment on the subject of the distribution of incomes, which would appear since 1970 to have become more unequal.[16] The interpretation of the figures has been disturbed by the *bête noir* of the left, the Minister of Finance and Vice-Chancellor Hannes Androsch, but this has not reassured those in the party who regard Androsch as living evidence of the government's tolerance of privilege and inequality. The business affairs of Androsch received great publicity before the Viennese municipal elections in 1978, when it was revealed that his accountancy firms were making enormous profits. Many questioned the compatibility of his position as Minister of Finance with his business interests and he was subsequently obliged to delegate their management to trustees while he remained in office. Anton Benya gave strong support to Androsch, whom he associated with stability and full employment. The controversy surrounding Androsch reappeared in 1980 when firms associated with him were suspected of being implicated in dubious financial transactions. The OeVP recalled parliament in the summer recess to bring a motion of no confidence in the Finance Minister. Kreisky successfully defended Androsch with noticeable brevity, and has indicated that life for the SPOe would be easier without this particular embarrassment.*

The Androsch affair was regarded as being symbolic of a loss of contact with ordinary people by a party grown complacent through security in office. Many in the SPOe, besides its avant-garde, are coming to the conclusion that the Government must introduce redistributive measures if it is to possess any credibility. The new programme seeks to rectify these disparities by preparing a reform of the taxation system, capital creation for workers (*Vermoegensbildung*), and democratic control of privilege and incomes in both the private and public sectors.

*The Chancellor finally announced Androsch's resignation from the government in December 1980.

Discontented murmurings from the Left have been fairly tame compared with the aggressive activity of young Socialists in the German SPD. The student demonstrations of the late 1960s left Austria comparatively unscathed. Ten years later a section of the youth is clearly disillusioned with the party, especially in its positive attitude to nuclear power, against which feeling is strong among the young. The result of a referendum in 1978, rejecting the commissioning of Austria's first reactor near Vienna, shocked the SPOe. Although prepared to support the party in a general election six months later, many voted against its recommendation to put the reactor on stream. The SPOe had alienated potential supporters, and had to work hard to regain their confidence by frequently stating that it would respect the voter's will on this issue. The government now has to deal with Austria's energy problems within a non-nuclear framework, or hope for a change in public opinion. The SPOe, while not underestimating the difficulties it faces, views the future with confidence. Kreisky declared before the last election: 'We have solved the problems of the 1970s; we shall also master the problems of the 1980s.'

REFERENCES

1. H. Hautmann and R. Kropf, *Die oesterreichische Arbeiterbewegung vom Vormaerz bis 1945*, Europaverlag, Wien, 1974, p.194.
2. *Das Grosse Erbe*, SPOe, Wien, p.43.
3. J. Braunthal, *The Tragedy of Austria*, Gollancz, London, 1948, p.121. Braunthal, a Jew, was in exile at the time.
4. E. Winkler, *Die Oesterreichische Sozialdemokratie im Spiegel ihrer Programme*, Verlag der Wiener Volksbuchhandlung, 1971, pp.70–81.
5. For further details on the election of 1979, see M.A. Sully, 'The Austrian Election of 1979: a Socialist Victory', *Parliamentary Affairs*, Autumn 1979, pp.437–47.
6. Figures on party membership have been compiled from the *Jahrbuch 1978* and *Jahrbuch 1979* of the SPOe.
7. H. Fischer, *Das politische System Oesterreichs*, Europaverlag, Wien, 1977, p.129.
8. See R. Klucsarits, 'Die Freidenker—gestern und heute', *Geist und Gesellschaft*, nr.1, 1977, p.17.
9. See F. Kaufmann, *Sozialdemokratie in Oesterreich*, Amalthea-Verlag, Wien, 1978, p.459.
10. E. Winkler, *op. cit.*, p.102.
11. See F. Kreissler, 'Vom Austro-Marxismus zum Austro-Sozialismus', *Revue d'Allemagne*, vol.V, Jan.–March 1973, p.17.

12.   E. Maerz, 'Systemkorrigierende oder systemveraendernde Reformen', *Die Zukunft*, nr. 5, March 1972, pp.14–17.
13.   *Das Neue Programm der SPOe*, SPOe, Wien, 1978, p.38.
14.   Quoted from an interview conducted by T. Lessing, *Austria Today*, Winter 1977, p.31.
15.   *Das Neue Programm . . .*, *op.cit.*, p.83.
16.   G. Chaloupek, 'Die Verteilung der persoenlichen Einkommen in Oesterreich', *Wirtschaft und Gesellschaft*, nr.2, 1978, p.200. See also H. Fischer (ed.), *Rote Markierungen '80*, Europaverlag, Wien, 1980.

3

THE PEOPLE'S PARTY

(a) Historical Background

The People's Party of Austria (OeVP) was founded in April 1945, and was to become a dominant political force in the Second Republic. It was the leading partner in the coalition government which lasted until 1966, and provided the Chancellor throughout this period. In 1966 it was still able to form a government without needing to rely on the Socialists, but since 1970 it has been in opposition and has suffered the humiliation of four election defeats. The OeVP recognises that this cannot all be attributed to the brilliance of Kreisky, and it is currently examining its own organisation to make it more attractive to voters. One of the main problems for the party is the predominance of centrifugal forces which make it difficult to present a united image to the public. It hopes that a centralisation of its structure will overcome this, but not all in the party agree that this is the most desirable way forward.

Unlike the Socialists, the OeVP was not keen to stress its historical continuity with its predecessor, the Christian Social Party. The latter was identified with the Catholic-conservative *Lager* which had developed in the late nineteenth century, influenced by the anti-semitism of Karl Lueger. Lueger's flair for organisation and oratory helped to create a mass party based on the petit-bourgeoisie in Vienna and its environs. The movement was characterised by radical anti-Socialist and anti-liberal ideas. It originated outside the parliamentary system and only slowly won political respectability; later it gained the support of the big industrialists and landowners whose interests often conflicted with those of the small tradesmen and peasantry.

In the 1920s, the Christian Social Party was the core of a series of anti-Socialist 'bourgeois blocks' which formed the government under the guidance of a Catholic priest, Ignaz Seipel. The intransigence of both Seipel on one side and the Social Democrat Otto Bauer on the other contributed to the lack of communication between the political *Lager*. The civil war found the 'Christian Socials', backed by the Fascist paramilitary *Heimwehr*, confronting the workers. Superiority of weapons and organisation led to a suppression of the workers' movement and the establishment of the authoritarian regimes of Dollfuss and Schuschnigg. These paved the way for the relatively easy annexation of Austria by Hitler and the inauguration of a thoroughgoing totalitarian system. The successors to the Christian Socials did not want to emphasise too many aspects of this tradition.

Discussions on the formation of a new party began in the closing stages of the war. It was decided that a strong commitment to democracy should be made explicit and that authoritarianism should be rejected. Acknowledgement was to be made of the independence of Austria, and the new party was to demonstrate faith in the ability of the country to survive without the assistance of its German neighbour. Unlike the Christian Socials, it was not to be enmeshed with the hierarchy of the Catholic Church. The inspiration for the new movement came from those who had suffered in Nazi concentration camps or who had been active in the illegal underground movement. They included members of the workers' wing of the Christian Socials, and they were prepared to co-operate with leading Socialists to find common ground through discussion. This positive approach to political rivals had been absent in the old Christian Social Party.

(b) The Second Republic

One of the leading figures to emerge in the new People's Party was Leopold Figl, who had been director of the pre-war Peasants' League. Although he had been a local leader of Schuschnigg's paramilitary organisation, he was acceptable to the SPOe because of his imprisonment in Dachau. Figl was chosen to be the OeVP's representative in Renner's provisional cabinet, and in September 1945 he became chairman of the party. His support came from the farmers of Lower Austria, at that time still an important element in the party. From the beginning the OeVP was a combination of competing interest groups including industry, agriculture and employees. In the immediate post-war period, seven out of the nine *Laender* were OeVP-dominated, and in five of these the Farmers' League reigned supreme. Figl was the national deputy leader of the Farmers' League (OeBB) of the OeVP until 1947. From November 1945 until 1953 he was Chancellor of the coalition Government , and established good working relations with the Socialist Vice-Chancellor, Schaerf. He served as Foreign Minister of the Republic in 1953–59.

The OeVP moved to the right while Figl was still Chancellor, when in 1952 he was replaced by Julius Raab as party chairman. Raab succeeded Figl as Chancellor in 1953, a post he held until 1961. Supported by the industrialists' wing in the party, he was leader of its

Business League (OeWB) from 1945 till 1963. Like Figl, his regional support came from Lower Austria; he had been a cabinet minister in Schuschnigg's last Government and had led the *Heimwehr* in Lower Austria. His accession to the leadership was the result of a feeling in the party that Figl was being too emollient to the Socialists, and the party's loss of the presidential election in 1951 reinforced the belief that it should assert its authority. The rise of Raab was also an indication of the increasing power of business in the party and the declining importance of the agricultural element. Raab's Minister of Finance, Reinhard Kamitz, directed the economy on a neo-liberal course which frequently conflicted with the priorities of the Socialists for high government expenditure and full employment. Although Raab had a more strained relationship with the SPOe than Figl had done when he was in control, he developed amicable relations with the president of the Trade Union Federation, Johann Boehm. This dialogue formed the basis for the development of 'social partnership', industrial peace and economic stability.

Austrian politics in the 1950s were dominated by Raab, who established a paternalistic and authoritarian style as Chancellor. The highlight of his career came with the signing of the State Treaty in 1955: this, combined with his sense of humor and his realism, made him a popular figure. Under his leadership the internal conflicts of the OeVP were held in check, but he was unable to stop the growth of a major crisis in the party after its setback in the 1959 election. His handling of the negotiations with the SPOe on the renewal of the coalition was not regarded as very astute, and his failing health led many to sense that the 'Raab era' had ended. At a party conference in 1960, Alfons Gorbach, the leader of the Styrian party, took over from Raab as chairman, and in 1961 he also took over Raab's duties as Federal Chancellor—showing more readiness to consult his colleagues than his predecessor. Raab continued in political life as president of the Chamber of Commerce. He stood for the Federal Presidency in 1963 against the Socialist Schaerf, but could only win 40.6 per cent of the votes, compared with his opponent's 55.4 per cent.

Gorbach had been the leader of the Fatherland Front in Styria under Dollfuss and Schuschnigg, and was among the first group of prisoners the Nazis sent to Dachau. This background made him acceptable to the older 'core' group in the OeVP, and for a time he was supported by the younger 'reformers' in the party. The 'new men' were in favour of a more aggressive attitude to the SPOe and a relaxation of the restrictions of the 'red-black' coalition.[1] However, Gorbach did not fulfil their plans; in 1963 Josef Klaus, one of the leading 'reformers', took over as party chairman, although Gorbach continued as Chancellor until 1964. Klaus was supported by the general secretary of the party, Hermann Withalm, and his regional base was Salzburg. He was a member of the new generation in the party who had not been in a concentration camp and his rise to the leadership signified a defeat for the 'old guard' in the OeVP, centred in Vienna and Lower Austria, and meant that the party was less predisposed to reach an understanding with the SPOe. Klaus managed to remain as Chancellor and leader of the party until 1970. In 1966 he formed the first OeVP single-party cabinet, but found it difficult to balance the rival claims of the competing interests and regions in the party.

The first break with the coalition did not bring any radical departure from the post-war style of consensus politics. Of the 515 new laws introduced during the legislative period 1966–70, only sixty-two were passed by the votes of the OeVP alone. The party proceeded very cautiously, unaccustomed to the experience of single-party government. Most of the attention was focussed on education, housing and reconstruction of the nationalised industries, and on problems which had been inherited from the coalition days. Little thought was given to the future strategy of the party or to how it should win the support of the growing numbers of salaried employees. Raab had neglected this phenomenon, preferring to tailor the party to the requirements of the 'small man'. In the 1960s it was becoming clear that reliance on this section was insufficient for electoral success.

Klaus ran into difficulties in his own party, and the 1970 election defeat quickly made him *persona non grata*. After a short interregnum under Hermann Withalm, he was succeeded by Karl Schleinzer, a member of the Farmers' League from Carinthia, who however was killed in a car crash just before the election of 1975. The party now looked to a young, dynamic banker, Josef Taus, but crushing defeats of the OeVP in 1975 and 1979 caused demoralisation, and again calls for reform were voiced. In the ensuing debate Taus resigned and was replaced in 1979 by Alois Mock of the Workers' and Employees' League (OeAAB) in the OeVP. The party seems to have no great expectations of Mock, which is probably to his advantage. No one is seriously relying on him suddenly to reverse the *Genosse Trend*, especially as long as Kreisky remains leader of the SPOe. So Mock has a short breathing space to reorganise the party on more modern lines and tackle the problem of internal disunity. The frequent changes in leadership have not helped to establish a clear identity for the party in the public's mind. After some stability under Raab it seems that the OeVP has not been able to unify around an acceptable figure. This contrasts sharply with the

Leaders of the OeVP		*Leaders of the SPOe*	
Leopold Kunschak	April–Sept. 1945	Adolf Schaerf	1945–57
Leopold Figl	1945–52	Bruno Pittermann	1957–67
Julius Raab	1952–60	Bruno Kreisky	1967–
Alfons Gorbach	1960–3		
Josef Klaus	1963–70		
Hermann Withalm	1970–1		
Karl Schleinzer	1971–5		
Josef Taus	1975–9		
Alois Mock	1979–		

stability of leadership in the SPOe: (see comparative lists). Election defeats have clearly contributed to the rise and fall of leaders of the OeVP, and Mock will have to discover some method to usurp the 'Chancellor party', the SPOe, if he is to survive politically. At the moment it seems that the best he can hope for is that the Socialists will start making mistakes.

(c) Organisation

The internal diversity of the OeVP finds expression in its controversial structure. The party consists of the six sub-organisations (*Teilorganisationen*) listed below, each of which is represented in the nine *Bundeslaender*. This means that the OeVP is composed of fifty-four separate units, each with its own specific identity thus making co-ordination extremely difficult. The six components of the OeVP are made up of three powerful leagues (*Buende*) and three other organisations, all nominally with equal status though with varying power and influence. The Union of Senior Citizens led by Withalm, the former party leader was promoted to become a constituent part of the OeVP in 1977.

1. The Farmers' League (OeBB)
2. The Business League (OeWB)   *'The Leagues'*
3. The Workers' and Employees' League (OeAAB)

4. The Women's Movement (OeFB)
5. The Young People's Party (JVP)
6. Union of Senior Citizens (OeSB)

Members are recruited to the party indirectly through the appropriate sub-organisations, which are financially autonomous. Direct party membership is possible but not numerically significant. Membership is open to those over the age of sixteen, and the youth section exists for those under the age of thirty. It is possible to be a member of more than one sub-organisation, and exact figures of the party's total membership are difficult to acquire. According to the OeVP's own report for 1980, the figures in that year were as shown in Table 3.1.

Table 3.i. PARTY MEMBERSHIP, 1980

OeBB	388,863
OeWB	152,906
OeAAB	271,995
OeFB	76,565
JVP	104,475
OeSB	172,783
Individual Members	301
Total	1,167,888

These figures include the so called 'family members' (*Familienmitglieder*), who are dependents of the members of the Farmers' and Business Leagues. In contrast to the ordinary members (*Hauptmitglieder*), they do not pay the full fees. The numerical preponderance of the OeBB is gained from the incorporation of the 'family members', which enables it to account for 49.7 per cent of the total membership of the three leagues. It is estimated that around 17 per cent of the members of both the OeBB and OeWB are 'family members'.

It is possible, according to the party's statute, to be a member of one of the sub-organisations while not taking membership of the OeVP. This adds to confusion about the OeVP's precise membership numbers, but it is clear that for a conservative party it is high. On the basis of these figures, taking into account membership of the three leagues alone, 41.0 per cent of voters were also party members in 1979. The three leagues together account for 70 per cent of the total membership.

The Farmers' League has an absolute majority of league members in Lower and Upper Austria. The OeAAB possesses 69 per cent of the combined league membership in Vienna where, not surprisingly, the OeBB is weakest. From the regional figures (Table 3.ii) it is clear that Lower Austria is still important for the OeVP and, if the leagues only are considered, it provides 40 per cent of the national membership.

From 1945 till 1953, the Farmers' League provided the Federal Chancellor, but its authority in the party was subsequently eroded

Table 3.ii PARTY MEMBERSHIP OF THE LEAGUES IN THE
LAENDER 1980

Province	OeAAB	OeBB	OeWB
Burgenland	9,391	8,740	3,953
Carinthia	11,859	8,658	6,500
Lower Austria	95,244	167,783	61,159
Upper Austria	42,915	106,295	13,738
Salzburg	14,708	14,764	8,698
Styria	39,360	56,233	28,071
Tyrol	15,674	18,992	14,274
Vorarlberg	5,587	3,623	3,790
Vienna	37,257	3,775	12,723

Source: *Bericht*, OeVP, 1977–80.

by the Business League during the Raab era. The Business League wields proportionately more influence than its numbers would suggest because of its powerful financial connections. Friction is inevitable between the three leagues because of their representation of such diverse interest groups. The structure of the OeVP contrasts strongly with that of the highly centralised and less complicated SPOe. Each of the three leagues has produced a Chancellor as well as a leader for the party.[2] The present leader Mock, like his predecessor, comes from the OeAAB and was its chairman from 1971–8. The three league chairmen (Herbert Kohlmaier, OeAAB, Roland Minkowitsch, OeBB, and Rudolf Sallinger, OeWB) have an unquestioned right to act as deputy leaders of the party, but from 1980 this will no longer be an automatic process, and deputy leaders will have to be elected by the party conference. This is part of a systematic attempt to reduce the power of the leagues, and is a reform particularly welcomed by the youth organisation.

Like the SPOe, the OeVP has a number of auxiliary associations to cater for different needs and interests. These include the League of Academics, with 8,900 members, which is concerned with the philosophy of the party.[3] A women's organisation, devoted specifically to provide help in times of natural disasters (*Katastrophenhilfe Oesterreichischer Frauen*), was established in 1965 in response to the severe flooding that had occurred in Austria. It now has 10,000 members and under the leadership of Dr Elisabeth Schmitz has been a consistent opponent of the Socialist abortion laws and of nuclear power. A Tenants' League, formed in 1946, has 60,000 members, represents the interests of tenants and landlords, and advocates the restoration of old accommodation in preference to random demolition. The OeVP also has an organisation dedicated to the education and welfare of children, and a welfare service which is engaged in social work and home help activities. The functionaries of the auxiliary associations are required to be members of the OeVP.

Unlike the pre-war Christian Social party, the OeVP does not have direct links with the numerous Catholic organisations. It was the declared policy of the Church after 1945 to avoid active participation in party politics; it wished to be independent of any political party, while reserving the right to speak out on matters of religious significance, such as the protection of 'unborn life'. The members of the OeVP, for their part, were keen to avoid the unfortunate integration of the Church with politics which had existed in the inter-war period and contributed ultimately to civil war. The position of the Church was made clear in 1952 in the Manifesto of Mariazell, which was based on the philosophy of a 'free Church in a free society'. Before the 1949 election, the Catholic Action organisation (not officially connected with the Church but containing many Church dignitaries and, at present, the Federal President) had asked Austrians, where possible, to vote 'Catholic', which could only be interpreted as supporting the OeVP. Almost 90 per cent of the population describe themselves as Catholic, and pronouncements of the Church are important, especially in small communities and the Alpine provinces. Since the Manifesto, the Church has gradually adopted a more neutral stance and has become resigned to the fact that increasing numbers of Catholics are voting Socialist. This new accommodation between Catholics and Socialists has proceeded more smoothly in Vienna where the archbishop, Cardinal Koenig, has developed friendly relations with the agnostic Kreisky and his Government. Koenig interprets his duties in the following way: 'I am not a bishop of the OeVP or of the SPOe; nor bishop of employers nor of trade unionists; I am not a bishop of those living on the land or of those in the towns. I am a bishop of all Catholics.'[4]

Despite the official disengagement of the Church from party politics, the great majority of all practising Catholics still identify with the OeVP (see Table 3.iii). Due to the fact that an average of 34 per cent of Austrian Catholics attend Church on Sundays, the religious commitment of members of the OeVP is high. This is confirmed by a survey of the religious background of parliamentary deputies which shows that 80 per cent of OeVP deputies regard themselves as Catholics. Only 30 per cent in the FPOe made such an acknowledgement, and the latest figures for the SPOe put this figure at just over 47 per cent.[5] One important link between the OeVP and the Church is the association of Catholic fraternities, (OeCV). This has 10,000 members, of whom roughly a quarter are students. It serves as an important recruitment centre for the top positions in the

Table 3.iii. CONFESSIONAL STRUCTURE OF THE PARTIES (%)

| | Sympathisers of the | | |
	OeVP	SPOe	FPOe
Go to Church			
Several times a month	57	16	16
Once a month	10	7	5
Once a year	21	32	31
Never	12	44	48

| | Members of the | |
	OeVP	SPOe
Go to Church on Sundays		
Regularly	63	6
Occasionally	86	23

Source: A. Pelinka in J. Raschke (ed.), Die politischen Parteien in Westeuropa, Rowohlt, 1978, p.417.

party. With the sole exception of Karl Schleinzer, all the post-war leaders of the OeVP have been members of the OeCV. Its influence was traditionally strong in the civil service and particularly the 'black' Ministries of Finance and Education in the coalition era. It finds competition harder at élite level since the SPOe has been in power, and many have been replaced by members from the socialist League of Academics (BSA).[6]

The federal structure of the party increases the diffusion of power and has further institutionalised intra-party conflict. Of the nine provinces, six still have governors who are members of the OeVP. These *Landeshauptmaenner* are regarded with respect within their own mini-empires. Often, being absorbed in the provincial affairs, they seem disinclined to follow the central party organisation. This is more likely to occur when, as in 1979, the federal party suffers an electoral defeat while making some gains in *Land* elections. Personalities are an important factor and the OeVP's leader in Tyrol, Eduard Wallnoefer, has become as revered a father-figure in that region as Kreisky is nationally.

While Figl and Raab were at the helm, the party was dominated by the regions of Lower Austria and Vienna. Government positions were monopolised by these two *Laender*, and until 1961 no representative from Upper Austria, Salzburg or Burgenland obtained a place in the cabinet. Between 1961 and 1966, under the influence of the 'reformers', the balance shifted to the southern and western provinces. The Governments of Klaus attempted to construct a very precise federal *Proporz*, and his cabinet of 1964, for the first time, assigned a cabinet post to each of the *Laender* (see Table 3.iv).

Klaus lacked strong connections with Lower Austria and Vienna, and ran into difficulties when he tried to gain the co-operation of the whole party. Integration was further weakened by the need to consider the leagues' *Proporz* claims. The Klaus cabinet of 1966 achieved a neat balance between the OeAAB, OeBB and OeWB in a ratio of 4 : 2 : 4. Some ministries were a traditional preserve of one league, and accordingly the Ministry of Agriculture went to a member from the OeBB and the Ministry of Trade to the OeWB. The OeAAB became more important after the end of the coalition in 1966, because it claimed some of the traditional Socialist ministries such as Social Affairs, Transport and Home Affairs.[7] The task of accommodating league and regional interests has weakened the authority of the party leadership. Reform of this structure has been the subject of debate in the OeVP throughout the 1970s, but influential vested interests in the existing arrangements made radical changes difficult to achieve.

According to the statute, the interests of the federal party take precedence over those of the sub-organisations. That this has not always been observed is evident from the phrase 'league egoism', which has come to be applied to the behaviour of these separate units. Not only the leagues but the other organs of the party frequently display an independence which can cause embarrassment to the federal party. During the election campaign of 1979, for example, the leader of the Women's Movement, Hertha Haider, announced that if returned to office the OeVP would not reverse the Socialist laws on abortion, and Josef Taus was consequently saddled with the job of pacifying Catholics in the party who could not accept this view. Shortly after the 1979 election rout, Taus put forward proposals for a thorough restructuring of the party. These envisaged a demotion of the leagues to 'fractions' of the party, without financial supremacy. Application for membership was to be made, in the first instance, through the OeVP then through a subsidiary sub-organisation. This provoked the opposition of the Farmers' League, and Taus resigned, leaving discussion on the reform of the party still unsettled. The debate continued under his successor, Alois Mock, and a party conference was called to decide on the most appropriate measures.

The party conference meets every three years and is officially the highest decison-making organ in the party. It is composed of delagates from the *Land* sub-organisations, and the auxiliary associations. The sub-organisations are entitled to one delegate for every 10,000 members, but a minimum of twenty-five delegates are entitled to attend from each. The auxiliary associations can send twenty delegates altogether, of which at least two must be from each

Table 3.iv DISTRIBUTION OF CABINET POSTS IN THE OeVP TO THE PROVINCES

Governments	V.	L.A.	U.A.	S.	T.	Vor.	St.	C.	B.
Figl 1945–9	3 Min.	Chanc. 1 Min.	–	–	1 Min.	–	–	1 Sec.	–
Figl 1949–53	3 Min.	Chanc. 1 Min.	–	–	1 Min.	1 Min.	2 Min.	1 Sec.	–
Raab 1953–6	3 Min.	Chanc. 1 Min.	–	–	1 Sec.	1 Sec.	2 Min.	1 Sec.	–
Raab 1956–9	2 Min.	Chanc. 1 Min.	–	–	1 Sec.	1 Sec.	2 Min.	1 Sec.	–
Raab 1959–61	3 Min.	Chanc. 1 Min.	–	–	1 Sec.	1 Sec.	–	1 Sec.	–
Gorbach 1961–3	2 Min.	1 Min.	1 Sec.	1 Min.	1 Sec.	–	Chanc.	1 Min.	–
Gorbach 1963–4	3 Min.	1 Min.	2 Sec.	–	2 Sec.	–	Chanc.	1 Min.	1 Sec.
Klaus 1964–6	2 Min. 3 Min.	1 Min. 1 Min.	1 Sec.	Chanc. Chanc.	1 Sec.	1 Sec.	1 Min.	1 Min.	1 Sec.
Klaus 1966–8	1 Sec.	1 Sec.	1 Min.	1 Min.	1 Min.	1 Sec.	1 Min.	2 Min.	1 Sec.
Klaus 1968–70	3 Min. 1 Sec.	3 Min. 1 Sec.	1 Min.	Chanc.	–	1 Sec.	1 Min.	2 Min.	1 Min.

Min. = Minister, Chanc. = Chancellor, Sec. = State Secretary.

Source: H. Maier, 'Die OeVP 1945–1970', unpublished dissertation, Salzburg, 1971, p.197.

separate association. The *Land* organisations can send one delegate for every 10,000 votes that went to the OeVP in that area in the preceding general election, but at least ten delegates are assigned to each of the *Land* parties. Members of the party in the Government, the *Nationalrat* and the *Bundesrat* are all entitled to attend. The conference is empowered to determine the ideological orientation of the party and its statute, and to elect the party chairman, general secretary and financial manager.

A party council (*Parteirat*) meets annually to give advice and compose resolutions on the current political situation. It selects candidates of the OeVP for the Federal Presidency on the basis of proposals from the party directorate (*Parteileitung*). The party council is composed of members of the directorate, OeVP members of the Government, deputies from Parliament, members of the OeVP in the provincial governments, leaders of the sub-organisations in the provinces, and representatives from auxiliary associations. (The party council was abolished in statute changes which came into force in 1980. At the same time, conference was given the power to elect four deputy leaders.)

The party directorate consists of about fifty members and includes nine provincial leaders, members on the party executive, and leading politicians of the OeVP in the *Nationalrat* and *Bundesrat*. The general secretaries of the sub-organisations attend as well as a member of the party's 'fraction' in the three main chambers and the OeGB. The directorate convenes and carries out the decisions of conference, and can take decisions on matters not covered by other party organs. It decides on the party's position on current topics, runs its financial affairs, and fixes the rate of membership dues. It meets monthly, but its large membership reduces its effectiveness as an important organ.

More powerful in the hierarchy is the party executive which meets every fortnight and deals with the current business of the directorate. It is responsible for the co-ordination of the activities of the federal party, the sub-organisations and the provincial parties. Its members include the leader of the party and his deputies, who until 1980 were always the chairmen of the sub-organisations. In addition up to eight members from the directorate, the party's general secretary, its financial manager and the leader of the parliamentary party constitute the executive.

The leader is supported in the fulfilment of his duties by the general secretary. Since 1976 this post has been occupied by Sixtus Lanner, a former director of the Farmers' League. The general secretary is in charge of the publicity of the party and co-ordinates this work in the provinces and the six sub-organisations. Lanner came under attack in 1979 for his weak handling of the election campaign. Some have questioned the need for a general secretary when the leader of the party is not at the same time concerned with the duties of the Federal Chancellor. In 1977 the general secretary possessed a deputy concerned with organisation, publicity and information, but after the 1979 campaign, it was argued that the work of the deputy duplicates that of the general secretary. The duties of the deputy manager of the party (*Bundesgeschaeftsfuehrer*)[8] were taken over in 1981 by the general secretary.

The selection of candidates for general elections comes within the sphere of influence of the *Land* organisations. They must consider the strength of the individual leagues in the *Land* when deciding the order on the party list. The federal party, in contrast to the SPOe, plays a minor role in this process, and has to be content with the right to name 5 per cent of the places on the party list. In May 1975, the OeVP experimented with primary elections (*Vorwahlen*) in all provinces except Tyrol, the aim being to offset the predominance of anonymous party lists by introducing a personal element into the system. Proposals for candidates were drawn up by the district organisations and sent to the provincial party directorate. Voters could write in a candidate's name if it did not appear on the voting slip, or put a cross by the preferred name if it did—generally voters confirmed the choice of candidates already proposed. The constituency organisations were bound to take note of these decisions in formulating and determining the order of candidates on the party list. The result was considered to have been only partly successful, and this procedure was not repeated before the 1979 election. In 1975 only 16 per cent of the electorate participated in the preliminary election (this represented 41 per cent of party voters and 63 per cent of party members). The OeVP's attempt at increasing inner-party democracy received a mixed response from the country (see Table 3.v).

The federal and league structure of the OeVP not only weakens the political authority of the central party, but also reduces its financial independence. The subscriptions to the sub-organisations are collected at *Land* level and only a small amount finds its way to the federal party. The OeVP does, however, also receive donations from industry, and the state helps to finance its activities and its educational and research centre, called the Political Academy, in Vienna. Like the SPOe, the OeVP relies heavily on membership fees for economic viability (Table 3.vi, p.83).

Table 3.v PARTICIPATION IN THE PRIMARIES, 1975 (%)

	Party Members	Party Voters	Total Electorate
Burgenland	80	57	26
Carinthia	26	11	3
Lower Austria	59	58	27
Upper Austria	85	70	29
Salzburg	31	18	7
Styria	70	33	14
Vorarlberg	34	14	7
Vienna	43	19	6
Austria	63	41	16

Source: A Khol and A. Stirnemann (ed.), *Oesterreichisches Jahrbuch fuer Politik, 1977*. Verlag fuer Geschichte und Politik, Wien, 1978 p.6.

(d) Electoral Support

The OeVP lost its absolute majority in the *Nationalrat* in 1949 and only regained it in 1966, when it was able to form a single-party cabinet. Generally, especially since the *Machtwechsel* of 1970, the trend has been to the SPOe (see Figure 2.i). As an official historian of the OeVP has noted, 'On 1 March 1970 the Austrian People's Party did not only lose a battle but a war.'[9]

One of the main reservoirs of support for the OeVP, the peasant farmer, has been declining in numbers. In 1950, 30.7 per cent of the working population were employed in farming but by 1978 this category had shrunk to only 9.5 per cent. It is estimated that by 1990 this figure will have fallen to just 5 per cent, representing a severe loss for the OeVP. The SPOe has achieved increasing success in small communities and rural areas (see Table 2.iv),which is thus a particularly disturbing trend for the OeVP. The OeVP will have to appeal to voters outside its core group, such as the salaried employees who cannot be regarded as the monopoly of any one party (see Table 2.vii). An additional problem for the OeVP is the presence of another party on the right, the FPOe. In 1979, the OeVP lost votes to the FPOe as well as to the SPOe (see Table 2.iii).

The wealthy farmers and staunch Catholics remain faithful to the OeVP and in the 1979 election it won 55 per cent of the vote in both Vorarlberg and Tyrol. Apart from these strongholds, the party seems to be on the defensive. One of the greatest shocks for it in 1979 was the result in Lower Austria where the SPOe gained more votes than the OeVP for the first time since the war. In this province the SPOe has benefited from the drift of agricultural workers to the

Table 3.vi. PARTY FINANCE 1976 (%)

Source of Income	OeVP	SPOe	FPOe
Membership contributions	47.7	53.4	13.6
State	25.1	30.3	59.0
Donations	14.8	2.4	16.0
*Party Tax	12.4	13.9	11.4

*Those who owe their position in politics or the financial world to a party are obliged to pay a 'party tax'.

Source: A Pelinka, *op. cit.*, p.419.

towns and from the increasing numbers of those who continue to work on the land but seek additional employment in the factories. These workers lose their traditional identification with the OeVP, and seem especially attracted to the SPOe because of its promise to maintain full employment. It is considered that a reform of the OeVP is particularly urgent in Lower Austria: discussion is taking place on how best it should adapt to these changes and modernise its image. The Farmers' League has always been predominant in the OeVP of Lower Austria but has been criticised for failing to keep pace with these developments. In the debate on the rejuvenation of the party, the OeBB is being challenged by the OeAAB, which argues that it can represent the new needs of voters in the area. Election results for the OeVP (Table 3.vii) indicate that some remedial action is required.

The *Landtag* election of 1979 confirmed this trend to the SPOe in the province. The OeVP lost two seats to the SPOe, and for the first time its share of the vote fell below 50 per cent. Results of other provincial elections in 1979 provided the OeVP with some comfort, just after the SPOe's greatest victory in a general election. In the *Landtag* election in Tyrol the OeVP increased its vote by 2 per cent to 63.1 per cent, which was mainly attributed to the popularity of the local candidate. In the general election the SPOe had made its greatest gains in Upper Austria to win, for the first time, over 50 per cent of the vote. In the *Landtag* election which took place five months later, the SPOe hoped for similar successes and campaigned with the declared aim of unseating the OeVP for the governorship. Far from achieving this, the SPOe lost votes and one seat to the OeVP. The result (Table 3. viii) shows the discrepancies in voting behaviour which can occur between regional and national elections.

The *Landtag* elections in the Autumn of 1979 indicate that some voters who had supported the SPOe at federal level (most likely the

Table 3.vii GENERAL ELECTION RESULTS IN LOWER AUSTRIA
SINCE 1966 (%)

	OeVP	*SPOe*
1966	54.03	41.42
1970	50.92	45.21
1971	48.63	47.02
1975	48.12	47.98
1979	47.28	48.40

Table 3.viii VOTING PATTERNS IN UPPER AUSTRIA (%)

Party	*Landtag* *1973*	*Landtag* *1979*	*General Election* *1975*	*General Election* *1979*
OeVP	47.68	51.62	43.68	41.81
SPOe	43.36	41.42	48.75	50.25
FPOe	7.67	6.37	6.74	7.21
KPOe	0.89	0.59	0.83	0.73

'Kreisky voters') switched to the OeVP in provincial elections. At the same time elections were also held in Carinthia where the SPOe has an absolute majority. There the OeVP lost and the SPOe increased its share of the vote to 54 per cent. These figures suggest that the electorate was prepared to confirm the position of the ruling party, and in each case the strongest party gained. It underlines the inherent conservatism of Austrian voters and the reluctance unnecessarily to cause a radical alteration in the balance of power between the parties. This was apparent in Upper Austria where the SPOe had set out to change the political colour of the province and had frightened some voters into defending the OeVP. There is a tendency for the electorate to construct different sets of checks and balances between the two main *Lager*. The 'red-black' coalition of the pre-1966 days would seem to have given way to a 'red' federal government parried by 'black' provinces. The OeVP accounts for six out of the nine provincial governors and the deputy mayor of Vienna. The power of these governors is restricted by the limited nature of Austrian federalism, but they have considerable influence in mobilising the population. In this way they can put pressure on the Federal Government as well as their own party. The personality of the provincial governor is an important factor in determining voting behaviour.

The deputy mayor of Vienna, Dr Erhard Busek, provides the OeVP in the capital with a young, dynamic leadership. Busek has accused the SPOe of major weaknesses—arrogance, tolerance of bureaucracy, and disregard for the ordinary people—which he has attempted to exploit. In the last *Landtag* election of 1978 he snatched four seats from the SPOe, which was temporarily thrown off balance. Busek is keeping up the momentum in the wake of the OeVP's national defeat. His line is to stress the importance of 'people over cars, and gardens over concrete'. Wherever a 'citizens' initiative' is under way to protest against a new bridge or road, Busek can be found energetically supporting the cause. Busek, who is a member of the OeVP's Business League, has been accused by the left and the youth in the SPOe of insincerity and opportunism. It is not yet clear whether Busek's trendy image will yield any long-lasting dividends to the OeVP. If it does, then the party may be tempted to adopt these ideas and, with them, their progenitor. In 1980 Busek took over as one of the deputy chairmen of the party.

The OeVP is represented in the three main chambers by each of the leagues respectively. The Business League dominates the chamber of Commerce and the Farmers' League the chamber of Agriculture, while the Workers' and Employees' League lives in the shadow of a Socialist majority in the Chamber of Labour (AK). The 'fraction' of Christian trade unionists (FCG) finds itself in a minority position in the predominantly Socialist OeGB. The FCG does not have direct links with the party, although there is a close overlap in membership with the OeAAB. Johann Gassner was elected leader of the FCG in 1975 and had, until then, been the general secretary of the OeAAB. The FCG is regularly represented on the presidium of the OeGB and is the second strongest fraction on the OeGB executive.

In elections to the Chamber of Commerce in April 1975, the Austrian Business League (OeWB) gained 86.3 per cent of the vote and won an increase of sixty seats. The Free Business League of the Socialists won 12.7 per cent of the vote and 9.3 per cent of the seats. Results of elections to the Chamber of Agriculture (Table 3.ix) show a similar stable monopoly for the Farmers' League over the group affiliated to the Socialists.

The Farmers' League (OeBB) has overall 84.24 per cent of the votes in the Chamber of Agriculture compared with 8.71 per cent for the SPOe and 1.77 per cent for the FPOe.[10] The SPOe consistently obtains on average around 10 per cent of the seats and its support outside Burgenland and Carinthia is negligible. The chairman of the OeVP Farmers' League, Minkowitsch, is a leading figure in the Chamber of Agriculture; he represents the party in the *Nationalrat* as the second President and deputy to Benya. The close links between the leagues and the major interest groups is further emphasised by the fact that the head of the Business League,

Table 3.ix RESULTS OF ELECTIONS TO THE CHAMBER OF AGRICULTURE

		OeVP		SPOe		FPOe	
		Votes	Seats	Votes	Seats	Votes	Seats
Burgenland	1973	43,470	24	15,378	8	–	–
	1978	38,846	23	15,675	9	1,121	–
Carinthia	1971	17,413	14	6,697	5	2,820	2
	1976	20,175	21	8,120	8	3,546	3
Lower Austria	1970	165,837	30	15,325	1	–	–
	1975	159,685	31	9,767	1	–	–
Upper Austria	1973	101,357	30	4,205	1	–	–
	1979	94,809	31	5,420	1	–	–
Salzburg	1970	21,380	22	1,078	1	–	–
	1975	20,799	24	970	1	1,666	1
Styria	1971	110,090	35	14,361	4	4,639	–
	1976	101,530	37	11,273	4	3,213	–
Tyrol	1973	20,891	16	–	–	128	–
	1979	18,604	16	–	–	–	–
Vorarlberg	1971	11,786	11.	–	–	2,385	2
	1976	13,363	12	–	–	1,627	1
Vienna	1973	1,265	17	225	3	–	–
	1978	1,144	18	190	2	–	–

Sallinger, is also President of the Chamber of Commerce. At the time of writing, twenty-one OeVP members of parliament are officials in the Chamber of Agriculture, nineteen hold important positions in the Chamber of Commerce and the industrialists' federation, and thirteen have close connections with the OeGB and the Chamber of Labour.

The Workers' and Employees' League (OeAAB) puts up a list of candidates for election once every five years to the Chamber of Labour. At the last election, in 1979, it won 31.0 per cent of the votes, making some gains mostly at the expense of the employees' wing of the FPOe. In Vorarlberg, where it is particularly well organised, the OeAAB won 64.9 per cent of the vote compared with 54.2 per cent in 1974. The OeAAB captured the presidency from the SPOe in Vorarlberg in 1974 and had hoped to do the same in Tyrol in 1979. The OeAAB is closing the gap between it and the Socialists in the Tyrol Chamber of Labour, and the SPOe now only has a 0.5 per cent advantage. Elsewhere the Socialists are firmly in control and their overall share of the votes amounts to 64.3 per cent. The OeAAB has been steadily improving its position in this Chamber since the war (Table 3.x). It hopes to build on this success and believes that it could have an important role to play for the party in winning votes in federal elections. Any upgrading of the OeAAB is likely to meet with opposition from the other leagues, which like as far as possible to maintain a status of parity. One proposal for reform is that in all the elections to the Chambers, the OeVP should put up lists in which, somewhere, the party's name appears. Some believe that the existence of the separate leagues weakens the party and confuses voters; this was one of the reasons why the 'Austrian Youth Movement' (OeJB) of the party changed its name in 1972 to Young People's Party (JVP).

The 'fraction' of Christian trade unionists (FCG), although it values its autonomy, works closely with the OeAAB in representing the interests of employees. The FCG's strength in the Trade Union Federation (OeGB) amounts to about 17 per cent, and one of its

Table 3.x ELECTIONS TO THE CHAMBER OF LABOUR (%)

	OeAAB	SPOe	FPOe	KPOe	Others
1949	14.8	62.3	14.4	6.9	1.6
1954	17.2	70.1	2.3	7.3	3.1
1959	19.9	69.5	3.8	4.9	1.9
1964	22.1	68.6	3.3	4.6	1.4
1969	23.5	68.0	5.0	2.6	0.9
1974	29.1	63.4	4.6	2.4	0.4
1979	31.0	64.3	3.2	1.2	0.3

members is the chairman of the Public Service Employees' Union. Johann Gassner is one of the vice-presidents of the OeGB, Chairman of the FCG and a deputy of the OeVP in the *Nationalrat*. The OeVP has three active trade unionists in the *Nationalrat*, and one of its members in the *Bundesrat*, Rudolf Sommer, is the chairman of the Public Service Employees' Union.[11]

In elections for the Federal Presidency, the OeVP has put up a candidate every time without success. It decided not to contest the election of 1980, and left it to the FPOe to oppose the choice of the SPOe. Members of the OeVP were divided on which candidate to support in 1980, lacking clear recommendations from the federal party.

(e) Ideology

The unsatisfactory electoral performance of the OeVP has been attributed to weaknesses in the structure of the party. There are less demands for major changes in the party's ideological position, which is currently based on the Salzburg Programme of 1972. This was the last of five main programmes adopted by the OeVP since the war:

1945   Programmatic Guidelines
1952   'Everything for Austria'
1958   'What we want' (the Innsbruck Programme)
1965   The Klagenfurt Manifesto
1972   The Salzburg Programme

As early as June 1945, before the first post-war elections (held in November), the OeVP had drawn up fifteen points to serve as a programmatic foundation. In these it made clear that, although it was a new party, it belonged to a heritage which defended democracy and Austrian independence. The preoccupation of this programme was with how to reconstruct a viable economy based on justice and freedom. The principle of a comprehensive old-age insurance scheme was included at the request of the employees' wing in the OeVP. An extension in the power of the state was recognised as necessary, provided it was compatible with the requirements of the whole economy. Great prominence was given to safeguarding the position of the peasantry and religious freedoms. The party was prepared to make concessions to its trade unionists by supporting social reforms; it hoped in this way to enlist the co-operation of the SPOe and to stunt the growth of National Socialism or Communism.

The defeat of the OeVP in the elections for the Federal Presidency

in 1951 inaugurated a major reassessment of its position. An extraordinary party conference was called for January 1952 which
adopted the programme, 'Everything for Austria'. It described the
party as the political home for all Austrian patriots who wished to
realise the 'Christian occidental' cultural values which were embodied in the OeVP's philosophy. Selfless service for the fatherland
and for the good of the Austrian people was commended. Federalism and 'solidarism' were elevated to be essential components of
this creed: 'solidarism' stressed the importance of the community
and rejected divisive concepts such as class. It argued for a growth in
the understanding of the need for individuals to work together in an
altruistic society for the good of all. It involved the notion of
Christian morals pervading society but did not endorse any further
political influence in this sphere: the Church was to remain independent. The programme stood for the protection of hard-earned
property, but added that ownership brought with it obligations and a
consideration of the common good. A property-owning society was
believed to be a precondition for freedom: 'The abolition of the proletariat, that is those groups who have nothing to call their own
property other than their labour power, forms an essential part of
the programme of the Austrian People's Party.'[12]

The 'backbone of society', the peasantry, once again received
inordinate attention in the programme; the general welfare of the
economy was considered to be inextricably linked with the fate of the
rural community. A limited role in the economy for the state was
grudgingly recorded but a clear distrust emerged of unnecessary
intervention. The most efficient and hardworking members of
society were to be justly rewarded. With Kamitz as the Minister of
Finance, the OeVP in the 1950s followed the West German CDU's
model of the 'social market economy'. The programme showed a
wish to emphasise the OeVP's willingness to co-operate with other
positive forces in society, but at the same time it betrayed a more
distinct *Abgrenzung* from the SPOe than was apparent in 1945:
'Marxism results in the proletarianisation of the property owners;
the Austrian People's Party aims to de-proletarianise the non-
property owners'. The explicit anti-Marxism of the OeVP was
designed to attract votes from the German nationalist camp, which
had been allowed to contest the 1949 election.

Slight modifications were necessary to the party's programme
after the debate on 'revisionism' in the SPOe and after the signing of
the State Treaty. These were made at a conference in Innsbruck in
November 1958 under the title of 'What we want'. This programme
was more detailed than the basic principles which had been drawn up
in 1952. Some anxiety was apparent about the growth in the modern

world of totalitarian systems and the erosion of personal liberty. The OeVP did not accept that the Austrian Socialists had changed as a result of their new programme, and believed that they were still wedded to the obsolete ideas of Marxism and materialism. Chancellor Raab had described the new programme of the SPOe as 'old wine in new bottles', and the OeVP rejected the idea that the two main parties were becoming ideologically more similar. The programme expressed the view that further extension of state control in the economy was incompatible with democracy. It welcomed an increase in the ownership of property by individuals instead of the state as a means of guaranteeing freedom. The OeVP felt the need to preserve the traditional family unit which it feared was being undermined by materialistic values. It looked forward to a society based on harmony, a sense of responsibility and a partnership between capital and labour.

With the end of the Raab era, debate on the party's ideological orientation increased. Gorbach, who had taken over from Raab in 1960, was himself replaced by the 'reformer' *par excellence*, Josef Klaus, at a party conference in Klagenfurt in 1963. At the same time a draft manifesto was formulated and circulated for internal discussion. An extraordinary party conference was convened in April 1965 in Vienna, and this adopted the 'Klagenfurt Manifesto'. The 'reformers' became associated with a new style of politics which they liked to describe as objective and free from the fixation with the coalition mentality:

'The Reformer does not like to do politics with a wineglass, but rather with a slide rule in his hand.' The new men prefer the efficiency of long-range calculation based on survey-research data to the intuitionist politics of their predecessors. They are, in short, rational managers, who use all the qualities such a label implies in their choice of goals and methods.[13]

The new mood found little expression in the Klagenfurt Manifesto of 1965. The traditional Christian and cultural values were reiterated, and the party pledged its support for the concepts of democracy and 'solidarism'. It emphasised its pro-Austrian commitment and hoped to achieve a stable, peaceful and prosperous society in unison with other interested groups. In practice the party became absorbed with the cool, rational approach to the solution of awkward problems. The programme of the party remained within the old idealistic framework of Christian Social theory.

The new course of the 'reformers' was exemplified in a project called 'Action 20', sponsored by Klaus. The idea was to foster an objective approach to politics by fusing it with science. For this purpose the advice of numerous academics and experts was sought on many topics including education, health,· economics, law and sociology. Ralf Dahrendorf was enlisted from the West German Free Democratic Party (FDP) to demonstrate the 'openness' of the OeVP to those with different political opinions. The iniative 'Action 20' was to examine these topics with a view to assessing and overcoming problems in the period 1965–75. It was not universally welcomed by the party functionaries, and met with the distrust of the leagues, who feared a diminution of their influence on the central decision-making process.[14] Despite the election success of 1966, the OeVP was not united on how best to deal with the problems of the 1970s. The Salzburg Programme of 1972 tried to remedy this, but clarity was often sacrificed for the sake of synthesising league interests.

Changes which took place in the SPOe after Kreisky became leader disorientated the OeVP. The old spectre of Marxism had now become incongruous even though Kreisky had been a member of the Revolutionary Socialists; he was sufficiently bourgeois and respectable for fears of a red take-over to be allayed. His modernisation of the party and interpretation of social democracy gave the SPOe a new, attractive image; it was an attempt—and a successful one—to compete with the OeVP by outmanoeuvring it on the right and not the left. The OeVP, in reply, had little to offer voters—it could either be purely pragmatic or recite the old precepts. Much of its philosophical basis seemed, to many, increasingly archaic. A non-interventionist stance in economics was blatantly at odds with the reality of the situation in Austria. With so many key industries nationalised and a well-developed system of 'social partnership', it seemed absurd to rely on individual ownership of property and market forces to show the way forward. The party's Christian puritanism and protective attitude to the sanctity of family life was finding less response, particularly among the young and among women. The growth of the consumer society with its materialism and emancipation challenged the traditional tenets of the OeVP.

Members in the OeAAB and FCG argued for a restyling of the party, which would overtake the SPOe on the left, but a radical shift of this nature was not likely to find much sympathy from the industrialists in the party. They feared that this would leave the Freedom Party (the FPOe) with a free rein on the right to siphon off support from the OeVP. Despite this the OeVP has refrained from identifying itself fully as 'conservative' which it considers inadequate to describe its dynamic policies.[15] It prefers to associate itself with the 'international community of Christian Democratic parties'. Salvation was finally sought in the idea of the party as a force in the 'progressive centre' of the political spectrum. It seemed to accommodate the different interests in the party but this label had the disadvantage of having already been taken over by the SPOe. Confusion persisted in the People's Party on the most suitable way to approach the SPOe—while some favoured co-operation, others advocated more aggressive opposition. An attempt to embrace both these methods characterised the OeVP's election campaign of 1979, but brought little success. So long as the OeVP trails behind the Government in opinion polls, it must avoid alienating any potential coalition partner. This inevitably restricts a concerted, unqualified attack on the Government and obliges it to be polite and tolerant to the FPOe. The OeVP's current programme is eclectic enough to allow it to pursue most of these options.

Discussion on the reform of the party began in May 1971 and continued in earnest after the election defeat in the autumn. Because of the plethora of ideas put forward, a draft programme had to be substantially modified before receiving unanimous acceptance at a party conference in November 1972. In this, the Salzburg Programme, the OeVP described itself as a party of the 'progressive centre' and of 'social integration', uniting different groups. Partnership and a peaceful resolution of conflict were preferred to the class struggle. The concept of 'solidarism' was still present in the party's thinking, and the individual was reminded of obligations to society; in return, the community would ensure the possibility for self-development of the individual. It was a rejection of both unrestrained collectivism and unrestrained individualism in favour of a Christian vision. The OeVP, although it upheld Christian values, recognised the independence of the Church and of all groups with an overtly religious purpose—Protestant as well as Catholic; it categorically rejected any alliance with a particular confession. In the same way as the SPOe has evolved to work with Christians sharing its beliefs, so the OeVP is prepared to realise its aims with all who share its fundamental principles. A new 'openness' is apparent in both parties which contrasts with the rigidity of their antecedents in the First Republic.

The party guaranteed to maintain basic freedoms and to secure the right to work and to a just share in the fruits of labour. The possession of private property was to be encouraged along with an awareness of the social obligations that it entailed and consideration of the common good. In this spirit the programme condemned private land speculators as anti-social and argued for a modern land reform. The OeVP wanted to see all in society in a position to own property, but warned: 'Property should make its owners free and not enslave others.'[16] Social justice found a place in the programme, which promised to provide assistance for the weak and infirm. The party recorded its opposition to discrimination and all forms of ethnic and religious prejudice. It indicated a desire to change society by abolishing existing inequalities and privileges and giving an equal chance in life to all. The programme stressed that personal effort would be rewarded, and this should be the criterion for determining levels of income, promotion and social recognition. The party accepted the need for a welfare state, but combined this with an exhortation to self-help wherever possible. Decentralisation was favoured as one way of achieving this and freeing the state from unnecessary burdens.

The Salzburg Programme endorsed the idea of the social market economy, which it believed contributed to prosperity and to an increase in the standard of living. Preoccupation with economic growth alone was rejected: the 'quality of life' and environmental protection also featured in the programme. It showed evidence of a social conscience and a desire to create a new humane society. The idea of a participatory democracy was a new element in the OeVP's theory and the programme advocated the active involvement of citizens in political education. It supported the idea of spontaneous groups and an increase in the dissemination of information to facilitate participation. Co-determination was regarded as a positive step in this process and was to be implemented by individuals directly in their own factories. The party supported the notion of capital creation for workers (*Vermoegensbildung*), believing that this would lead to an increase in commitment and so ultimately benefit industry. The Salzburg Programme stated that women were entitled to the same educational and career opportunities as men, and should receive equal pay for equal work. The programme also wanted a clear recognition of the role of women who did not go out to work but preferred to bring up their families. The programme maintained that the family had an important function to fulfil in the education of the young, and that everything should be done to ensure its viability as an independent unit. Abortion was rejected as a method of birth control, although education and advice in family planning were supported.

From 1973 till 1975 the OeVP continued its programmatic discussion with the publication of four booklets under the general heading of 'The Quality of Life'. The first was primarily concerned with health, housing and the environment, and built on many of the ideas outlined in the Salzburg Programme. This recognised the role of the state in the provision of an efficient health system and acknowledged that some illnesses were the outcome of an industrialised society. Small groups and individual initiative were encouraged to help overcome the problem of a lack of communication in the modern world; this would also militate against the growth of an anonymous bureaucratic apparatus. The second plan of the OeVP 'social progress for all' was concerned with co-determination and *Vermoegensbildung*, stressing the importance of partnership in industry and a feeling of involvement by workers. These two plans bore the mark of the employees' wing in the party.

In 1974 the third plan, 'a qualitative social market economy', was produced. This aimed to restrict state activity in economics; competition and not state regulation was supported as the best way to keep prices from rising. It was highly critical of the Socialist government's toleration of large deficits and subsidies to the Federal theatre and railways. This plan condemned the government's policy of deficit financing and recommended cuts in the civil service as one measure to promote rationalisation. The last plan in this series, on education, was put forward in 1975 and envisaged increased expenditure to provide better opportunities for all. The party's attitude to social welfare and the provision of a modern educational system was welcomed by the SPOe, but considered impractical, given the OeVP's negative views on government expenditure. Kreisky continually emphasised this contradiction in the opposition's policies during the 1979 election campaign. He was successful in convincing voters that it was preferable to tolerate high taxation and an increase in state interference in exchange for the reassurance of job security and relative affluence.

The OeVP tried desperately to update its image, and in provincial elections before 1975 it aped the slogans of the SPOe which had been so successful at federal level. The result of the 1975 election brought only disillusionment for the OeVP, which set off once more to communicate its ideas in a series of pamphlets entitled 'New ways for Austria'. They were to form the policies for an alternative to the SPOe, and promised to provide jobs, help the elderly, families, farmers and women. They were strangely similar to the policies already being put into practice by the SPOe. The OeVP continued with its mission to save the budget and protect the citizen from the monster, Socialist state. No. 14 of 'New Ways' suggested cutbacks (apart from the security forces) on unnecessary, wasteful expenditure. Accordingly school buildings were to be constructed on the basis of demographic indicators. Subsidies to the theatre, railways and postal services were to be cut. Neither 'New Ways' nor the 'Quality of Life' series brought the OeVP electoral success. The post-mortem of 1979 has been conducted mainly on the structure of the leagues rather than on the ideology of the party. Many in the OeVP believe that the Salzburg Programme does not need amending. They criticise the party for failing to put its ideas into practice where it has been in power in the provincial and local communities. They believe that this contributes to popular distrust of the party and a belief that it does not practice what it preaches.

In their basic programmes, the two main parties show a growing tendency to converge. Both stress the importance of freedom, equality, democracy and social justice. The need to create a humane society and to control economic growth in order to save the environment is recognised by both parties. Similarly wider participation in the decision-making process, to overcome a feeling of helplessness and alienation of individuals finds a prominent place in the programmes. In foreign policy a large degree of consensus has developed between the two main parties in the Second Republic, and both emphasise the necessity to safeguard neutrality. The parties still vary in the amount of stress they place on the desirability of state intervention, on the importance of the family's role and on modes of co-determination and self-help. A survey of 1975 showed that 42 per cent of the population found it increasingly difficult to detect major differences between the SPOe and OeVP. This left a majority of 56 per cent convinced that 'in many basic questions, as well as in their practical policies,' the two strongly differed.[17] It is questionable whether most of the electorate are sufficiently well-informed to appraise the growing ideological similarity between the two political parties from programmes, policy statements and suchlike. Just two-thirds of Austrians were aware that the SPOe had drawn up a new programme in 1978, but only one-third had even a vague idea of its essential points.[18]

The main driving force of ideological debate in the OeVP has come from the Workers' and Employees' League, the OeAAB. The intellectuals from this wing in the party tend to be receptive to many of the policies of the SPOe, especially on social reform and an improvement in working conditions. The OeAAB supported the SPOe's proposal to introduce a minimum of four weeks' annual holiday for all workers, which provoked the hostility of the OeVP's Business League(OeWB). The latter is mainly an interest organisation and is not predisposed to the articulation of grandiose ideological schemes.

Several middle-class-based groups exist outside the OeVP which are antagonistic to the OeAAB and wish to see the party move decisively to the right. Among these is the 'Association of the Free Self-employed' an organisation which campaigns against the 'Moscow course' of the SPOe. It is directed by Karl Steinhauser, produces a magazine called *Blitz* and is believed to have around 14,000 supporters. In the summer of 1978, Steinhauser was active in encouraging a blockade of Austria's borders by lorry drivers as a protest against the increase in the transit levy. This mobilisation alarmed many who were not used to such disruptive tactics in the Second Republic. It is considered that in the long run such militancy can only be counter-productive, and the OeVP is reluctant to become too involved: it has a large stake in the 'social partnership' model, and the adoption of radical politics could only serve to paralyse this highly successful mechanism. The Business League in the OeVP can have little interest in damaging this informal partnership, which continues to provide it with benefits. These considerations act as a brake on the party lurching too far to the right in response to electoral defeat. Clearly the party will have to present a sharper ideological profile to voters in addition to introducing organisational changes if it is to become a credible alternative to the SPOe.

REFERENCES

1. For the position of the 'reformers', see H. Andics, *Die Insel der Seligen*, Molden Verlag, Wien, 1976, pp.276–93.
2. Figl—OeBB; Raab—OeWB; Gorbach—OeAAB; Klaus—OeWB; Withalm—OeWB; Schleinzer—OeBB; Taus—OeAAB; Mock—OeAAB.
3. Membership figures and details taken from *Bericht zur Parteiarbeit 1974-1977*, OeVP, Wien.
4. Cited by P.M. Zulehner in H. Fischer, *Das politische System Oesterreichs*, Europa-verlag, Wien, 1977, p.634.
5. A. Pelinka in A. Khol and A. Stirnemann(ed.), *Oesterreichisches Jahrbuch fuer Politik 1978*, Verlag fuir Geschichte und Politik, Wien, 1979, p.49.
6. For a history of the OeCV see G. Hartmann(ed.), *Der CV in Oesterreich*, OeCV—Bildungsakademie, Wien, 1977.
7 For details see L. Reichhold, *Geschichte der OeVP*, Verlag Styria, Graz, 1975, p.475.
8. See *Bundesparteiorganisationsstatut*, OeVP Linz, 1977, pp.19–25.
9. L. Reichhold, *Die Chance der OeVP*, Verlag Styria, Graz, 1972, p.53.
10. Figures taken from *Bericht zur Parteiarbeit, op. cit.*, p.58.
11. Information supplied by the *Nachrichtendienst*, OeGB, 8 November 1979. See also, A. Pelinka, 'Die oesterreichische Volkspartei', *Austriaca*, May, 1980, pp.33–5.
12. K. Berchtold, *Oesterreichische Parteiprogramme 1868–1966*, Verlag fuer Geschichte und Politik, Wien, 1967, p.383.
13. Cited in W.T. Bluhm, *Building an Austrian Nation*, Yale University Press, New Haven and London, 1973, p.111.
14. L. Reichhold, *Geschichte der OeVP*, Verlag Styria, Graz, 1975, pp.383ff.

15. *Grundsaetze fuer die Praxis*, Vereinigung fuer politische Bildung, Wien, 1976, p.29.
16. *Das Salzburger Programm*, OeVP, 1972, 4,5.
17. M.Fischer-Kowalski and J. Bucek(ed.), *Ungleichheit in Oesterreich*, Jugend und Volkverlag, Wien, 1979, p.210.
18. *Journal fuer angewandte Sozialforschung*, no.4, 1978, pp.29–30.

4

THE FREEDOM PARTY AND THE RIGHT

(a) Historical Background

The Freedom Party of Austria (FPOe) is a new party which has come into being in the Second Republic. The persistence of a marked German-nationalist wing places it to the right of the FDP in West Germany. During the days of the Great Coalition it was excluded from power, and had little influence on the decision-making process. It has increased in importance as a bargaining partner since the formation of single-party governments, although it has not been able to exploit this potential fully. Internal ideological disputes and leadership squabbles have blunted the effectiveness of the party as a political force. Associations with anti-clericalism arouse distrust in the OeVP, while the SPOe continues to suspect pro-Nazi leanings. The FPOe has many difficulties to overcome before it can, for the first time, qualify for consideration in a cabinet after a possible close-run election. Its chances are not at present rated very high, and some have even speculated that it may be eclipsed altogether from Austrian political life.

The FPOe regards itself as part of a national-liberal tradition stretching back to the nineteenth century. It rejects ties with the period between 1938 and 1945, but otherwise stresses a continuity with the past. The FPOe considers that its predecessors fought against the internationalism of both Catholicism and Marxism, and that in the Second Republic it is continuing with a similar struggle against the red-black *Proporz* system. In this sense the party sees in its history a consistent fight against absolutism and for freedom.

The FPOe is a descendant of the pan-German nationalist *Lager* which was militantly anti-Habsburg and anti-Slav. Its strength lay in Lower Austria, Vienna and areas where a threat to German culture was felt. Under the inspiration of Georg von Schoenerer, (1842-1921), who became a parliamentary deputy in 1873, it became a radical exponent of anti-liberal and anti-semitic ideas. The slow pace of industrialisation in the empire retarded the development of a liberal urban bourgeoisie. Schoenerer failed to create a mass basis for his movement, although his anti-establishment views were popular among students and declassé elements. One of the early followers was Victor Adler, who later founded the Social Democratic Party; he was attracted by Schoenerer's social reform programme, but increasing anti-semitism made it difficult for him to work in the movement.[1]

Adler's social democrats and Lueger's Christian Social Party gradually contributed to the waning support, particularly in Vienna, for the pan-Germans. Schoenerer's overt anti-Catholicism alienated many who would otherwise have sympathised with his philosophy. This third *Lager* could not compete as a coherent mass movement, but in its challenge to the existing order it remained an influential force.

In the First Republic several groups joined together to form the Pan-German People's Party. A Peasants' Party in Styria remained apart from this, later forming a section of the Agrarian League (*Landbund*), which was strong in Protestant areas. Both contributed to the lack of pro-Austrian national consciousness by their support of the idea of *Anschluss* with Germany, which typified the political parties and associations of the First Republic. The pan-German nationalist *Lager* never secured a co-ordinated central direction, and provincial leaders tended to be important in dictating their party's ideological position. Despite this weakness, the pan-German nationalists occupied a pivotal position between the two main *Lager*, neither of which was able during the First Republic to win an absolute majority in Parliament (See Table 4.i); but the pan-German nationalists' internal feuds paralysed all efforts to operate as an independent political force and negated this advantage. Their participation in the anti-Socialist bourgeois coalitions was an important factor in keeping the Christian Socials in power. In the early 1930s many pan-German nationalists drifted to the National Socialists, while members of the Agrarian League gave guarded support to Dollfuss before finally disbanding themselves.

Table 4.i PARLIAMENTARY REPRESENTATION IN THE FIRST REPUBLIC
(*seats*)

Year	Christian Socials	Social Democrats	German Nationalists	Other
1919	63	69	24	3
1920	82	66	26	1
1922*	85	69	28	1
1923	82	68	15	–
1927	73	71	21	–
1930	66	72	19	8

*Figures amended to include results in Burgenland 1922.

Source: M. Welan, *Parteien und Verbaende in Oesterreich*, Verlag fuer Geschichte und Politik, Wien, 1970, p.6.

The various permutations of alliances attempted on the right led a fragile existence, plagued by religious and political cleavages. The unyielding strength of the 'Austro-Marxist' camp was the spectre which promoted the acceptance of radical extremism as a political solution. After the Second World War, the successors to the *Lager* showed a willingness to co-operate with each other in the parliamentary system. Even if founded on mutual distrust, the Great Coalition represented a break with the previous rigid polarisation. This new climate reduced the scope for a third *Lager*, and the domination of the Second Republic by the OeVP and the SPOe has brought difficulties for the successors to this tradition.

(b) The Second Republic

The remnants of the former Agrarian League decided in 1945 to join forces with the OeVP, providing it with an additional source of support in rural areas. A pan-German nationalist party was not allowed to re-form for the elections in November 1945, but with support from the Socialists, a successor to this *Lager* —the League of Independents (VdU)—was granted a license to contest the next election in 1949. The OeVP protested, and accused the Socialists of scheming to split the bourgeois *Lager,* but once this fourth party had been formed, both the OeVP and the SPOe were concerned to woo its members for their own advantage.

The VdU was formed by two journalists Dr Herbert Kraus and Viktor Reimann in Salzburg, which was chosen as its base since it was outside the Soviet Zone, and because, together with Graz, it had been a centre for Nazi activities before 1938. It fought the 1949 election under the name 'Electoral Party of Independents' (WdU) and won sixteen seats, representing 12 per cent of the vote. It did particularly well in the western provinces and, to the surprise of the SPOe, gained seats at the expense of the left. During the campaign the WdU complained of sabotage and reported that evidence had been found of interference with its mail.

The first leader of the VdU was Kraus, who had concluded in 1945 that pan-Germanism was a spent force.[2] He had served in the German army but had not been a member of the NSDAP. In place of pan-Germanism, Kraus adopted the idea of a united Europe which was to become a substitute concept for many ex-pan-German nationalists. However, his main interests lay in economic affairs rather than with nationalist theories. His collaborator, Reimann, had originally been in the NSDAP but left it in 1939 to join a Catholic group. Reimann subsequently spent over four years in a concentration camp, and after the war could claim to have a German nationalist background in addition to being a victim of Nazism. He became editor of the party's paper *New Front* in 1949. He possessed a more romantic vision of the German nation than Kraus, but because of his concentration camp background, he was not trusted by the right in the VdU.

Kraus aimed to integrate into his party those returning from the war who found readjustment difficult. He campaigned against laws which he believed to be 'undemocratic' because they discriminated against former Nazis. He estimated that support for such a party could be in the 7–20 per cent range, and never envisaged the growth of a mass membership party. The idea of the VdU as a 'third force' or check on the power of the main parties and the *Proporz* system figured prominently in the philosophy of Kraus. He had hoped to establish a broad 'liberal' basis for the VdU, since it was clear that purely pan-Germanist elements had been decimated, but this was not accepted by all in the party and the VdU quickly degenerated into a multiplicity of rival factions. Regionally the party showed wide variations and while in Upper Austria it was more 'social-liberal' in orientation, in Tyrol it was conservative and built on a former component of the *Heimwehr*.

The leader of the party in Vienna was a radical pan-German nationalist, Fritz Stueber. In 1949 Stueber entered Parliament as a VdU deputy, and announced his pride in following the tradition of von Schoenerer.[3] He became a controversial figure, repeatedly making provocative speeches which amounted to apologetics for the Third Reich. He was fully in agreement with the decision to seat VdU deputies on the extreme right in parliament. In 1956, under pressure from the party, this was revoked, and the FPOe deputies in the *Nationalrat* now occupy a central position. Stueber operated independently of the Salzburg leadership and launched attacks on its 'careerist' policies. After the Presidential elections of 1951, Kraus resigned as leader of the VdU and in October 1952 was replaced by Max Stendebach, who initiated a more right-wing course. In the elections for the Federal Presidency in 1951, a candidate of the VdU put up a good performance in the first round. He nevertheless had to withdraw, and in the second round Kraus supported the OeVP's candidate who lost to the Socialist Koerner. The nationalist wing under Stueber had protested against this engagement of the VdU for the 'black' candidate, believing that it reduced the credibility of the party in the eyes of its own voters.

After the general election of 1953, Kraus pressed for discussions with the OeVP. Stueber opposed all such moves, and was expelled in November 1953 for breach of discipline and for damaging the VdU by continual opposition. He had scorned Kraus' idea of a 'loyal' and 'constructive' opposition, and advocated an uncompromising attack on the parliamentary system and the 'red-black' *Proporz*: 'Our struggle is not about participation in the system but in overcoming it.'[4]

Although the WdU had lost seats in 1953, Stueber was heartened by the results in Vienna, where he managed to make some gains. He attributed this to his concentration on a nationalistic campaign. Stueber was not unanimously expelled, and his ideas had greater roots in the party even though his projects were not especially successful. Stueber stayed in Parliament as a maverick, and was the only deputy refusing to vote for the ratification of the State Treaty in 1955. He decided in 1956 not to seek re-election to Parliament; although his old party adopted a more right-wing attitude, he was unable to come to an agreement with the new leadership. He founded his own movement, the Freedom Group of Austria (FSOe) which was supported by some members of the VdU in Vienna, but this failed to make any electoral impact and by the mid-1950s had become an insignificant force. Stueber dissolved the organisation and replaced it with a similarly luckless 'Democratic National Workers' Party' (DNAP) which lasted for two years. Both parties were intended to induce respect for the ideas of National Socialism but found little support. Stueber failed to attract many former Nazis, who regarded him as an intellectual dreamer rather than a serious activist.

These internal feuds did little to help the fortunes of the VdU and it began losing support in regional elections. In 1955 a right-wing 'Free Party' (FP) was founded by Anton Reinthaller, an ex-Nazi who had been Minister for Agriculture in the cabinet of Seyss-Inquart formed after the *Anschluss* in 1938. After lengthy negotiations, the FP merged with the VdU in 1956, thus creating the FPOe, over which Reinthaller assumed control. Kraus dissociated himself from the new FPOe believing that it had fallen under the domination of right-wing extremists and former Nazis.[5] He claimed that it had never been his intention to create a successor to National Socialism, but that he had merely tried to regenerate the movement and provide it with a social-liberal dimension. Reimann, the co-founder with Kraus of the VdU, refused to ally with the new FPOe although most members of the VdU joined it. The FPOe fared even worse in elections than its predecessor. The signing of the State Treaty increased the popularity of the Great Coalition, and both the main parties were striving hard to integrate frustrated ex-Nazis. This deprived the FPOe of its *raison d'être*, and left it little to offer to the majority of voters.

Reinthaller died in 1958 and was succeeded by Friedrich Peter, who was to lead the party for twenty years. Peter, hitherto the leader of the FPOe in Upper Austria, was a former SS officer, and at first he continued to direct the party in Reinthaller's style. He dismissed the idea of Austria as a 'nation', and advocated a positive appraisal of the efforts made by soldiers who had defended the fatherland in the Second World War. His vision was of Austria as a free German state in a united Europe. Peter represented the 'Front' generation in the third *Lager*, consisting of those who, unlike Kraus and Reimann, had been actively committed to Nazism during the war. Paradoxically it was Peter who initiated a reform of the FPOe which sought to make it more respectable in the Second Republic. He tried to transform it from its purely oppositional role and to integrate it into the existing system. He fostered relations with the SPOe and particularly with Kreisky but was handicapped by his 'brown' past. Shortly after the 1975 election, Peter was accused of complicity in the extermination of Jews and Gypsies during the war. Kreisky became involved in the affair by defending Peter's position in public life; this was unpopular with many in the SPOe who believed that Peter should not hide behind the theory of collective guilt.

Peter steered the party through a series of dismal election results. His survival as leader was an example of stamina, good luck and an absence of other willing contenders. In the autumn of 1978, the FPOe looked to a new leader, Dr Alexander Goetz, who had been quietly gaining some fame in the province of Styria. In April 1973, with the support of the OeVP, Goetz had become mayor of Graz, the second largest city in Austria. The party hoped that the 'Graz model' could be repeated on a national scale, but was disillusioned by the results in 1979 which confirmed the supremacy of the SPOe. Goetz came from the right wing in the party and his associates during his student days were members of pan-German nationalist groups. He had been a member of the Hitler Youth and imprisoned by the British occupation authorities for over a year at the end of the war. He differed from Peter by launching an attack on Kreisky, arguing for more confrontation in politics.

The aggressive style of Goetz was not welcomed by all in the FPOe, and a crisis developed in the party just one year after he had assumed the leadership. He was now in Parliament and mayor of Graz. It seemed increasingly unlikely that he could combine these two functions, and at the same time keep firm control of the party in Vienna. It was no secret that he felt more at home in Styria, and during the 1979 election campaign he forsook the capital, leaving his general secretary in charge. Peter was still leader of the parliamentary party and as such presented a potential threat to Goetz's authority; Goetz intimated that he wanted Peter's post in addition to the leadership, but he could not carry the party with him, especially the members in Vienna. Furthermore, his opponents in the party believed that he should fulfil his duties in the *Nationalrat* free from additional responsibilities as mayor. He chose to withdraw from the *Nationalrat,* and returned to Graz, where at first he intended to continue his leadership of the federal party, arguing that this was a gesture the FPOe could make to demonstrate that it favoured decentralisation, and hinting that future meetings would occur more in the provinces, which would have a greater influence on the party.

Criticism of Goetz's behaviour mounted: his irresolution was considered bad publicity for the party. It was arranged that the party's general secretary would enter Parliament in his place, but he suddenly announced his resignation from his post and declined the offer. Unable to subdue the criticism of his incompetence and remoteness from colleagues, Goetz resigned as leader. The party was left in a state of utter confusion and hastily found an interim leader from Upper Austria, an ex-son-in-law of Peter. Meanwhile, the party executive proposed that the next party conference should adopt Dr Norbert Steger from Vienna as the new leader.

Steger is associated with the liberal wing in the FPOe, and had been a constant critic of the economic policies of Goetz, which, in his view, had pushed the party too far to the right and had weakened its employees' wing. This was reflected in the losses it sustained in elections to the Chamber of Labour in 1979. Steger believed that this damage could not compensate for any bonus the party had received in the way of increased donations from industry. Shortly after his designation as the new leader, he announced that he saw the FPOe as essentially a 'national-liberal' party; it was obvious from this statement that he was obliged to appease both wings in the party, and that it is difficult to eject the ideological ballast of German nationalism. Steger, who was born in 1944, has more credibility than many in his party in disowning the negative aspects of the nationalist tradition.

Just before the party conference was due, Goetz intervened to propose his own protégé, Dr Harald Ofner, leader of the Lower Austrian party, for the leadership. This was a clear indication of the rifts in the FPOe, which make it difficult for it to present to the public a picture of strength. It is believed by many, especially in Vienna, that the 'Goetz course' has damaged the party and brought it into disrepute. Ofner represents those in the FPOe who are mistrustful of the urbane intellectual, Steger, with his fanciful ideas on social policy. The adoption of a pronounced liberal course could split the party and cripple the electoral chances of rival successors. The weakness of the two opposition parties, the FPOe and the

OeVP, is a source of jubilation and often amusement for members of the SPOe, but in the long run, it cannot be considered desirable for democracy in Austria.

At the party conference in Linz in 1980, Steger was elected leader with 247 out of 451 votes. His opponent Ofner obtained 199 votes, an indication of the strength of the nationalist wing and of the difficulties which Steger faces in uniting the party.

(c) Electoral Support

In the first election which it contested in 1956, the FPOe lost eight of the fourteen seats which had been held by the VdU. Since then it has gained on average just over 6 per cent of the vote or roughly half the support originally mobilised by the WdU in 1949, when it gained votes outside the reservoir of former National Socialists. The WdU's regional strength was similar to that of the pan-German nationalists before the war, although support dwindled in the eastern areas under Soviet occupation. Yet it benefited in the west, and particularly in Upper Austria, from the shift in the population from the Soviet zone. The WdU lost some ground in Styria where Alfons Gorbach, later Chancellor and leader of the OeVP, was sympathetic to the national camp and had integrated many potential members into the OeVP. The engagement of the former leader of the Agrarian League, who came from Carinthia, for the OeVP encouraged others to follow his example. His decision deprived the WdU of a significant agrarian base, and sections of the Protestant peasantry in Burgenland, who had once supported the Agrarian League, switched to the OeVP.[6]

In 1953 the WdU lost support in Upper Austria among sections of the working class who abandoned it for the SPOe, and in the 1956 election the FPOe incurred further losses to the main parties. The

Table 4.ii REGIONAL VOTING STRENGTH OF THE THIRD *LAGER* (%)

	1930	1949	1953	1956
Vienna	10	7	11	6
Lower Austria	8	4	5	3
Upper Austria	7	21	12	7
Salzburg	13	18	19	15
Styria	17	14	14	7
Tyrol	12	17	13	6
Vorarlberg	21	22	19	10
Carinthia	22	20	17	15
Burgenland	16	4	4	3

exodus of the 'liberal' wing under Kraus left the party with a shallow bourgeois base. It became identified with negative policies and picked up protest votes from those disillusioned with the OeVP-SPOe coalition.

The strength of the FPOe is concentrated in the small towns and among the self-employed. Salaried employees and civil servants are over-represented in the social composition of its support (see Table 2.vii). The FPOe's electoral base is similar to that of the OeVP, with the difference that its adherents are manifestly areligious (see Table 3.iii). Most of the gains the FPOe made in the 1979 election were at the expense of the OeVP (see Table 2.iii). Its greatest support came from Salzburg (11.41 per cent in 1979), but otherwise only in Carinthia and Vorarlberg was it able to poll more than 10 per cent. This voting pattern is reflected in *Landtag* elections, where the party can rely on 15 per cent of the vote in Salzburg, 12.5 per cent in Vorarlberg and 12 per cent in Carinthia. Least support in the 1979 election came from the eastern *Bundeslaender* of Burgenland (2.73 per cent), Lower Austria (3.56 per cent) and Vienna (4.73 per cent). Research has indicated that the FPOe had, on average, greater success in areas with a high proportion of pensioners. Academics continue to show a preference for the FPOe, and constitute one section of the population which is showing more resistance to the trend towards the SPOe; the proportion of total SPOe supporters who are academics has increased from 0.9 per cent in 1971 to 1.2 per cent, but this still lags behind 3.4 per cent for the OeVP and 6.5 per cent for the FPOe. Since the percentage of academics in the total population is estimated at 2.4, it is clear that this group has an above-average affinity with the third *Lager*.[7]

During the 1979 campaign, the SPOe set out to revive fears of a 'bourgeois block', something which retains negative connotations from the First Republic. The strategy was successful in ensuring a clear majority for the Socialists and seems to have damaged the OeVP more than the FPOe. Possibly the combination of Taus and Goetz helped to prompt young voters to opt for the more progressive SPOe. One survey showed that 40 per cent of those questioned suspected that the OeVP would form a coalition with the FPOe if no party possessed an absolute majority. Only 13 per cent considered this desirable, whereas 50 per cent found the Great Coalition the preferable system of government under these circumstances.[8] The FPOe has shown little promise of being a reliable partner in a small coalition. In the 1950s it tended to favour relations with the OeVP when the latter was in command. After the narrow result of 1953 election, the VdU entered into discussions with the OeVP, but these were abruptly cut short by the intervention of the Federal President. The isolation in domestic politics of the newly-formed FPOe continued into the 1960s. Before the 1962 election it seemed hopeful of forming a 'black-blue' coalition with the OeVP, but it was disillusioned by the survival of the Great Coalition. It subsequently explored the possibility of coming to an arrangement with the Socialists. This seemed a viable enterprise after the FPOe allied with the SPOe in 1963 in defeating the efforts of the OeVP to allow the return to Austria of Otto Habsburg. This rapprochement was severely damaged by the 'Olah affair' which revealed dubious financial support of the FPOe by the Socialist trade unionist.

The fall of the Great Coalition in 1966 ended the lone opposition of the party, and gave it renewed aspirations to act as a mediator. The FPOe calculated that the OeVP would lose its absolute majority in 1970, and hinted that it did not rule out a 'black-blue' government. Unwisely the FPOe rejected an alliance with the SPOe, which won a relative majority. From the spring of 1970 until the next election in the autumn of 1971, the FPOe gave qualified support to Kreisky's minority Government. The impact of the 'third force' was never greater than during these months, and the FPOe won some concessions from Kreisky, including consideration of its taxation proposals in the budget. One of the most important benefits was a reform of the electoral system which meant that the FPOe needed to win roughly the same number of votes to obtain a seat as either of the two main parties, instead of twice as many under the old procedures. The absolute majority of the Socialists since 1971 has frustrated the FPOe's quest to hold the balance of power. Its internal difficulties further restrict its activities and reduce its influence with the other two parties. The present apparent disintegration of the party will not inspire much confidence in it as a future coalition ally.

In the Presidential election of 1951, the VdU's candidate gained more than 15 per cent of the vote and did particularly well in the city of Salzburg, where he polled 48 per cent. In 1957 the FPOe put up a joint candidate with the OeVP, who was unsuccessful against the Socialist Schaerf. Many FPOe supporters preferred Schaerf because of his anti-clerical image, and the OeVP blamed th FPOe for the defeat. The FPOe fielded a candidate for the 1980 Presidential election, who benefited from the absence of a rival from the OeVP. Some members of the latter openly declared their support for Willfried Gredler, a Catholic from the Tyrol and former member of the OeVP. One problem for the FPOe was that the right-wing neo-Nazis contested the election, forcing Gredler to clarify his role in the Resistance Movement. Gredler was reluctant to stress his activities as a Resistance fighter but was keen to glean votes from liberals. He was evasive on his attitude to Nazism for fear of losing the pan-German nationalist vote: 'In 1938 I was certainly no supporter of the *Anschluss,* but I was by no means unsympathetic to National Socialism.'[9] Gredler describes himself as a 'man of the centre' and appealed to those who were in disagreement with the Socialists' monopoly of power. He was critical of the passivity with which Kirchschlaeger had conducted the Presidency, although it was not clear how he would seek to reinterpret these duties if elected. The presence of a rival from the extreme right deprived Gredler of votes he would otherwise have picked up from malcontents. The FPOe has found it difficult in elections to mobilise 'liberal' voters, who in recent years have given support to Kreisky. The stability and economic prosperity of the Second Republic has contributed to a positive acceptance of 'Austria', which was absent before the war. The tendency of the FPOe to play down the achievements of an independent Austria identifies it as a party of the past.

The FPOe has very weak links with the major interest groups which in Austria are dominated by the two main parties. In the Chamber of Commerce the adherents of the FPOe do not form an independent group, but often collaborate with the Business League of the OeVP. Support for the party in the Chamber of Agriculture is negligible (see Table 3.ix). In the Chamber of Labour the employees' wing of the party polled 3.2 per cent of the votes in 1979, and sustained losses in every province, mainly to the OeVP's advantage (see Table 3.x). A separate FPOe *Fraktion* is not explicity recognised in the OeGB, although since 1972 FPOe members have nominal representation on the executive board. Loose connections with the interest groups enable the FPOe to criticise the oligarchical nature of what it regards as an essentially Chamber and Trade Union state.

(d) Organisation

The FPOe does not publish membership figures but these are estimated to be around 35,000. Membership, as in the SPOe, is direct and individual. Compared to the other three main parties, it has a low percentage of members in relation to voters, just over 12 per cent. It can be described, in this sense, as the only voter-based party of any significance in Austrian politics. It depends, more than either the SPOe or the OeVP, on financial support from the state (see Table 3.vi).

The Federal conference of the party meets every two years and elects a leader and his deputies. It consists of members of the party directorate and delegates from the provinces. The conference also elects the party directorate and the FPOe executive. The leader of the party chairs the conference as well as the party directorate and

Table 4.iii
ELECTIONS TO THE STUDENTS' UNION (%)

	RFS	*VSSTOe	*OeSU
1953	32	17	49
1955	31	12	56
1957	29	12	60
1959	27	14	58
1961	27	14	57
1963	27	12	55
1965	29	12	58
1967	30	13	49
1969	29	12	49
1971	25	11	54
1974	21	13	42
1975	15	17	36
1977	8	17	48
1979	7	18	38

*The VSSTOe is the Socialist students' organisation; the OeSU is supported by the OeVP. Both the OeSU and the RFS have lost ground in recent years to a rival right-wing group of 'Young Europeans' (JES), also sponsored by the OeVP, which won 14 per cent of the vote in 1979. Participation has dropped from 60 per cent in 1953 to 33 per cent in 1979.

executive, and he is empowered to call these organs into session. The FPOe leader is entrusted with the supervision of the entire activity of the party, and he must prepare for meetings of the executive and carry out its decisions. In consultation with the party executive, he appoints the manager and top posts in the secretariat.

The party directorate is composed of almost ninety members and includes members of the executive, the party's members in the provincial governments and the party's parliamentary deputies. It meets at least four times a year and determines general guidelines for the party. It prepares and carries out the decisions of conference, and can set up committees and working parties. It is entrusted with the administration of party funds and fixes membership fees. The party executive consists of about nineteen members including the leader and his deputies, leaders of the provincial parties and the chairman of the party's group in Parliament. According to the party's statute, at least one member of the executive must be a woman. The occupational background of the party executive is largely public service (42.1 per cent); self-employed account for the next largest group (31.5 per cent), while salaried employees and workers (each 10.5 per cent) and farmers (5.2 per cent) make up the rest of the party's executive.[10] The executive prepares and carries out the decisions of the directorate, and in emergencies can fulfil the directorate's duties. It further has the responsibility to deal with all matters not specifically designated to another organ. The presidium of the party is a smaller organisation consisting of the leader, his deputies and the chairman of the party's group in Parliament. It is concerned with the current administration of the FPOe, and has to deal with duties assigned to it by the executive. Local groups play an important part in the decision-making process of the party, and enjoy relative independence. It has not been the intention of the FPOe to create a large centralised organisation. In comparison with the statute of the OeVP and the SPOe, the FPOe's is a very short document.

The party has its own weekly newspaper, the *Neue Freie Zeitung*, and produces a quarterly theoretical magazine, *Freie Argumente*. Since 1972 it has had a research organisation, the Political Academy, based in Baden near Vienna, which holds regular meetings and seminars.

The FPOe does not have the extensive network of auxiliary associations which is a feature of the two main parties. But it does not have a youth organisation, the Ring of Free Youth (RFJ) with its headquarters in Salzburg; this caters for those under thirty, and membership is believed to be about 5,000. It is overtly pan-German nationalist and rejects the idea of an Austrian 'nation'. The Association of Free Academics also exhibits pronounced right-wing and pan-German nationalist sentiments. It produces a magazine *Die Aula* in which references to the unity of the German fatherland are common. The students' organisation of the party (RFS) publishes a magazine, the *Ring,* which shows a similar bias: it is rooted in the Cold War mentality and publishes frequent gruesome accounts of attacks on human rights in Eastern Europe. But support for the RFS in the universities has been declining, and in the 1979 elections it could not muster much more support than the parent-party gained in the Federal election (Table 4.iii, p.109). In addition to these groups, the party has an association for teachers, who figure prominently in the party, and an organisation for pensioners centred in Linz, the capital of Upper Austria.

(e) Ideology

The revival of the national-liberal *Lager* in 1949 was accompanied by a programmatic statement. This was chiefly inspired by Herbert Kraus and assigned an important role to the rule of law, moral purity and individual effort. The autonomy of the state was accepted, although an allegiance to cultural and racial links with the German *Volkstum* was emphasised. It was considered that a United States of Europe would be a contribution to peace and economic progress. The VdU's first programme made clear its opposition to the party *Proporz* and to corruption in administrative life. It defended the right to private property, and rejected nationalisation and the promotion of class hatred in society. It wished to establish a progressive system of social legislation, and organise welfare to cater for the needs of 'victims' of the war. Kraus hoped to appeal to former Nazis by ensuring their integration in the new state, and aimed to reduce punitive measures which worked to their disadvantage.

A new programme was formulated by the VdU in Bad Aussee in May 1954, in which more prominence was given to the 'nationalist' aims of the party:

Austria is a German state. Its politics must serve the entire German people and should never be directed against another German state. We demand the unity of European nations on the basis of full equality of rights.[11]

The VdU considered that the nations of Europe should have learnt from the experiences of 1945 that problems could only be overcome jointly. Within a new European community it was understood that the uniqueness of the individual nations would be guaranteed. The VdU pledged to strengthen the German *Volk* in Austria by fostering a feeling of belonging together with all Germans (*Zusammengehoerigkeitsbewusstsein*). It hoped to create a physically and intellectually healthy youth whose education would be based on a community spirit, self-discipline, a sense of responsibility and readiness to make sacrifices. The programme supported the idea of the 'social market economy' and free competition. It objected to the growth of monopolies, cartels and restrictions on the free development of individuals through increasing collectivism. The injection of a stronger dose of ideology was designed to integrate the party, but this was unsuccessful and the VdU collapsed soon after the Bad Aussee programme.

Discussions between different groups that were forming the embryo of the future FPOe led to the formulation of a common platform at the end of 1955. This was not very detailed and reiterated many of the third *Lager*'s earlier criticisms of the influence of political parties in the state. It renewed its commitment to the German *Volk* and cultural community. A party conference of the newly-formed FPOe was convened in Klagenfurt in 1957: this was concerned with the organisation of the party, its statute and the formulation of an official programme. 'Freedom' was claimed to be the principal concept in the party's philosophy, and this was being threatened by Communism and by the internal governmental system. In the FPOe's opinion the domination of partisan interests in political life, described as '*Proporz* dictatorship', made a sham of democracy.

One of the foremost duties of the party was considered to be resistance to any drifting apart of Austria from the German *Volk;* the idea of Austria as a separate 'nation' or a mixture of different races and nationalities was summarily dismissed. The programme declared that the Germanic nature of Austria could not be disputed, and that if it was to be claimed that 'Vienna was not a German city, then Paris could no longer be described as French and London could not be accepted as an English city.'[12] The family was regarded as a vital element in transmitting the feeling of belonging to the *Volk* and of a special cultural community. The party's opposition to 'Bolshevism' was unequivocal; it believed that harmony in society and a peaceful relationship between capital and labour could be brought about.

At the beginning of the 1960s, the FPOe decided to try and change its image and to portray itself as a more 'liberal' party. The continuance of the Great Coalition, even though tensions were apparent, reinforced its political isolation. At the party conference in Salzburg in June 1964, it adopted a new programme under the motto 'freedom and progress'. Present at the conference were representatives from the West German FDP, and Peter declared that nationalism and freedom were the twin principles of the FPOe. The party showed an awareness of links with a 'liberal' tradition which had its origins in the nineteenth century. This was a new development in the FPOe, and was connected with an attempt to break out of its 'ghetto' and to make it acceptable for governmental office. The party continued to doubt the effectiveness of a democratic system based on an ossified obsession with the Great Coalition. The programme declared readiness to provide an alternative by sharing governmental responsibility with one of the big parties. It reaffirmed the party's faith in the German *Volk* and cultural community, and promised to keep Austria 'German', though without elaborating on these ideas as the previous programme had done. Great emphasis was placed on the 'Europeanism' of the party, and it advocated the participation of Austria in the EEC.

With the dissolution of the coalition in 1966, much of the FPOe's programme relating to attacks on this system became obsolete. Work began on the formulation of a new basic programme, which was accepted at a party conference in Bad Ischl in 1968. This programme opened with the words, 'We wish to see a European federal state.' It accepted the 'democratic republic of Austria' and the German *Volk* and cultural community. Mostly the programme contained brief platitudinous comments on freedom and democracy. It had little claims to rank as a major contribution to theoretical debate, a weakness that was acknowledged, and during 1972 a study group worked on a fresh draft programme. This was the first time that different proposals were discussed by ordinary party members as well as the leadership, and culminated in the adoption in 1973 of the most detailed and thorough set of principles the party had ever devised. It was ostensibly limited to questions of social policy and named accordingly, since it was considered that other topics such as foreign policy and defence had been covered in the Bad Ischl programme.

The terms of reference of the 1973 'manifesto on social policy' were interpreted more flexibly than the title suggests. The manifesto envisaged the development of a free society based on strictly ordered relationships. The party was to encourage individuals to strive for self-improvement and progress according to their own capabilities. The document referred to an 'active element' in society, not necessarily based in any specific class; these people showed a strength of character, forcefulness and self-confidence which compelled them to aim for the 'higher things' in life (*Streben nach Hoeherem*).[13] It was thought that the party's concept of personal freedom would appeal to these people more than to the 'passive element' of the population. This 'active element' would be more inclined to accept risks and uncertainty, which the manifesto regarded as inevitable companions of an increase in freedom; the party was to ensure that these members of society would have the best conditions possible to develop their potential free from the restrictions of any stifling bureaucracy. The weaker members of the community should be encouraged to try harder and aim higher, and it was clear that the fate of the entire community rested with the 'active element' described as the 'motor of society': if this was throttled, no progress would be possible and all development would eventually come to a standstill. The FPOe deduced from this that it had a moral duty to ensure that the 'active element' could flourish freely.

The *Volk* was described in the manifesto as a natural community of those sharing a common language, history and culture. The German language and European culture were to be preserved. The right of other peoples to their own cultural heritage was respected, and accordingly there was rejection of the idea of assimilation in the German culture of the *Gastarbeiter* whose right to return to their respective homelands was supported. The FPOe believes that the family has a duty to ensure that hereditary diseases are not transmitted to its offspring, and so it encourages, where necessary, voluntary sterilisation.[14] The family was understood in the manifesto to be an important organic link between the individual and society, so by instilling the correct values it could provide the individual with an identity and a feeling of belonging to a community. It is characteristic of the main parties in Austria that in some way they show a concern to provide the individual with a home and a sense of meaning in life. The SPOe responds to this by the creation of its numerous organisations, the OeVP is supported by the teaching of the Church, and the FPOe stresses the *Volk* and the family. The integration of the individual into one of these sub-cultures was formerly more important and an essential component of the *Lager* mentality, but since the war overlapping membership and cross-pressures have weakened the exclusive absorption of the individual by one political camp.

The FPOe manifesto supported the 'social market economy' and dynamic policies to aid farmers and the middle class. The party's desire to protect private property and keep state interference to a minimum has an affinity with the ideals of the OeVP. The FPOe wishes to facilitate individual initiatives and to reduce dependence on the state; it is opposed to wasteful subsidies and abuses in the social security system, and is anxious to tame the activities of anonymous, powerful institutions in society which threaten to become a 'state within a state'. It wishes to see a separation of Church and state and tends to regard the power of the Church as representing a possible infringement of personal liberty. In the 1979 election, the FPOe campaigned against the continued politicisation of society by the perpetuation of the 'party book' system. It considers that party members should not be given preferential treatment when applying for jobs, accommodation or bank credit.

The party's division of society into the resourceful 'active element' and the 'rest' contains an implied acceptance of élitism. The FPOe is critical of the Socialist philosophy which attempts to provide all with similar rewards regardless of personal effort, believing that this produces a pampered society whose members gradually lose all creativity and incentive, and can only be the harbinger of a reversal in historical development.

The party had omitted from the Bad Ischl programme and the manifesto some of its earlier *deutschnational* sentiments, yet it had not developed into a fully-fledged liberal party. A new generation in the party continued with a discussion of concepts, after the adoption of the 1973 manifesto, influenced by the programmatic activity of the West German liberals. A group known as the *Atterseekreis* had been established at the beginning of 1971 to act as a kind of ginger group. It is estimated to have around 500 members, mainly intellectuals, and holds on average five meetings a year. It acted as an antidote to the right-wing Reinthaller circle which had been based in Lower Austria. Members of the *Atterseekreis* had mostly been involved with the student organisation (RFS) in the late 1960s and wished to develop the party's ideology, which had been much discussed in the universities. These young academics were instrumental in formulating the major tenets of 1973 manifesto, and have continued to consider ways of modernising the party. Norbert Steger has been closely involved with this group.

Pan-German nationalist nostalgia remains very much in evidence in the FPOe. A survey carried out in 1976 revealed that 51 per cent of party supporters questioned thought that Europe would now be a better place if Germany had won the war.[15] Of the remainder, half disagreed with this statement, and the rest were not sure. A change has been slowly taking place in the party and more of its supporters now accept the idea of Austria as a nation (Table 4.iv); its stress on Austria as part of the German *Volk* is becoming less popular and this nationalist element is not likely to increase its electoral support. In 1956, 46 per cent of the population believed that Austria belonged to the German *Volk*. In 1964, only 15 per cent were of this opinion, and by 1970 this had declined to 8 per cent.[16] In 1973 it was estimated that 90 per cent of the population had a positive attitude to neutrality, which the VdU had originally voted against and the FPOe only reluctantly came to accept. The great majority of the party's supporters reject the idea of an *Anschluss* with Germany, but some suspect the FPOe's strong European commitment to be a way of achieving this by devious means.[17] The consistent defence of 'German' interests in the South Tyrol and the FPOe's fear of Slav domination in the province of Carinthia indicate that it has followed a pan-German nationalist course. While accepting the possibility of an Austrian 'state', it continues to deny the existence of a distinct nation and this bias has strained its relations with both the OeVP and SPOe. Pronounced *deutschnational* tendencies linger on in the FPOe, although some in the party feared that under Friedrich Peter it was drifting

Table 4.iv ACCEPTANCE OF AUSTRIA AS A NATION (%)

	1964	1970
FPOe	16	36
OeVP	50	66
SPOe	58	70

Source: H. Konrad (ed.), *Sozialdemokratie und 'Anschluss'*, Europaverlag, Wien, 1978, p.109.

away from these fundamental principles. Those who saw no future in working in such a party could choose to support an extreme right-wing organisation which had been established in the mid-1960s, the National Democratic Party (NDP).

(f) Parties on the Right

The National Democratic Party was founded in July 1966 and consisted of many ex-followers of the FPOe. By 1970, it had 1,803 members whose average age was thirty.[18] Its leader is a former member of the FPOe, Norbert Burger, who achieved some notoriety in the 1960s from his imprisonment following terrorist activities in South Tyrol—this was part of his philosophy of 'active' and radical politics. Burger formed a committee to support him as President in the election of 1980 and he campaigned under the slogan 'Austria must stay German'. He stands for the reintroduction of the death penalty, the abolition of abortion, and the withdrawal of civil rights from conscientious objectors. His election meetings in Salzburg and Linz were disrupted by anti-Fascist demonstrators.

The NDP is opposed to the presence of foreign workers and believes that the Turks are once again threatening Vienna. Its members refer to the 'Auschwitz lie' and glorify the deeds of German soldiers in the war: the party believes that their contribution in the fight against Bolshevist attempts to dominate the world should be acknowledged. The NDP reserves a particular hatred for the SPOe Minister of Justice Christian Broda, regarded as a Communist sympathiser, for his reforms of the penal code. It has maintained contacts with some members in the FPOe, and Otto Scrinzi, once an FPOe member of Parliament, has addressed its meetings. Scrinzi, once a leader in the Nazi SA, frequently made inflammatory speeches against the Slovenes in Carinthia. His views on racial hygiene have provoked criticism from members of the Austrian Resistance because of their similarity to National Socialism.

The NDP remains an insignificant force and the authorities have not been inclined to stop its activities and provoke any more sympathy for the party than it would acquire from its appeal to like-minded people. Article 4 of the State Treaty obliges Austria to 'prevent the existence, resurgence and activities of any organisations having as their aim political or economic union with Germany, and pan-German propaganda in favour of union with Germany'. Article 9 refers to the duty to 'dissolve all Fascist-type organisations existing on [Austrian] territory, political, military and para-military, and likewise any other organisations carrying on activities hostile to any member of the United Nations or which intend to deprive the people of their democratic rights'. Until now it has not been considered that the existence of the NDP poses a threat of this nature or that its activities warrant the party's dissolution. Terrorist acts of violence outside Carinthia and South Tyrol have only been sporadic, and most of the energies on the right seemed to be directed into various mystic rituals and ceremonies. The NDP fought the general election of 1970, but only managed to gain 0.07 per cent of the vote. The Second Republic has relatively little cause for alarm-given the continuation of economic prosperity.

The resilience of the democratic system was put to the test in 1965 with the 'Borodajkewycz affair'. Taras Borodajkewycz had been a member of the Nazi party in Vienna before the war and had enthusiastically supported the ideas of the Third Reich. In 1943 he was expelled from the party after he had ceased to believe in a German victory, but successfully appealed against the verdict. He became a professor at the College for International Trade in Vienna and even after the war continued to propound Nazism. His lectures frequently included references to the 'Jewish' SPD of Weimar Germany and praised the oratorical brilliance of Hitler.[19] His anti-semitic comments provoked demonstrations from the anti-Fascist student committee, which demanded his dismissal. Some SPOe members in the *Nationalrat* supported these protests, but the Minister of Education (a member of the OeVP) was reluctant to consider the case. A demonstration by the Austrian Resistance Movement was organised in March 1965 and culminated in a violent clash with students sympathetic to the professor. In the melée a demonstrator against Borodajkewycz—Ernst Kirchweger, aged sixty-seven—was killed and became the first victim of Neo-Nazism in the Second Republic. It took the relevant authorities more than a year to decide that the professor would be best advised to accept early retirement. The affair had led to a tragic death and the revival of unpleasant memories. More than 25,000 people attended Kirchweger's funeral including prominent trade unionists, Socialists and members of the OeVP. The feeling of solidarity between those of different parties provided some hope that the mistakes of the past could be avoided.

The police have restricted the operations of a more militant right-wing organisation, the *Aktion Neue Rechte* (ANR) led by Dr. Bruno Haas. It was formed in January 1974 and claims to have around 500 members based on the schools and colleges in Vienna, although this is considered an exaggeration. In elections to the University Central Committee in 1977, it was only able to poll 1.2 per cent of the vote. The Students' Union protested against the intentions of the group to contest the university elections in 1979. The ANR decided in May

1979 to disband its organisation and work clandestinely.
The ANR claims to be more radical and 'active' than the NDP. In
1978 the two movements decided not to duplicate activities and it
was agreed that the NDP should concentrate on electoral activity
while the ANR should carry on with extra-parliamentary work. The
members of the ANR wear Nazi-type uniforms and are well
equipped with dangerous weapons. The ANR glorifies the racialist
ideas of the Third Reich and believes talk of an Austrian 'nation' to
be a Communist lie. It adopted a basic programme in June 1976
which stated a belief in innate biological differences between races.
The programme demanded recognition of the entire German nation
and unity including existing 'occupied territories'. It declared a
constant struggle against all foreign influences which sought to
undermine the Germanic homeland. The ANR advocated, in the
programme, education on élitist principles to select the most talented
for leadership. It wanted to see the mass media and culture free from
corrupt, left-wing influences. The aim was to develop a healthy
species by discouraging the perpetuation of hereditary defects. In the
economic field, the programme stated that self-sufficiency was
desirable.

The ANR has been challenged by other groups on the right and
there are signs of increasing fragmentation. These organisations
include:[20]

Bund Volkstreuer Jugend. Youth group which is officially dissolved
but still in operation.

Kameradschaft Babenberg. A para-military organisation which
holds regular training exercises, although banned in 1980 by the
authorities.

Volkssozialistische Arbeiterpartei. Led by a former member of the
SA, this group is anti-capitalist and particularly concerned with the
protection of the environment.

Nationales Ideologiezentrum. Consists mainly of former members
of the NSDAP. Fritz Stueber, who was expelled from the VdU, was
active in this organisation until his death in 1978. Contributors
to its publications have included the controversial Professor
Borodajkewycz.

Aktionsgemeinschaft fuer Politik. Arranges meetings on 'national'
politics, which are attended by members from other extreme right-
wing groups. A meeting of 1976 received a cable with good wishes
from the FPOe member of Parliament, Gerulf Stix. A member of the
Spanish falange addressed this meeting in uniform, and extolled
fascism in Spain. Harald Ofner, candidate for the leadership of the
FPOe in 1980, was also present. *Oesterreichischer Turnerbund.*
Successor to the German Gymnasts' League which was pro-Nazi at

the time of the *Anschluss* in 1938. Allegedly it has 75,000 members, but not all are believed to share the political views of the organisation. It is led by a former leader of the Hitler Youth from Linz and exalts *deutschnational* sentiments and apartheid. It is not accepted as a member of the Austrian federal sport organisation.

Kameradschaft IV. An association of former SS members.

Oesterreichischer Kameradschaftsbund. The largest war veterans' association in Austria. It is believed to have around 300,000 members of whom 50,000 are under thirty. Its influence is particularly strong in the Federal army, and it agitates against those refusing military service. It organises marches and memorial services for those who died as 'heroes' in the war.

Kaerntner Heimatdienst (KHD). A pan-German organisation in Carinthia. Estimates for membership figures vary between 8,000 and 110,000, but its influence, especially in the main parties in the province, is indisputable. It aims to keep Carinthia 'German' and reduce what it considers to be 'Slovenisation'. Its activities frequently provoke protests from Yugoslavia. Periodically violent clashes occur between the KHD and the Slovene organisations (see Chapter 6).

Precise membership figures for these numerous groups on the radical right are difficult to obtain. Many of their basic values find a sympathetic response from the population, even though most are not actively involved. A survey of 1976 found that 20 per cent of those questioned in Vienna were confirmed anti-semites. Although many had never met a Jew, it was generally accepted that Jews were dominant in the financial world. Most thought that Jews constituted about 10 per cent of the population—the actual figure is 0.1 per cent.[21] Authoritarian opinions are particularly strong among those in the professions including teachers, doctors, priests, the police and politicians. A study made at Linz University showed that members from these groups considered Fascism more desirable than Communism. Over 50 per cent of those questioned believed that a Hitler Youth type of education was desirable, and 37 per cent believed that Jewish influence in finance was increasing.[22] In 1976 an opinion poll found that 34 per cent of supporters of the FPOe thought that Austria should have more *Lebensraum*, and 42 per cent of respondents considered it desirable for a nation to have a single politician to take decisions.[23] Although democracy in the Second Republic has become established on a relatively firm foundation, it appears that many old prejudices persist.

REFERENCES

1.   R.S. Wistrich, 'Victor Adler: a Viennese Socialist against Philo-
      semitism', *Wiener Library Bulletin*, vol. XXVII, no. 32, 1974.
2.   H.A. Kraus, *Oesterreich zwischen 1945 und 1955*, Freiheitliches
      Bildungswerk, Wien, 1979, p.7.
3.   F. Stueber, *Ich war Abgeordneter*, Leopold Stocker Verlag, Graz,
      p.126. This is Stueber's personalised account of his activities and dis-
      putes with Kraus. It contains some illuminating interpretations of
      Nazism and of the value of parliamentary democracy.
4.   *Ibid.*, p.234.
5.   R. Staeuber, *Der Verband der Unabhaengigen (VdU) und die
      Freiheithiche Partei Oesterreichs (FPOe)*, OK Organisation Kolb, St.
      Gallen, 1974, p.145. This is a very detailed and interesting assessment
      of the survival of the German nationalist element in the party since
      1945.
      A recent well-documented analysis of the 'third force' in Austrian
      politics can be found in M.E. Riedlsperger, *The Lingering Shadow of
      Nazism: the Austrian Independent Party Movement since 1945*,
      Columbia University Press, New York, 1978.
6.   R. Staeuber, *op. cit.*, p.91.
7.   K. Blecha, *Die Nationalratswahl 1979*, Dr. Karl Renner-Institut,
      Wien, 1979, p.37
8.   R. Kruspel, 'Der 6 Mai 1979—Daten und Motive', *Oesterreichische
      Monatshefte*, 5/6, 1979, p.16.
9.   Interview in *Profil*, 4 February 1980.
10.   M. Fischer-Kowalski and J. Bucek (ed.), *Ungleichheit in Oesterreich*,
      Jugend und Volkverlag, Wien, 1979, p.215.
11.   K. Berchtold, *Oesterreichische Parteiprogramme 1868–1966*, Verlag
      fuer Geschichte und Politik, Wien, 1967, p.489.
12.   *Ibid.*, p.497.
13.   *Freiheitliches Manifest zur Gesellschaftspolitik*, FPOe, Wien, 1973,
      p.13.
14.   *Ibid.*, p.45.
15.   Sozialwissenschaftliche Studiengesellschaft (Fragebogen nr. 160) 126
      Bericht, May 1976.
16.   J. Weidenholzer, 'Rechtsextreme und autoritaere Tendenzen im
      Bewusstsein der oesterreichischen Bevoelkerung', in *Rechtsex-
      tremismus in Oesterreich nach 1945*, Oesterreichischer Bundesverlag,
      Wien, 1979, p.394.
17.   R. Staeuber, *op. cit.*, p.208.
18.   *Ibid.*, p.186.
19.   See K. Horak and F. Klar, *Hitler ist nicht tot*, Verlag Jungbrunnen,
      Wien, 1968.
20.   Full details of all organisations are contained in W. Neugebauer,
      Gefahr von rechts, Dr Karl-Renner-Institut, Wien, 1979, and *Recht-
      sextremismus in Oesterreich nach 1945, op. cit.*

21. 'Anti-semites in Austria', *Patterns of Prejudice*, May-June 1977, pp.13ff.
22. *Extrablatt*, June, 1978.
23. H. Konrad (ed.), *Sozialdemokratie und 'Anschluss'*, Europaverlag, Wien, 1978, pp.111ff.

5

THE COMMUNIST PARTY AND
THE LEFT

(a) Historical Background

The Communist Party of Austria (KPOe) was founded in Vienna on 3 November 1918. Unlike the Communist Party in Germany it was never to offer a serious challenge to the unity and strength of the Social Democrats. In the first Republic the party's electoral support was negligible and it never won a parliamentary seat. Throughout the 1920s it was torn by many factional rivalries, and in 1933 it was banned (after the Civil War in 1934 it won the support of some disillusioned Social Democrats). In the Second Republic the KPOe had hoped to benefit from the presence of the Soviet forces, but after an initial improvement it reverted to its weak position. The prospects for the party in the 1980s are not encouraging and its impact on domestic politics is insignificant.

The party's formation came at a turbulent time in the history of Austria and was rooted in the despair of obtaining revolutionary leadership from the Social Democrats. Shortly afterwards the First Republic was proclaimed amid a badly organised attempt to establish a proletarian dictatorship on the Soviet model. Fears of a Bolshevik take-over persisted throughout the winter of 1918–19 as unemployment and starvation became acute. The Social Democrats (SDAP) managed to maintain discipline among their followers and successfully helped to repel a Communist putsch in 1919. Friedrich Adler, who enjoyed considerable mass support after his assassination of the Prime Minister Stuergkh in 1916, remained true to Social Democratic principles and urged caution instead of revolution in 1919. He declined to assume the leadership of the Communists and shared Otto Bauer's belief that Austria was too weak and vulnerable to experiment with a workers' dictatorship. The Social Democrats retained some sympathy with and understanding of Soviet Russia's progress to socialism; this strong intellectual tradition of Austro-Marxism provided them with powerful arguments to keep those attracted to the KPOe within their fold. The Communists, lacking a dynamic leadership, consisted mainly of the unemployed, former prisoners-of-war and a few intellectuals. Its support among the mass of industrial workers was small.

Throughout the 1920s the Social Democrats steadily constructed 'Red Vienna' with fine municipal apartment blocks, modern schools and hospitals, all financed by a progressive taxation system. This helped to create a sense of identity between the workers and the party which was to survive even during the years of Fascist dictatorship. For many, Social Democracy was not just a political movement but a family and even a religion. The party had built up numerous organisations to cater for all types of hobbies and recreational interests. With Otto Bauer as the revered leader and a general tolerance of leftist ideas, the Communists found it difficult to penetrate the Social Democratic colossus. The verbal radicalism of the Social Democrats and their ambiguous reference to a dictatorship in the Linz Programme of 1926 helped the bourgeoisie to identify them as the main 'Bolshevist' party. The KPOe managed to gain some support when the economic and political situation deteriorated at the end of the 1920s, and in the first half of 1931 its membership increased from 3,508 to 6,813.[1] This compares with a membership at the time of around 650,000 for the Social Democrats.

An important opportunity for the Communists came with the defeat of the Social Democrats by Dollfuss in the battles of 1934. Despite its apparent strength, the SDAP was unable to stop Fascism, and many of its members criticised its indecision and lack of revolutionary spirit. Some were even prepared to sever links and endanger the unity of the party, which had always been considered sacred and had formerly kept potential dissidents in line. Among the most illustrious recruits to the KPOe at that time was Ernst Fischer, who in 1945 became for a short time Minister of Education and one of the party's leading theoreticians. Having been banned in May 1933, the KPOe was more prepared for underground activity than the Social Democrats although it suffered many losses through arrests. A minority in the SDAP operated under the name of Revolutionary Socialists (RS), and some attempts were made by them before the *Anschluss* to work together with the Communists.[2] However, lasting co-operation proved difficult since many in the RS retained an admiration for Otto Bauer and the 'old' party, and were suspicious of Communism. The RS was accordingly denounced by the KPOe as reformist and then, during the Moscow Trials, as 'Trotskyist'.[3] The Communists continued with underground activity after the Nazis occupied the country, while the RS disbanded its organisation, leaving its members to work on their own or with the KPOe.

The reluctance of the RS to surrender its independence and subordinate itself to the Moscow-oriented KP strained relationships between them between 1934 and 1938. The RS was proud that a mass drift to the Communists had been averted, and by stressing a 'revolutionary' strategy it had provided a home for those who did not want to make the break with Social Democracy but who were nonetheless critical of the SDAP's past. It helped to provide a bridge between the old party and the Socialist Party formed in 1945. After the war the Communists were again to play a secondary role in the shadow of the SPOe, which continued to enjoy the confidence of the majority of workers.

(b) The Second Republic

Towards the end of the war the Communists were optimistic about their future prospects. They hoped that their heroic role in the Resistance and their contribution to the liberation of Austria by participation in the Yugoslav Partisan movement would be rewarded. In April 1945 Koplenig, the pre-war chairman of the party, and Fischer returned from Moscow. Together with other Communists returning from Yugoslavia, they began to prepare the party for participation in a new political system. The policy of the KPOe at this time was to support the idea of an independent Austria, and it was proud that its patriotic stance and endorsement of an Austrian nation had been formulated even before the war and the Moscow Declaration (see above, p.31). The party stressed the importance of a broad anti-Fascist front and hoped thus to gain the co-operation of non-Communists. An important aspect of this was the formation of unified, all-party trade union and youth organisations. Although the OeGB, a unified, organisation, was founded in 1945, Socialist, Christian and Communist fractions were formed within the trade unions, which forestalled domination by the KPOe. In May 1945 the KPOe formed the Free Austrian Youth (FOeJ), which was originally intended to be an all-party organisation, but when other parties established their own youth sections, it soon became the KPOe youth movement. The Communists blame the SPOe for allegedly splitting the workers' movement by founding its own youth organisation as a rival to the FOeJ.[4] Some contacts existed between the small left wing in the SPOe and the KPOe, but the Socialist leadership discouraged close links. The SPOe was more interested in co-operating with the OeVP and winning the trust of the Western Allies.

The presence of the Soviet forces in Eastern Austria and their unpopularity thwarted the development of the KPOe. The party hoped to make substantial gains in the election of 1945, but it was disappointed by the results which gave them only four seats. Apparently it had expected to pick up around 20 per cent of the votes, but instead it gained a mere 5 per cent. The KPOe had been members of the Provisional Government, and had provided the Vice-Chancellor and the important Ministers of the Interior and Education. But after the election the party had to be content with one post, the Ministry of Power, which it surrendered in 1947 after a disagreement on the currency reform law. Another factor which contributed to the resignation of the one Communist Minister was that originally he had agreed with the rest of the Government to accept Marshall Aid, which was later rejected by the Soviet Union. This put the party in an embarrassing position, and resignation seemed a logical move. The KP also found itself in difficulty over the question of German assets in Austria. The Government had passed nationalisation laws designed to salvage as many industries as possible from the Soviet Union. The opposition of the Soviet Union, which had a claim to these 'assets', obliged the KPOe to voice criticisms of the nationalisation measures. In this way it became labelled rather disparagingly as the 'Russian party'. Immediately after the war, the KPOe had asserted a belief in the possibility for different countries to find their own way to Socialism, but after the Soviet break with Yugoslavia it followed the Soviet line and concluded that the road to Socialism was inextricably bound to the path followed by the Soviet Union.[5]

Members of the SPOe sympathetic to the idea of closer links with the Soviet Union soon found themselves isolated. Among the most important of these was Erwin Scharf, the SPOe's central secretary. At the SPOe's conference in 1947 he introduced a motion calling for a more energetic attack on the OeVP instead of regarding the KPOe as the main enemy. Soon afterwards Scharf last his position as central secretary and was suspected of being a Communist agent; those with similar beliefs either modified their opinions or found themselves pariahs in the party. Scharf considered that his support for a more closely-knit workers' party was in the spirit of Otto Bauer.[6] He thought that the SPOe's pathological fear of Communism was misplaced in a country where it was insignificant, and pointed to the greater danger of an enslavement of Austria by Western capitalism. Scharf's disagreements with the SPOe finally led to his expulsion in 1948 and a consolidation of the right-wing dominance in the party which had already been apparent in 1945. Scharf founded his own Socialist Workers' Party, which was not very successful; finally, in 1956 he joined the Communists and at the time of writing he is the party's central secretary and a member of the politburo. The consistently anti-Communist line of the SPOe has continued throughout the Second Republic, condemning the KPOe to a peripheral existence. The Scharf case had effectively destroyed any possibility of a reconciliation between the two parties, and the KPOe frequently attacked the 'traitors' and the 'reactionary clique' in the socialist leadership. The Communists were particularly unhappy that the Socialist Minister of the Interior, Helmer, was gradually eroding their influence in the police force. One of the KPOe's complaints was that former Fascists were finding their way back into public life with the blessing of the SPOe.

The elections of 1949 did not bring any consolation to the KPOe, and faced with the steady decline in its influence, the party became embroiled in an attempt to recoup some of its losses by extra-parliamentary means. The parlous economic situation, which was causing great hardship among the lower paid, forced it to take some action: it criticised the increase in gas, electricity, public transport and grain prices, and found the workers more than receptive. In September 1950, workers in Upper Austria decided on a general strike, and the unrest soon spread to Lower Austria and Vienna; its extent apparently took the KPOe by surprise.[7] The SPOe temporarily lost its traditional hold on the working class but quickly regained its authority, appealing for the restoration of order.

In the second strike wave which took place in October 1950, the SPOe and trade unions warned the workers of the dangers of drifting into a 'People's Democracy'. The KPOe attempted to disrupt communications by force, but was met with opposition from many workers, now acting in the belief that they were defending the Republic from dictatorship. The Communists failed to mobilise the masses at a time of economic crisis partly because of the historic strength of Social Democracy in Austria and partly because of their identification with the Soviet occupying forces, who hesitated to provide them with adequate support. After 1950 Communists in the trade unions and serving in the police force were replaced by more 'reliable' elements, further undermining their weak position. The existence in Austria of this 'foreign enclave', as the Communist Party was regarded, helped to develop a policy of consensus between the two major parties.[8]

(c) Electoral Support

The party lost its remaining three seats in the 1959 general election and since then has not been represented in the *Nationalrat*. At the election in May 1979 it won 0.96 per cent of the vote, and only managed to top 1 per cent in Carinthia (1.1 per cent), Styria (1.1 per cent) and Vienna (1.5 per cent). Least support for the party came from Burgenland (0.4 per cent) and from Salzburg and Tyrol (both 0.6 per cent). Its only gains came from Vorarlberg where it won 0.9 per cent of the vote. There it had put forward a distinctly Euro-Communist position.

Table 5.i ELECTORAL PERFORMANCE OF THE KPOe IN GENERAL
ELECTIONS 1930–1979

	Votes	%	Seats
1930	20,951	0.6	–
1945	174,257	5.4	4
1949	213,066	5.1	5
1953	228,159	5.3	4
1956	192,438	4.4	3
1959	142,578	3.3	–
1962	135,520	3.0	–
1966	18,636	0.4	–
1970	44,750	1.0	–
1971	61,762	1.4	–
1975	55,032	1.2	–
1979	45,280	1.0	–

In the 1966 election the KPOe only contested one constituency in
Vienna, and elsewhere recommended its supporters to vote for the
SPOe. This appears to have been a suicidal tactic, and the party has
never recovered. The KPOe's best hope of winning a basic seat is in
Vienna, although in the 1979 election it suffered losses there and was
only able to gain 1.5 per cent of the vote compared with 2 per cent in
1975. To win a basic seat and thus be eligible for parliamentary
representation in 1979, the party would have needed 25,825 votes in
Vienna, but fell short of this by over 10,000 votes. Nonetheless, the
capital provides the party with over one-third of its total votes. In the
Bundesrat, the KPOe was represented with one seat from 1949 until
1954. In *Landtag* elections (see Table 5.ii), the KPOe lost its last seats
in Vienna in 1969 and in Carinthia and Styria in 1970. The party had
once possessed seven seats in the *Landtag* in Vienna, and its losses
there are symptomatic of its general decline (see Appendix D).

The KPOe lost its last seats in the *Landtag* of Salzburg in 1949, in
Burgenland in 1956 and in Lower Austria in 1959. The only time it
put up a candidate for a Presidential election was in 1951 when it
won 219,969 votes—5 per cent of the total. The level of Communist
representation in the Chamber of Labour is a further indication that
the party is unable to capture working-class support, which remains
faithful to Social Democracy. In the Chamber's election in June
1979 (Table 5.iii) the Communists lost six of their ten seats while the
Socialists took a total of 534 out of 810.

The KPOe's position has not been helped in the Chamber of
Labour by the formation of a rival list originally composed of
members critical of the party's position on Czechoslovakia. In 1974
this group (GE) gained one seat in Vienna, which it lost in the 1979

Table 5.ii ELECTION RESULTS OF THE KPOe IN THE VIENNESE
LANDTAG

	Votes	%	Seats
1945	69,820	8.0	6
1949	89,646	7.9	7
1954	89,161	8.2	6
1959	53,575	5.2	3
1964	52,002	5.0	2
1969	27,357	2.9	–
1973	22,093	2.3	–
1978	14,771	1.8	–

Table 5.iii CHAMBER OF LABOUR ELECTION RESULTS, 1979 (%)

	Socialists	OeAAB	FPOe	KPOe	GE
Vienna	72.0	23.1	2.6	1.4	0.8
Lower Austria	64.3	32.7	1.3	1.3	0.4
Burgenland	63.3	35.8	0.8	0.1	0.0
Upper Austria	65.2	29.2	4.6	1.0	0.0
Styria	69.9	26.2	2.2	1.4	0.3
Carinthia	68.2	24.3	6.0	1.5	0.0
Salzburg	58.2	32.9	8.1	0.8	0.0
Tyrol	48.7	48.2	2.8	0.3	0.0
Vorarlberg	30.1	64.9	4.5	0.5	0.0
Austria	64.3	31.0	3.2	1.2	0.3

Note: 1,970,025 were entitled to vote and in 1979 the turn-out was 61.1 per
cent.

elections. Currently the KPOe is represented in the Chamber of
Labour with two seats from Vienna, one from Lower Austria and
one from Styria. The Communists are also split in the Trade Union
Federation, and their influence remains extremely small compared
with the monopoly enjoyed by the Socialist fraction. Of the fifty-
four members on the OeGB's executive, two are Communists,
compared with thirty-nine Socialist trade unionists. Soviet action in
Hungary and Czechoslovakia and a lack of clarity in the KPOe's
own position, especially in its attitude to the SPOe, has contributed
to its loss of support. The KPOe believes that its poor electoral
performance is partly the result of successful pre-war Fascist and
Nazi indoctrination, which instilled into the masses a hatred of
Communism. The relative affluence of the working population in
recent years has also worked against any potential appeal of
Communism.

(d) Organisation

The party has been steadily losing members, and exact figures are no longer published, although the total is believed to be well under 20,000. The KPOe has a high ratio of members to voters: in 1979,44 per cent of Communist voters were also party members. No less significant than the overall decline in numbers is the high average age of members. In 1974, 49 per cent of them were over sixty, 20 per cent between fifty and sixty and only 6.6. per cent under thirty.[9] The party's future prospects do not look encouraging on the basis of these figures. The party supports a large bureaucracy consisting of some 300 paid functionaries, has its own publishing house, and produces its own daily paper, *Die Volksstimme*. The small amount collected in membership dues could not finance all the KPOe's activities, and the party is heavily dependent on the 'goodwill' of the Soviet Union. In return the Soviet Union expects and obtains ideological solidarity, a stance which does not appear to be receiving a sympathetic response from the people.

The decline in readership of the party press (see Table 5.v) and the general weakness of the party apparatus have been a cause for concern, and recent party conferences have called for a rejuvenation of the party and an increase in contacts with the rank and file. At the party conference of 1977 Karl Reiter, a Politburo member, admitted that insufficient progress had been made, and deplored the fact that only 15–20 per cent of members attended meetings. Many members had no contact with the organisation or the party's newspaper, and gained most of their information from radio and television.[10]

The organisation of the KPOe is based on the principle of democratic centralism, with the main organs of the party elected and obliged to report regularly on their activities. Decisions of the leadership are considered binding on all party members, of whom the necessary revolutionary discipline is expected.[11]

Table 5.iv MEMBERSHIP OF THE KPOe

1945	*ca.* 150,000
1961	42,500
1965	36,500
1969	33,000
1970	20,500
1974	20,200
1977	*ca.* 20,000

Source: W.Lindner, *Der Grosse Verrat*,
Verlag Alois Wieser, 1978, p.33.

Table 5.v CIRCULATION FIGURES OF THE KPOe's PRESS

	Weekdays	*Sundays*
1953	124,000	187,100
1954	124,900	187,100
1956	86,400	139,000
1957	66,800	106,600
1958	54,982	90,223
1959	54,746	91,800
1960	54,148	91,468
1961	49,530	87,700
1965	50,249	88,081
1968	51,213	90,190
1970	47,706	85,500
1971	44,901	81,607
1974	44,209	82,000
1977	41,760	82,246

Source: W. Lindner, *op. cit.*, p.32.

The party conference is considered the KPOe's supreme body. Meeting once every three years, it has the responsibility to determine the general guidelines of party policy and to elect the central committee. Delegates with full voting rights are elected to conference at meetings of the party in the districts or relevant organisations. In 1977, 277 such delegates were present of whom 143 were classified as salaried employees, sixty-six as workers, thirty-four as pensioners, twenty-nine as academics, three as housewives, one as a farmer and one from a profession.[12] Other members of the conference are delegates from the district and provincial organisations and members of the central committee. When there are any, Communist deputies in the *Nationalrat, Bundesrat* and *Landtage* are entitled to attend. In addition, Communist members on the executive board of the OeGB and a further five delegates from the trade union movement, plus five from the Communist youth and two from the student organisation, are sent to the conference. These members possess a consultative vote and in 1977 numbered 125: seventy-five of them were salaried employees, twenty-five pensioners, fourteen academics, ten workers and one from a profession. The conference is run by a Presidium which it elects.

Between party conferences the central committee is regarded as the party's highest authority, and it can take decisions for which it must bear collective responsibility. It is responsible for convening and carrying out the conference decisions. The central committee must give an account of its activities to the conference and prepare a financial report. It is the task of the central committee to elect the

politburo, the party chairman and the central secretaries. The politburo is empowered to take decisions between meetings of the central
committee. The last party conference in December 1977 elected
seventy-four members to the central committee and eleven members
were elected to the politburo.

(e) Ideology

The KPOe describes itself as a Marxist-Leninist party defending the
interests of 'the working class and working people' in Austria. It
aims to establish a new Socialist order based on democracy and
peace. For this struggle it urges all workers, irrespective of their individual beliefs, to unite in a common cause. The KPOe has maintained unwavering loyalty to the Soviet Union, with the exception of
a brief spell in the 1960s, culminating in the crisis over Czechoslovakia, when it temporarily deviated.

Ideological questions assume a greater importance for Communists than for other political parties. A recent survey showed that
32 per cent of KPOe supporters considered that parties should
primarily concern themselves with ideological matters, compared
with 16 per cent of SPOe respondents.[13] Since the war, the KPOe has
formulated five main programmes:

1946   XIII party conference, 'Programmatic Guidelines'.
1954   XVI party conference, 'The Road to Winning and Secur-
         ing the Independence of Austria'.
1958   'Principles for Austria's Road to Socialism'.
1965   XIX party conference, 'Theses on Future Prospects'.
1974   XXII party conference, 'Political and Ideological Objec-
         tives'.

The first post-war conference in April 1946 outlined in an optimistic tone the KPOe's tasks in liberated Austria. The 'Programmatic Guidelines' emphasised that the KPOe represented not only
the working class but the middle class, the peasantry, intellectuals
and all who were victims of capitalist exploitation. The party
declared its aim to be the establishment of a genuine 'people's democracy' based on a union of all democratic and progressive forces; but
it pledged itself unequivocally to the idea of a free, independent and
democratic Austria. It considered that the best way to avoid a revival
of German Fascism and to fight economic imperialism was for the
workers of each nation to struggle for their own independence; in
this sense, the party considered its policy of national independence
as both 'Austrian' and 'internationalist'. The party saw the nationalisation of the banks and key industries as a necessary component

of the new system. It did not envisage a revolutionary upheaval, and stressed that a peaceful way to Socialism was possible. The KPOe seemed to imagine that after a period of competition between the two systems, the masses would be convinced of the overwhelming advantages of Socialism over capitalism.[14]

By the beginning of the 1950s, the KPOe had come to identify itself more explicitly with the policies of the Soviet Union. Of increasing concern to it was the four-power occupation and the negotiations for a State Treaty; discussions on this dominated the party conference in May 1954, at which a speech by the party chairman Koplenig was later adopted as the official policy. Koplenig accused American imperialism of attempting to destroy the economic and political systems of Communism in the 'people's democracies', in China and in the Soviet Union. He accused the United States of promoting a revival of German militarism which was intended to lead to the subjugation of Austria.

Not surprisingly, the KPOe supported a proposal made by the Soviet Union at the Berlin conference of 1954 which advocated a collective security agreement for all the countries in Europe and a withdrawal of occupation troops from Germany. The Soviet Union insisted on the maintenance of occupation forces in Austria until a satisfactory peace agreement had been reached with Germany. This was unacceptable to the Austrian Government, and little headway was made in concluding a State Treaty. The KPOe's programme reasserted its faith in an independent Austria which it considered would be best achieved in a government of all democratic forces including Socialists and Catholics. Such a government, it was hoped, would free itself from dependence on the Americans and follow the Soviet Union's plans for peace and economic progress. The KPOe, although surprised at the final signing of the State Treaty in 1955, nonetheless welcomed it maintaining that an earlier agreement could have been reached if the Western powers had not attempted to integrate Austria into NATO.

The withdrawal of the occupation forces created a new situation for all parties in Austria, but the KPOe, unlike the other parties, was obliged to react as well to developments in the Soviet bloc. Khrushchev's famous speech denouncing Stalin at the XX CPSU conference in February 1956 was declared in the KPOe's politburo to be false, but not all its members were equally happy with this position and Ernst Fischer called—unsuccessfully—for a translation of the text to be made available for the central committee.[15] The events in Hungary in October 1956 further unsettled the party which lost roughly one-third of its membership at this time. Many were beginning to think in the light of these developments that Khrushchev's speech had been a grave mistake. Leopold Spira, for many years a member of the central committee, comments:

The events of 1956 had dealt a hard blow to the KPOe. Just when the heavy burden of identification with the Soviet occupation power had faded through the conclusion of the State Treaty in May 1955, the Austrian Communists were once more encumbered by their identification with the acts of the Soviet Union—acts which were rejected by the majority of the population.[16]

At the XVII party conference in March 1957 Koplenig admitted that the development of the personality cult in the Soviet Union had led to serious mistakes, but added that Stalin's great service in building Socialism could not be effaced. In this way members were able either to justify their doubts or, if they wished, confirm their belief that the policies of the past had been correct. The majority in the party were content to accept Koplenig's neat compromise, but two members of the central committee resigned just before the conference over the Soviet Union's intervention in Hungary.

As a result of these traumatic events, the KPOe considered a new appraisal of its basic objectives to be necessary, and discussion on this began at the XVII party conference. In February 1958 a special party assembly was called by the central committee to adopt the new programme, 'Principles for Austria's Road to Socialism'. In the transition to Socialism, leadership from a Marxist-Leninist workers' party was considered necessary to establish a dictatorship of the proletariat which would be supported by the mass of the working people.

The party acknowledged that different economic and political conditions would mean that each country would use different tactics in finding its own way to Socialism. The peculiar conditions in Austria were considered to be its advanced industrial base and the fact that the large banks and important industries were already nationalised. This enhanced the possibility of a peaceful development to Socialism by consolidating the social and democratic rights already won to achieve a majority in Parliament which could be used to serve the people. In this struggle the party hoped for a union of the police and the military with the working population. The KPOe's tentative reflections on the possibility of a parliamentary road to Socialism were qualified at this stage by considerable reservations and preconditions.[17] Indeed, it was added that this possibility should not obscure the realisation that the bourgeoisie's power must be resolutely broken, and a warning was given against 'reformist illusions' which tried to avoid a social revolution. In the external field the party, influenced by Khrushchev's thinking, concluded that the struggle for international détene and peaceful co-existence was of prime importance.

A more decisive break with the past was to come at the XIX party conference in May 1965 with the formulation of the 'Theses on Future Prospects'. Franz Muhri, then aged forty, took over from the veteran Stalinist Koplenig as party chairman. Friedl Fuernberg, central secretary and one of the few surviving Stalinists in the leadership, was under the impression that Khrushchev's removal did not signify any dramatic change in Soviet policy and was prepared to accept the new orientation of the KPOe,[18] as set forth in the 'Theses' of 1965, which asserted that not only was a strategy based on a peaceful way to Socialism possible but that, because of changes in capitalist countries, it was necessary: capitalism had been obliged to modify, and could no longer be equated with the old system of the inter-war period and its deep economic crises.

The party envisaged that under Socialism existing freedoms would be extended, and it guaranteed to maintain a private sector for small traders and farmers. In the struggle to achieve Socialism the KPOe accepted the help of other parties, and for the first time relinquished its claim to play the leading role in any alliance: 'The peaceful road to Socialism will be taken by several parties, and will be linked with modifications and changes in the existing parties, which then together will arrive at socialism'.[19] Emphasis was laid on a piecemeal implementation of Socialism rather than an acceptance of the Soviet revolutionary example of 1917. The aim was gradually to reduce the power of capital by excluding its influence on the public sector and by nationalising key industries still in private hands. At the same time, so the 'Theses' declared, an extension of democracy throughout the whole economy would take place.

The 'Theses' criticised the SPOe not for its participation in a coalition but for its complicity in the system of 'social partnership' adding, 'We support every step of the SP which is in the interest of the working people and of progress'.[20] An attempt to reach an understanding with Socialist comrades was regarded as a prime political task. The Communists' lack of success in trying to regain parliamentary representation led them to accept the idea of a working arrangement with the SPOe to avoid total isolation from the working class. Later in 1965, the KPOe decided to support the SPOe in the *Landtag* election in Tyrol, and in the general election of 1966 they only contested one constituency and elsewhere recommended Communists to vote for the SPOe. These overtures met with an ambiguous response from the SPOe, which felt acutely embarrassed by such dubious backing. The 'Theses' also sanctioned an attempt to reach an understanding with left-inclined Catholics and the workers' wing of the OeVP, which would make an alliance of democratic forces more effective.

The conference accepted the principle of proletarian internationalism, but stressed that the KPOe was an autonomous party which would develop its political struggle according to the dictates of the situation in Austria. The party hoped that differences of opinion resulting from this policy would receive a sympathetic hearing and not lead to witch-hunts. The tone of the 'Theses' was a clear warning to the Soviet Union that the KPOe could not in future be relied upon to defend its policies and actions without question. The changes that this conference had inaugurated were followed by a wide-ranging discussion within the party, and not all members were entirely convinced of the correctness of the new perspectives. The painful process of re-thinking basic principles and pursuing a more independent course was abruptly interrupted by the events in Czechoslovakia in 1968. Thereafter, the KPOe, in a state of utter confusion, withdrew from following the spirit of the 'Theses', and has since consolidated this 'normalisation' with unflagging consistency.

(f) Years of Crisis 1965–1969

After the XIX party conference many controversial issues were debated, including alienation, 'false consciousness' (i.e. use of ideology to perpetuate powerful vested interests), the role of intellectuals and the relationship of democracy to Socialism. For some, the concept of 'dictatorship of the proletariat', even if understood —in the sense of scientific Socialism—as progressive, seemed ambiguous after the experiences of Nazism and Stalinism. At the conference Fuernberg had rejected the term as outdated and unsuitable as a description of the party's new aims. 'Socialist democracy' was favoured by the reformers in the KPOe, who also accepted the idea of a multi-party system in the Western sense, with tolerance of non-Socialist parties. This logical extension of the principles embodied in the 'Theses' met with a mixed response, but developments in neighbouring Czechoslovakia were soon to force members either to opt openly for the new course or resolutely to call a halt to further 'revisionism'.

At the beginning of 1968, the KPOe welcomed the Czech Communists' efforts to adopt their own road to Socialism based on democracy. For many the developments in Czechoslovakia seemed a vindication of their own cherished beliefs, and direct contacts existed between the reformers in the KPOe and the leaders of the Prague Spring. On the day of the invasion Franz Muhri, in a radio interview, supported the Czechs and considered the action of the

Soviet Union to have been unnecessary and damaging to the entire Communist movement. A press statement of the Politburo expressed disapproval of the invasion and its wish to see a 'political solution without military pressure on the basis of the full sovereignty of the CSSR'.[21] The Free Austrian Youth used stronger language, accusing the Soviet Union of having abandoned Socialism by resorting to tanks to repress the hopeful developments which had been taking place. Strong support for the Czechs also came from the Communist trade unionists, who called on their comrades in the Warsaw Pact countries to press for a withdrawal of troops.

The initial reaction of the KPOe was hasty, since the invasion had taken most of the leadership by surprise. Gradually, however, under pressure from Moscow and the 'conservatives' in the party, the KPOe toned down its original standpoint. In the process, Muhri tried to appease both wings in the KPOe and to avoid an open split in the party. On 22 August a meeting of the central committee took place, at which Muhri defended the XIX party conference. He deduced on the basis of this that it was logical to condemn the invasion and to hope for a withdrawal of troops and the restoration of Czechoslovakia's sovereignty. He continued by warning the KPOe against abandoning its solidarity with the CPSU, and referred to the invasion as a 'miscalculation'. For Muhri, the invaders had acted in all good faith and were not enemies of further democratisation. Ernst Fischer opposed this 'centrist' position and condemned Soviet aggression without qualification. After some debate, the central committee resolved to condemn the invasion and called for a withdrawal of troops but reinforced its solidarity with the Warsaw Pact and with the Soviet Union. The central committee hoped that 'normalisation' in the world Communist movement could be reached through a peaceful political solution. Just sixty-one of the eighty-four members of the central committee which had been elected at the party conference listened to the debate and only forty-six were present at the end. The leadership was by no means unanimous in its attitude to the invasion, and in subsequent months the 'conservative' wing of the party felt confident enough to assert its authority. The KPOe had, under Muhri's influence, avoided a total confrontation with the Soviet Union, leaving open the option of a retreat to a more orthodox position.

Among large sections of the youth and trade union movement, especially in Vienna, feeling against the invasion remained strong. Many felt that the central committee's resolution had not gone far enough and were critical of Muhri's intermediate position. They were backed by a group of intellectuals on the party's fortnightly magazine *Tagebuch* who were prepared to attack the degenerate

Soviet 'system' in addition to its actions. Ernst Fischer maintained his incessant onslaught on Soviet power politics, arguing for a complete break in relations with the Soviet Union. Not all among the progressives agreed with Fischer's outspoken criticism, and some thought that it even damaged their case by going too far and providing the leadership with an excuse to intervene and demand the total loyalty of the party to Moscow. The progressives shared a belief in the possibility of democratic, humane Socialism free from the stultifying influence of bureaucracy and repression. The existence of this element obliged the KPOe to maintain its criticisms of the intervention although with increasing reluctance.

The situation was further complicated for the KPOe by the approach of the XX party conference scheduled for January 1969. A discussion document, issued by the central committee in October 1968 in preparation for the conference, expressed the view that the invasion had been a setback for democracy and peace. It added that the KPOe did not anticipate a break with the Socialist countries and the Soviet Union, but hoped that differences of opinion could be overcome. The policy was still to endorse the Czechs' aim of finding their own way to Socialism, and there was no discovery yet of counter-revolutionary tendencies. About two-thirds of the membership of the party at this time were over fifty; they had been impressed by the victories of the Red Army in the Second World War and been strongly influenced by Stalin. Many could not bring themselves to accept continued friction with the Soviet Union. It was becoming evident that the decisions of the KPOe's XIX party conference could not be pursued without provoking opposition from Moscow, and the majority of members were not prepared for this.

At the XX party conference, attacks were made on the progressives and especially those in leading positions who were allegedly damaging the party's image. Complaints came from the progressives that the choice of delegates had been manipulated to favour a predominance of conservatives. The conservative attack extended to the leadership of Muhri, who insisted at the conference on the restoration of Czechoslovakia's sovereignty and the withdrawal of Soviet troops. Muhri was also unpopular with the progressives, for at the same time he welcomed 'positive' steps that the Soviet Union was making to find an amicable solution. For the progressive wing, the party was subtly moving away from its original denunciation of the invasion and seeking a route to reconciliation with the Soviet Union.

One of the tasks of conference is the election of a new central committee, a procedure normally completed smoothly. The difficulties this encountered at the XX party conference reflected the divisions in the KPOe. Ernst Fischer decided not to stand again, ostensibly because of his age, but four other progressives who were proposed failed to be elected to the central committee as a result of 'manipulations'. In protest twenty-five members of the new central committee, including members of the youth and trade union movements, threatened to resign and demanded a second election. Muhri indefatigably tried to overcome the open breach in the party, and it was finally agreed to approve a list of all candidates including the four who had been at the centre of the controversy.[22] The progressives had tenaciously resisted attempts to oust them from the central committee. The conference ended rather unsatisfactorily with no clear and agreed position on Czechoslovakia; however, one point was evident—that further developments stemming from the 'Theses' of the 1965 conference could no longer be expected.

Ernst Fischer continued to irk the party leadership, and soon after the conference, in a television interview, he referred to the Soviet Union's *Panzerkommunismus* (tank Communism). The central committee decided that the case should be investigated by a special arbitration committee, which some months later recommended his expulsion. The central committee, anxious to avoid further disruptions in the party, challenged the decision, and later, in October 1969, twenty-seven members on the central committee from the youth and trade union sections publicly voiced their opposition to the expulsion, but they did so in vain. Fischer came to represent a test-case for those in the party wishing to see it proceed along the lines of the 'Theses' of 1965. The order for his expulsion marked a significant step in eradicating these 'revisionist' tendencies in the KPOe.

(g) 'Normalisation'

The writers of the magazine *Tagebuch* had continued relentlessly to publish anti-Soviet articles and to plead the case for democratic Socialism with a human face. The party now stepped in to correct this deviationism, and assumed control of the magazine's operations. In response to this, the *Wiener Tagebuch* was formed, which from January 1970 appeared monthly, and today, with Leopold Spira a former member of the KPOe's central committee as its editor, it follows a Euro-Communist line. Spira took over from Franz Marek, an ex-member of the politburo and leading theoretician, who died in June 1979.

The party in late 1969 also decided to take action against the rebels in its youth movement, the Free Austrian Youth (FOeJ), which had been formed in 1945, and had become one of the main centres of opposition to the Soviet Union and its invasion of Czechoslovakia. The party decided to form in its place a reliable organisation, the 'Communist Youth of Austria' (KJOe): this was rejected by many in the FOeJ. A separate organisation was founded as a rival to the new KJOe, under the old name of FOeJ which was later changed to the 'Movement for Socialism' (BfS). It produces a monthly magazine *Offensiv links* and the number of its supporters is estimated to be between 200 and 300. Under the same name, *Offensiv links*, this group contested the general election in 1971 in Vienna only, where it gained 1,874 votes.

The party had still to deal with the twenty-seven 'revisionists' on the central committee who had protested against Fischer's expulsion. At an emergency meeting of the central committee in November 1969, Muhri once again tried, with various equivocal utterances, to maintain unity in the party. Although rejecting the invasion of Czechoslovakia, he stated his belief that the Soviet Union had been motivated by a deep concern for Socialism and the security of the Socialist countries. This was not enough for the 'conservatives' in the party, who proposed the replacement of a member on the politburo responsible for work in the youth organisation on the grounds that he was not prepared faithfully to represent the party's views. Immediately afterwards, many withdrew from active work on the politburo and the central committee, and the split that Muhri had painstakingly tried to avert actually occurred. Many who subsequently left the party did so reluctantly, realising the difficulties, both financial and political, of working in isolation. The final break had been provoked by the 'conservatives', although it was already becoming clear to the progressives that efforts to change the party from within were fruitless. Of the twenty-seven 'dissidents' on the central committee, a couple drifted back to the party but the remainder contribute to and follow the line of the *Wiener Tagebuch*. The youth representative whose proposed dismissal had caused the exodus became a passive member of the 'Movement for Socialism'.

The Communist fraction in the Trade Union Federation (OeGB) similarly split as a result of the normalisation process. Leading functionaries who did not conform were not re-elected to the central committee, and subsequently founded their own association (GE) in the OeGB, based mainly in Vienna. The GE trade unionists and the BfS work closely together with the circle around the *Wiener Tagebuch*. In this way the party forfeited many of its most prominent and experienced trade unionists.

By the time of the next party conference in May 1970, most of the progressives were no longer active in the party. Altogether thirty-one members of the central committee did not stand for re-election because of political differences with the party. In 1971 a delegation of the KPOe visited Prague and on its return issued the following statement:

The Austrian Communists recognise that the Soviet Union and the other Socialist countries have rendered the Communist Party of Czechoslovakia and Socialist Czechoslovakia great assistance in overcoming a crisis and repelling revisionist and anti-Socialist forces. The great majority of our party and of the central committee consider that the intervention of the five Warsaw Pact states on 21 August 1968 was a painful necessity.[23]

This was followed by a wave of expulsions of leading functionaries and of resignations, the extent of which prompted Leopold Spira, himself one of those expelled, to comment: 'There is no other example in Western Europe of such bloodletting in a Communist party in the post-Stalin era'.[24] With the public withdrawal of the KPOe's condemnation of the invasion, relations with the Soviet Union were once again harmonious and the party was pleased that purity had largely been restored in its ranks. Yet the KPOe's official programme, as outlined in the 'Theses' of 1965, was in clear contradiction to the current thinking. A more appropriate set of principles needed to be worked out to accommodate the changes which had occurred. This was the main task of the XXII party conference in January 1974.

(h) New Perspectives

The 'Political and Ideological Objectives' of 1974 did not mention a new type of capitalism which had been described in the 'Theses' but stressed the traditional crises inherent in the system. The historic role of the working class in achieving the transition to Socialism was considered more important than before. The KPOe had abandoned its conciliatory approach to other parties embodied in the 'Theses'. The OeVP was accused of being solely concerned with the preservation of capitalism and of embracing solidly anti-Socialist principles; no dialogue was considered possible with such an anti-Marxist party with a history of Austro-Fascism. The programme recognised that the OeVP included workers and small tradesmen, but considered that before being fully able to participate in achieving Socialism, they should be freed from bourgeois influences. The SPOe received harsher criticism than in 1965 for its complicity in propping up the capitalist system, especially during its period of office. The Socialist Government was attacked for perpetuating exploitation and, above all, the leaders and officials of the SPOe and of the OeGB were regarded as appendages of capitalism. Their integration in the system through social partnership and economic interests was regarded as total. The KPOe claimed that the interests of those workers who now belonged to the SPOe could not be represented by its leadership; it saw part of its task as being the ideological enlightenment of this section by the development of class consciousness. There was a need for unity between Communist, Socialist and Christian workers who shared the same class interests, but the KPOe saw the uncompromising anti-Communism of the SPOe as a big barrier to this being achieved. Efforts of the party should therefore be directed to winning Socialists to the cause by making clear to them the mistakes of the SPOe government—and by building a strong Communist party. Now, in 1974, there was no contemplation of lending electoral support to the SPOe as there had been in 1965, and it was clear that any alliance was to be dominated by the working class and the KPOe. The programme declared that only the Communist Party represented the class interests of the working population.[25]

Greater emphasis was placed than in 1965 on the importance of the Soviet Union, which was acknowledged as the main force in the anti-imperialist struggle and the chief power in the Socialist community. The KPOe looked outside Austria rather than inside, as in 1965, for favourable influences to support its own struggle. The programme accepted the policy of détene and peaceful co-existence, but only in so far as this served the class struggle. While admitting that there was a real possibility of avoiding a Third World War, the programme added that permanent peace would ultimately only be possible with the abolition of capitalism.

The attitude of the party to the peaceful development of Socialism was far more sceptical than in 1965. The programme recorded the desire of the KPOe to achieve Socialism without a civil war, but added that this depended on the willingness of the bourgeoisie to surrender its power. The new 'Perspectives' adopted a more aggressive stance than the 'Theses', and proclaimed that for the success of the Socialist revolution the mobilisation of the majority of workers was necessary under the leadership of a revolutionary party. Even if a civil war was avoided, the KPOe warned that the road to Socialism would not be achieved purely through parliamentary means. The strengthening of the party, particularly in its fight for socialism outside the parliamentary system, was of the utmost importance.

The aim of the KPOe was to break the power of capital through the implementation of a dictatorship of the proletariat. The reference to the leadership of a Marxist-Leninist party in the transition to Socialism implied a clear rejection of the philosophy of the 'Theses'. The 'Perspectives' of 1974 recognised that peculiar conditions in Austria would influence the development of Socialism, but preferred to see the country proceeding towards Socialism in unity and with the support of other Socialist states. Unlike the 1965 programme, there was to be no 'Austrian' road to Socialism. The KPOe had obediently returned to the Soviet fold.

The party conference in December 1977 further consolidated these changes. The central secretary, Erwin Scharf, decisively rejected 'Euro-Communism', and renewed the KPOe's enthusiastic support for the 'party of Lenin and the first Socialist state'.[26] One of the delegates addressing the conference could report some encouraging news for the party on the organisational front. The party's secretary for Vorarlberg, twenty-five year old Reinhard Farkas, spoke of success in winning new young members in that area, adding that the omnipotence of the central committee had not always helped and had occasionally hindered this development.[27] In the general election of 1979 Vorarlberg was the only province where the KPOe showed any gains. Later in the year, Farkas openly criticised the trials being held in Czechoslovakia as reminiscent of Stalinism: for this he was attacked in *Die Volksstimme*, which stated that only criminals and terrorists were being put on trial. Farkas had earlier attacked the banishment of Kohout from Czechoslovakia, which he considered incompatible with the Helsinki agreement. He and a few other comrades in Vorarlberg were also showing an unhealthy interest in the Euro-Communism of the Italian Communist Party. This met with strong opposition from the Viennese KPOe, who were unable to tolerate these lingering elements of 'revisionism', and expelled Farkas in the autumn of 1979. So long as the party continues to react in this way, it chances of winning young members seem slim. It appears that the party's fate in the foreseeable future will be to remain enclosed in its uncontaminated ghetto.

(i) Other Parties on the Left

The Sino-Soviet split produced difficulties for members of the KPOe, who at the same time were impressed by developments in China and anxious to remain loyal to the Soviet Union. Only a small minority broke with the party to join Maoist organisations. Among these was Franz Strobl who in October 1963 set up his own newspaper *Rote Fahne*, which proclaimed its intention to represent the views of 'Marxist-Leninists in the KPOe'. After the 'revisionist' party conference of the KPOe in 1965, the words 'in the KPOe' disappeared from the newspaper. Strobl concluded that the KPOe was no longer revolutionary, and in 1965 decided to form a new party. In the election of March 1966, his 'Marxist-Leninists of Austria' (MLOe) contested one constituency in Vienna, gaining 486 votes.

This was a poor result considering that the KPOe had not put up a rival list exhorting its supporters in the constituency there to vote for the SPOe.

This group, renamed the Marxist-Leninist Party of Austria (MLPOe), consists today of a handful of members who follow a pro-Albanian line. Towards the end of 1966 Strobl's group found it necessary to expel some members because of 'political unreliability and adventurism'.[28] Alfred Jocha, one of those expelled, formed a separate faction, the 'Union of Revolutionary Workers of Austria' (VRA), which produces a Maoist-Stalinist paper *Die Volksmacht*. Its active following consists of about a dozen members.

The largest Maoist organisation is the 'Communist League of Austria' (KBOe). This has its roots in the international student activity of the late 1960s, and was constituted in December 1972 in Vienna, originally as the Communist League (KB). In the middle of 1978 it was decided to rationalise the movement, which had formed groups in Linz, Salzburg, Graz and Klagenfurt, and form the KBOe. At its peak it was estimated to have around 1,000 members, but its support has recently been declining. The KBOe regards the KPOe as an agent of Soviet imperialism and attacks it for abandoning the revolutionary road to Socialism and for adopting a conciliatory attitude to capitalism. It regards the development of the KPOe, since it adopted its programme for 'Austria's Road to Socialism' in 1958, as revisionist. It also accuses the MLPOe and VRA of revisionist degeneration. It has a weekly paper, *Der Klassenkampf*, which publishes regular articles on the anti-nuclear campaign as well as foreign affairs reports and political polemics.

The most important Trotskyist organisation in Austria is the 'Group of Revolutionary Marxists' (GRM), founded in 1972, and with a membership considered never to have risen much higher than 100. It produces a monthly paper *Die Rotfront*, and describes itself as the Austrian section of the Fourth International. In the general election of 1975 it put up a list in Vienna and gained 1,024 votes, but in the 1979 election it was unable to obtain the 500 signatures necessary to put up a list, and recommended its supporters to abstain. In some local elections the group has given 'critical support' to the KPOe despite its 'Stalinism', because it is the only main party standing out against the system of 'social partnership'. The GRM has developed contacts with a few members in the Socialist students' organisation, who were disillusioned with the SPOe. The influence of all these groups is admitted even by their members to be negligible in a country whose working population solidly supports the SPOe and, in particular, Kreisky.

REFERENCES

1. *Geschichte der Kommunistischen Partei Oesterreichs, 1918–1955,* Globus Verlag, Wien, 1977, p.116.
2. See F. West, *Die Linke im Staendestaat Oesterreich,* Europaverlag, Wien, 1978.
3. *Ibid.,* pp.274–9.
4. *Geschichte der Kommunistichen Partei Oesterreichs, op. cit.* p.253.
5. L. Spira, *Ein gescheiterter Versuch,* Jugend und Volk, Wien, 1979, p.15. For post-war developments in the Austrian Communist Party see K.R.Stadler in D.Childs (ed.), *The Changing Face of Western Communism,* Croom Helm, London, 1980.
6. See E.Scharf, *Ich darf nicht schweigen,* Wien, 1948.
7. See H. Konrad, *Neues Forum,* 'Kein Putsch', October 1977, pp.39–43.
8. See A. Pelinka, 'Auseinandersetzung mit dem Kommunismus', in E. Weinzierl and K. Skalnik (eds.), *Oesterreich Die Zweite Republik,* Styria, 1972, vol. 1.
9. L. Spira, *op. cit.,* p.224.
10. *Parteitag der KPOe,* 1977, p.188.
11. *Statut der KPOe,* 1974.
12. *Parteitag der KPOe,* 1977, p.324.
13. Cited in A. Kadan and A. Pelinka, *Die Grundsatzprogramme der oesterreichischen Parteien,* Verlag Niederoesterreichisches Pressehaus, 1979, p.25.
14. See K. Berchtold, *Oesterreichische Parteiprogramme 1868–1966,* Verlag fuer Geschichte und Politik, Wien, 1967, pp.316–23.
15. L. Spira, *op. cit.,* p.19.
16. *Ibid.,* p.28.
17. K. Berchtold, *op. cit.,* pp.350–1.
18. L. Spira, *op. cit.,* p.52.
19. Cited in A. Kadan and A. Pelinka, *op. cit.,* p.43.
20. *Rote Fahne,* 15 May, 1965 p.19.
21. L. Spira, *op. cit.,* p.87. This is one of the best accounts of the internal conflicts in the party over Czechoslovakia, and the subsequent section is based in part on this book. Spira mentions disputes and impressions gained first-hand as a member of the Central Committee. He was eventually to leave the party in 1971 over disagreements on Czechoslovakia and the KPOe's rejection of Euro-Communism.
22. K. Devlin, 'Czechoslovakia and the crisis of Austrian Communism', *Studies in Comparative Communism,* July-October 1969, pp.22–5. See also T. Prager, *Zwischen London und Moskau,* Europaverlag, Wien, 1975, pp.210–14.
23. Cited in L. Spira, *op. cit.,* p.215.
24. *Ibid.,* p.217.
25. *Parteitag der KPOe,* 1974, pp.320–48.

26.   *Parteitag der KPOe*, 1977, p.210.
27.   *Ibid*., p.176.
28.   *Rote Fahne*, 1 December 1966, p.3.

6

THE ELECTIONS

(a) The Electoral System

The Second Republic adopted the main features of the electoral system which had been practised since 1929. This was modified by a law introduced by the Socialists in 1970 and passed with the support of the FPOe. The *Nationalrat* is elected in accordance with the principles of proportional representation. According to Article 26 of the constitution,

The number of deputies shall be divided among the qualified voters of a constituency (electoral body) in proportion to the number of nationals in the constituencies, i.e. the number of Federal Nationals who in accordance with the result of the last census had their domicile in the constituencies.

This provision means that the rural, western provinces with larger families have an advantage over the urban areas of the eastern provinces with smaller families. The distribution of seats is based on the number of nationals, including children, not on the number of voters. This bias has tended to favour the OeVP, and a two-thirds majority would be necessary to make any changes.

The reform embodied in the law of 1970 increased the total number of deputies from 165 to 183. These are distributed among the constituencies on the basis of the previous census. Alterations made after the last census reflect the decline in the population of

Table 6.i DISTRIBUTION OF PARLIAMENTARY SEATS BETWEEN
THE PROVINCES (ELECTORAL DISTRICTS)

	1961 Census	1971 Census
Burgenland	7	7
Carinthia	13	13
Lower Austria	36	35
Upper Austria	29	30
Salzburg	9	10
Styria	29	30
Tyrol	12	13
Vorarlberg	6	6
Vienna	42	39

Vienna (see Table 6.i). After 1970 each province became an 'electoral district' or constituency (*Wahlkreis*). Combinations of these formed two 'groups of electoral districts' (*Wahlkreisverbaende*), Burgenland, Vienna and Lower Austria constituting *Wahlkreisverband* I and the rest of the country the second (see Map 6.i).

Elections are conducted in two stages. In the first stage, seats are distributed in the nine *Wahlkreise* and calculated according to the Hare system. The total number of votes cast in each *Wahlkreis* is divided by the number of seats allocated to it. The resulting figure is the electoral quota, or the number of votes each party needs to gain a seat. The votes cast for each party list are divided by the electoral quota and this determines the number of seats to which each party is entitled in the electoral district. This gives the parties their *Grundmandate* or 'basic seats'. A party has to gain a 'basic seat' in this first stage before it can be eligible to qualify for seats in the second round.

The 'remaining seats' not distributed in the first round (*Restmandate*) are collected together in the two *Wahlkreisverbaende*. The votes which each party has remaining to it from the first stage—the *Reststimmen*—are counted (the votes of the parties who failed to win a 'basic seat' are not included). The distribution of seats in the second stage is determined according to the d'Hondt system. The electoral quota is calculated by the following process (illustrated by the example in the next paragraph). The number of votes remaining to each party is written down in order of size. Under these numbers are written the half, the third and the quarter; further divisions are continued if necessary. If, for example, there are three remaining seats, then the electoral quota must be the third-highest of these numbers. To calculate the distribution of seats to the parties the *Reststimmen* of each party are divided by this electoral quota. This then forms the parties' *Restmandate*.

This system can be illustrated by an example drawn from the 1979 election. In Electoral District no. 1 (Burgenland) the electoral quota was 25,817. The SPOe with 95,688 votes won three seats, which left 18,237 'remaining votes' and the OeVP with 79,394 votes also won three seats with 1,943 votes over. The FPOe and the KPOe did not poll enough votes to meet the quota. One seat was left over after this first stage in the distribution of 'basic seats'. Under the procedures for the second stage, Burgenland is included in *Wahlkreisverband* I with the electoral districts of Vienna and Lower Austria. These three electoral districts together had six 'remaining seats' (*Restmandate*) and 133,240 'remaining votes' (*Reststimmen*) which were split between the parties as shown below (p.149). These numbers were divided to find the sixth highest number which would form the electoral quota.

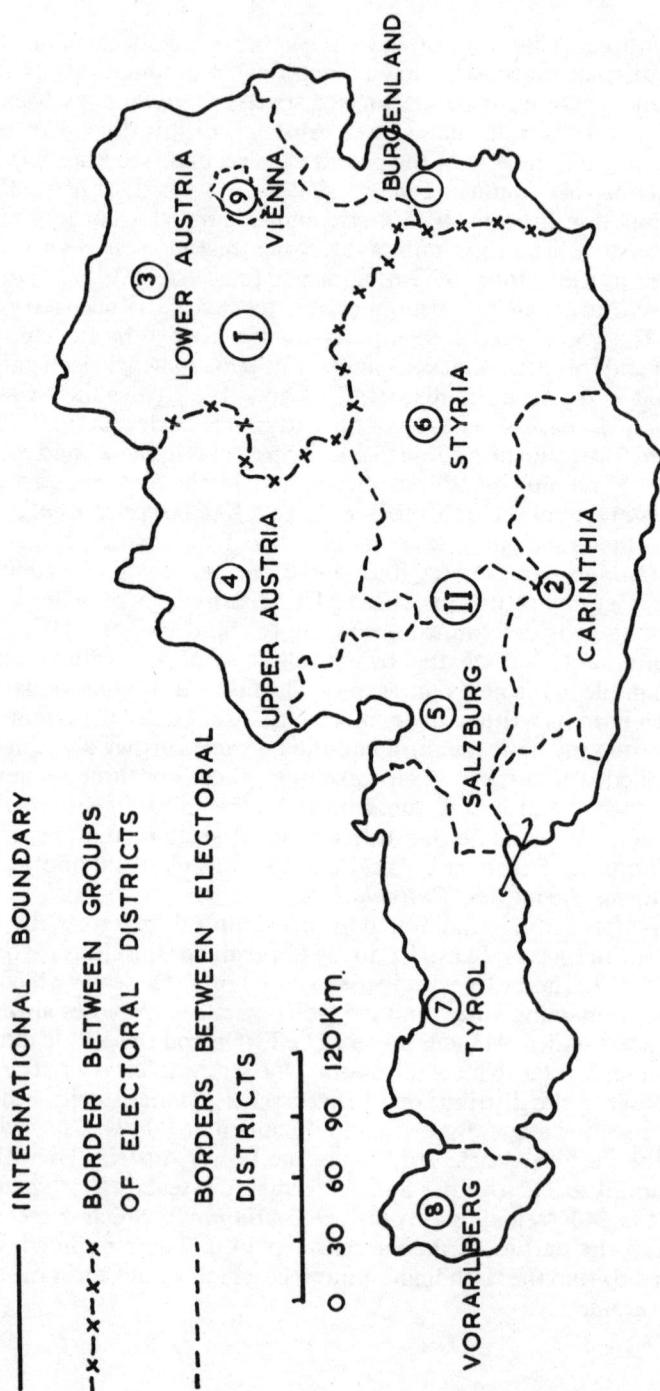

Map 6.i. THE DIVISION OF AUSTRIA INTO ELECTORAL DISTRICTS

Electoral District	'Remaining votes' of		
	SPOe	OeVP	FPOe
Burgenland	18,237	1,943	4,941
Lower Austria	24,764	14,447	6,466
Vienna	16,385	24,188	21,869
Wahlkreisverband I	59,386	40,578	33,276

SPOe	OeVP	FPOe
59,386	40,578	33,276
29,693	20,289	16,638
19,795	13,526	11,092

The six seats left over were allocated by dividing the parties' remaining votes by the electoral quota of 19,795 (arrived at as shown above).

SPOe	$59,386 \div 19,795 = 3$ seats	
OeVP	$40,578 \div 19,795 = 2$ seats	
FPOe	$33,276 \div 19,795 = 1$ seat	

The votes that are left over after this process are 'wasted'. After the 1979 election the SPOe had only three votes left over that had not been used in the calculations, the OeVP had 15,133, and the FPOe 30,889. The seats were distributed to the parties as shown in Table 6.ii. Thus the second stage benefits the Freedom Party which gained four of its eleven seats in this way. The east-west split is apparent from these figures. *Wahlkreisverband* I represents the three eastern electoral districts and in these the SPOe won forty-five out of a possible eighty-one seats. The other two parties have their strength in *Wahlkreisverband* II composed of the six more Western provinces. The regional distribution of the votes between the parties in 1979 is clearly shown on map 6.ii (p.152).

All Austrian citizens over the age of nineteen are entitled to vote. Votes are recorded on an official ballot paper which lists the names of the parties in consecutive order (see Fig. 6.i). 'List 1' is always allocated to the strongest party at the time. In the polling booth the voter puts a cross against the party whose list is chosen. Unlike the system in West Germany, the voter has only one vote.[1] Voters can also enter by the preferred party the name of a candidate who then receives points. The candidate must be a member of the party already selected by the voter so there is no opportunity for 'splitting the ticket'. In 1979 only 0.10 per cent of ballot papers for the SPOe also included the name of a candidate, 0.12 per cent of the OeVP's papers were marked with a candidate, 0.14 per cent of the FPOe's and 0.28 per cent of the Communists, had the name of a candidate

Table 6.ii DISTRIBUTION OF SEATS, 1979 ELECTION

Party	Stage in Distribution	Seats in Wahlkreisverband		
		I	II	Total
SPOe	First	42	47	89
	Second	3	3	6
OeVP	First	31	42	73
	Second	2	2	4
FPOe	First	2	5	7
	Second	1	3	4
All Parties	First	75	94	169
	Second	6	8	14
	Total	81	102	183

Source: Die Nationalratswahl vom 6. Mai 1979, Oesterreichisches Statistisches Zentralamt, Wien, 1979, p.35.

written down. Ballot papers with only the name of a candidate and no cross count as a vote for that party list. Candidates who manage to accumulate the same number of points as the electoral quota, qualify for a parliamentary seat. The order of candidates on the party lists is, in practice, decisive for the allocation of seats. Voting is compulsory in the 'federal *Laender* where this has been enacted by *Land* law'. This is the case in Styria, Tyrol and Vorarlberg and failure to vote can result in a fine of up to 3,000 Schilling. Turn-out in these electoral districts is slightly higher than in those where voting is not compulsory (see Table 6.iii). Voter participation in Austria is high and since the war has never fallen below 92 per cent. Some concern was expressed in the 1979 election that the turn-out was 'only' 92.23 per cent; but by most standards this appears a creditable achievement.

Voting always takes place on a Sunday, and shortly after the

Table 6.iii TURN-OUT IN THE ELECTORAL DISTRICTS, 1979 (%)

Burgenland	95
Carinthia	91
Lower Austria	94
Upper Austria	93
Salzburg	90
Styria	96
Tyrol	94
Vorarlberg	96
Vienna	86
Austria	92

Amtlicher Stimmzettel

für die

Nationalratswahl am . .6. Mai 1979. . .

Wahlkreis: . . .9. (Wien)

Liste Nr.	Für die gewählte Partei im Kreis ein **X** einsetzen!	Kurzbezeichnung	Parteibezeichnung	Bezeichnung eines Bewerbers durch den Wähler
1	⊗	SPOe	Sozialistische Partei Oesterreichs	**KREISKY BRUNO**
2	◯	OeVP	Oesterreichische Volkspartei	
3	◯	FPOe	Freiheitliche Partei Oesterreichs	
4	◯	KPOe	Kommunistische Partei Oesterreichs	
5	◯			
6	◯			
7	◯			
8	◯			
usw.				

Fig. 6.i.   EXAMPLE OF A BALLOT PAPER

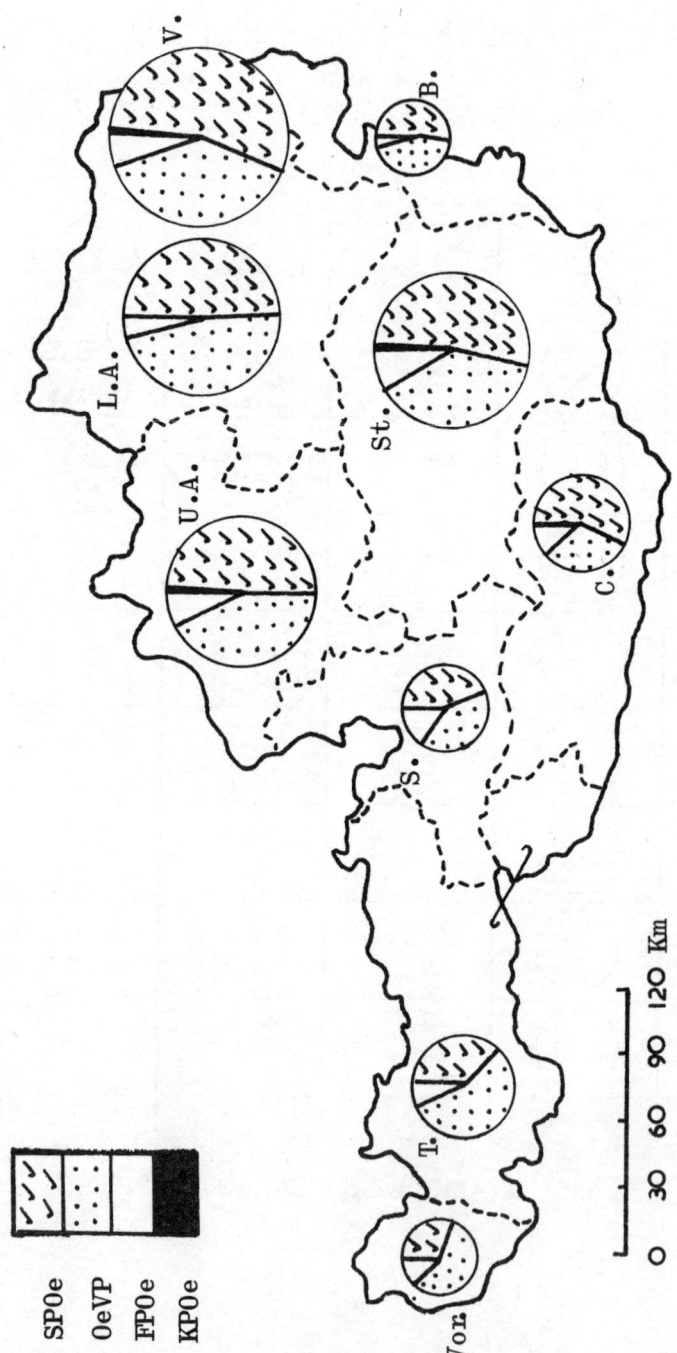

Map 6.ii.   THE DIVISION OF VALID VOTES BETWEEN THE PARTIES, 1979

booths have closed in the evening at 5 p.m. the first, usually accurate, predictions are made. These may have to be modified a few days later when the 'electoral cards' (*Wahlkarten*) have been counted: these are votes cast when a voter is to be absent on voting day from the constituency in which he is registered. They are handed to officials before the election but only counted afterwards. If the ballot paper is returned in another area of the same electoral district, it is included with the count in that region. If the vote is cast in an 'alien' electoral district, outside the one where the voter is registered, then this must be collected with others and transported back to the correct electoral district for inclusion in the count. In 1979 the addition of these votes meant that the SPOe just missed winning an extra seat in Vienna, and it was generally assumed that these *Wahlkarten* were cast by conservatives who had deserted the city on polling day for their country retreats. In the election of 1979 there were 280,503 *Wahlkarten*, of which 130,123 were cast in 'alien' electoral districts.[2]

The Freedom Party benefited from the reforms of November 1970, which made the price of a seat more equal. The number of seats was increased from 165 to 183, and the number of electoral districts was reduced from twenty-five to nine; the *Wahlkreisverbaende* were reduced from four to two.[3] These changes introduced more proportionality. Differences between the parties were not so exaggerated with, on average, twenty seats for each electoral district instead of seven, as before 1970. In the 1979 election the SPOe needed 25,402 votes for one seat, the OeVP 25,737 votes, and the FPOe 26,068 votes. There is no '5 per cent clause', as in West Germany, but small parties are still penalised by the stipulation that each party must win a 'basic seat'.

This has worked against the Communists, who have not won a 'basic seat' since 1956. In that year they gained less than 5 per cent of the vote but still managed to gain three seats, which indicates that the Austrian system is less harsh on minor parties than that of West Germany. The KPOe concentrates on trying to win a 'basic seat' in Vienna where it has most support. In 1979, just 2.6 per cent of the votes would have given the KPOe a 'basic seat', and with this hurdle cleared, it could have proceeded to qualify for parliamentary representation. But it mustered only 1.5 per cent of the vote in this electoral district and so fell a long way short of its target.

Anomalies have occurred in the past, as in 1953 and 1959 when the SPOe gained more votes but less seats than the OeVP. The insistence on distributing the number of deputies in Parliament on the basis of the number of citizens, including minors, had distorted the fairness of the system. Discussions have been taking place for years on a further revision of the electoral system, although this particular aspect is not under review. One proposal is to divide the country into 110 electoral districts and introduce more opportunity for voters to elect individuals. The West German model is particularly favoured. Proposals for change are viewed with suspicion by the parties since all are concerned with how their interests might be affected. The FPOe has voiced its objections to any 'manipulation' of the system which would strengthen the position of the two larger parties, the trend since the war having been for those parties to increase their share of the vote. In 1979 the SPOe and the OeVP together gained 93 per cent of the vote, compared with 83 per cent thirty years earlier. The 1979 election seems to have given a fair deal to the FPOe, which won 6.0 per cent of the seats in the *Nationalrat* with 6.06 per cent of the vote. In 1970, before the electoral reform, the FPOe had won 5.5 per cent of the votes but only gained 3.6 per cent of the seats. The first election held after the reform, in 1971, rectified this discrepancy, and with 5.5 per cent of the vote the FPOe won 5.5 per cent of the parliamentary seats (see Table 6.iv, p.156).

The domination of the two main parties results to some extent from their superior organisation and the resilience of *Lager* discipline. It is also a reflection of the weakness of the two other parties which normally contest elections (see Chapters 4 and 5). In 1979 only these four main parties fought the election in all constituencies. A fifth party put up a list in Tyrol, calling itself the *Christlich-Soziale-Arbeitsgemeinschaft*. The main recognisable policy of this party was total opposition to pornography. It gained 2,263 votes, which was 0.66 per cent of the valid votes cast in Tyrol. At least 500 signatures must be collected to put up a list in a general election. This is frequently a difficult barrier for the minor parties to overcome, since Austrians are reluctant publicly to identify themselves with the non-established *Lager*. The 'party book' system is a powerful factor in ensuring that proportional representation does not encourage a multiplicity of parties.

Before 1975, political parties received financial support from the national budget for their parliamentary and educational activities. In July 1975 a Party Law was passed which allowed for extra state finance for publicity and in particular for election campaigns. Each party in the *Nationalrat* with at least five deputies receives a lump sum. Additional finance is distributed to the parties every year in proportion to the number of votes acquired at the previous election. State finance is especially vital for the FPOe, which receives relatively little support from industry and membership fees (see Table 3.vi). Political parties not represented in Parliament but which have won 1 per cent of the valid votes in a *Nationalrat* election are entitled to financial support. The KPOe thus failed to qualify after the 1975 result, although it had never accepted anyway such finance from the bourgeois state. All parties must be officially registered with the Ministry of the Interior and possess comprehensive statutes outlining the rights and duties of their members. There is no stipulation that these statutes must conform to democratic principles. The legal recognition of a party under the 1975 Party Law has given right-wing groups some protection since there are no provisions for banning a party. Before 1975, the political parties had no specific legal basis in constitutional law. The new provisions established that 'for Austrian democracy the existence of political parties is not only a necessary evil, but an essential precondition'.[4] In addition to the four traditional parties, there are twenty-one splinter groups which have also claimed the status of political parties.

The Freedom Party gained most in relative terms from the Act, which provided each recognised parliamentary party with a fixed sum of 4 million Schilling. In 1980 this was increased to 5 million; in addition to this, the SPOe received, in 1980, 23.6 million Schilling, the OeVP 19.3 million, and the FPOe 0.8 million Schilling.[5] Supervision of the parties' expenditure in elections is conducted by a special commission of the Ministry of the Interior, whose task is to ensure that the parties have not exceeded their allowances by more than 10 per cent. Full details of sources of income and expenditure have to be published by the parties each year. Anton Pelinka, professor of political science at Innsbruck University, considers that the law is likely to promote the development of minor parties and act as a brake on the growth of a full two-party system; the FPOe receives the same basic amount as the two big parties. The Party Law has reduced the importance of traditional sources of income such as membership dues and contributions from individuals and interest groups; but despite this there have been demands for tighter controls on financial support from industry after a series of scandal and corruption charges in 1980. The Party Law and the electoral reform of 1970 have both provided more favourable conditions for the development of small parties. Despite this, the domination of Austrian politics by the SPOe and the OeVP, which has increased since the war, shows little signs of radical change in the foreseeable future.

(b) Elections to the Nationalrat 1945–1959

The two main parties established their monopoly in the frist elections of 1945. The campaign took place in unusual and difficult circumstances among the ruins of a war-scarred country with a starving electorate. The Communists were rudely disillusioned to discover that, despite these desperate conditions, only 5 per cent were prepared to turn to them for salvation (see Table 6.iv). The OeVP, with its slogan 'Freedom, Democracy and Independence', expressed the hopes of many, and won almost 50 per cent of the vote. The *leitmotiv* of election campaigns throughout the Second Republic was

Table 6.iv ELECTION RESULTS TO THE *NATIONALRAT* 1945–1979

	SPOe		OeVP		FPOe		KPOe		Others	
	% of votes	No. of seats	% of votes	No. of seats	% of votes	No. of seats	% of votes	No. of seats	% of votes	No. of seats
1945	44.60	76	49.80	85	–	–	5.42	4	0.19	–
1949	38.71	67	44.03	77	11.67	16*	5.08	5	0.51	–
1953	42.11	73	41.26	74	10.95	14*	5.28	4	0.40	–
1956	43.05	74	45.96	82	6.52	6	4.42	3	0.06	–
1959	44.79	78	44.19	79	7.70	8	3.27	–	0.05	–
1962	44.00	76	45.43	81	7.04	8	3.04	–	0.48	–
1966	42.56	74	48.35	85	5.35	6	0.41	–	3.32	–
1970	48.42	81	44.69	78	5.52	6	0.98	–	0.39	–
1971	50.04	93	43.11	80	5.45	10	1.36	–	0.04	–
1975	50.42	93	42.95	80	5.41	10	1.19	–	0.03	–
1979	51.03	95	41.90	77	6.06	11	0.96	–	0.05	–

*WdU.
The electoral reform of 1970 increased the number of seats from 165 to 183.

the quest for security and protection from external or internal dangers. The defence of Austria against the threatening spectre of Communism and absorption by the 'people's democracies' was a favourite election ploy of the OeVP, the Socialists usually being portrayed as in league with the Communists in their sinister and evil designs. The coalition of the OeVP with the SPOe was a product of *Realpolitik* and the need for survival—a marriage without love, but one which worked.

The election of 1949 restored the vote to many who had been disenfranchised in 1945 because of their Nazi past. A fourth party, the WdU, entered the fray dedicated to the integration of former Nazis and those returning from prisoner-of-war camps. The SPOe showed understanding and tolerance of the new party, clearly delighted by the prospect of divisions in the bourgeois camp. The dilemma which faced the OeVP was solved by a combination of vituperative attacks on the VdU and secret meetings which were designed to gain the support of ex-Nazis. The OeVP confessed that it had 'negotiated with representatives of various circles of National Socialists',[6] although it was publicly committed to oppose the creation of a new-Nazi party. The OeVP was accused of unscrupulously trying to win the votes of ex-Nazis while at the same time refusing to establish a separate party to represent these right-wing interests.

The spectre of the savage-looking Bolshevist 'red cat' (shown as a menacing creature sucking in Socialists—it has been part of the terminology of Austrian politics ever since) emerged in the emotive propaganda of the OeVP which was intended to scare off voters from supporting the SPOe and dictatorship in its new East European form. The OeVP exhorted Austrians to defend the country against the tyranny of the 'people's democracies' which were being established 'only 60 kilometres from Vienna'. There was not much subtlety in its campaign, which branded Socialists and Communists alike as the gravediggers of democracy and freedom. For good measure, it accused the WdU of being secretly in league with the Communists. In retaliation the SPOe claimed that it was, in reality, the OeVP that was manoeuvring behind the scenes with leading Communists. The KPOe, aware that its associations with Soviet Communism had not brought much success in 1945, renamed itself the 'Left Bloc' in an effort to win the voters' confidence.[7] The Left Bloc included dissident Socialists, among them Erwin Scharf, the former central secretary of the SPOe who had been expelled from the party. All the parties showed signs of nervousness bordering on hysteria during the 1949 campaign. It was one of the most bitter in the life of the Second Republic, rivalled only by that of 1966 in which the OeVP resurrected the Marxist 'popular front' bogey.

Both coalition partners sustained heavy losses to the WdU, which won eight seats from each. The SPOe lost a ninth seat to the Communists. The OeVP had lost its absolute majority and renewed the coalition with the SPOe. Clashes between the OeVP and the WdU during the campaign made any consideration of an alliance between these two unlikely. The WdU won almost 500,000 votes, which roughly corresponded to the number of 'less incriminated' Nazis who had been re-enfranchised. Regional variations show that not all the WdU's support came from this section. In Upper Austria, an area where there had only been 76,225 registered ex-Nazis, the party gained 124,520 votes. In Vienna only 79,149 votes went to the WdU, although the franchise had been restored to 112,945 former Nazis.[8] The party, with sixteen seats in the *Nationalrat*, was at its zenith. Any initial worries of a revival of neo-Nazism soon disappeared; the Communists, with five seats, had also peaked, and subsequent elections reinforced the stability of support for the two main parties.

In addition to the four parties in Parliament, seven others contested the election of 1953, but all remained insignificant. A group of monarchists gained just over 1,000 votes, slightly more than the Austrian National Republicans. The Communists hoped for better luck with yet another name, the 'People's Opposition', and they joined forces with a group which had fought the 1949 election under the name of the 'Democratic Union' led by Professor Dobretsberger who had once made a career in the *Heimwehr*; however, they lost the seat they had gained in 1949. In the propaganda of the OeVP, the 'red cat' scare of 1949 was replaced by the menace of a 'red spider' which appeared on placards to be encroaching upon most of the sacrosanct institutions of Austria.[9] The Socialists took advantage of their position as junior partners in the coalition, and blamed the OeVP for most of the prevalent economic ills and the increase in unemployment. They were less on the defensive than they had been in 1949, and portrayed the OeVP as a party which would insidiously deprive pensioners of their money and enrich itself at the expense of exploited tenants and starving workers.

The SPOe gained 36,740 more votes than the OeVP, but had one less seat in the *Nationalrat*. The WdU lost two seats but still had fourteen which could have provided the OeVP with a useful cabinet partner in a three-party government. This possibility was explored by the OeVP, well aware that Socialist fears of a new 'bourgeois block' would curb any ambitious demands for an alteration of the *Proporz*. The SPOe realised the danger and showed a willingness to renegotiate the two-party coalition. The Federal President Theodor Koerner, a former Socialist mayor of Vienna, coaxed the OeVP into complying with this move after he had ruled out the inclusion of the

VdU in a government. The SPOe gained two new State Secretaries for their efforts, the one in the realm of Foreign Affairs occupied by Bruno Kreisky. The results of the 1953 election were a sign that the electorate was beginning to show concern for social security and was not afraid of state influence in the economy. The continuation of the coalition was greeted in the United States and Britain as a defeat for extremism and an indication of Austria's political maturity. Despite underlying differences of opinion on budgetary policy, the two parties had peacefully resolved the electoral deadlock of 1953. It gave some reason to hope that crises could be contained within the system and resolved through discussion, even if tinged with a little backstairs intrigue.

The signing of the State Treaty and the restoration to Austria of major industries which had been nationalised had domestic implications. One of the most contentious issues was the control of these industries and the organisation of the economy. In 1949, jurisdiction over the nationalised industries had been assigned to the Ministry of Transport under the control of the Socialists. The OeVP believed that the Minister responsible, Karl Waldbrunner, had already accumulated too much power in his 'kingdom'; it wanted to denationalise industries which had been under Soviet administration, but this was vigorously opposed by the Socialists. Tension between the two parties increased, and it was agreed to hold an election in May 1956.

The OeVP continued with the theme of the 'red terror', personified by Waldbrunner who seemed to be leading Austria, and particularly its oil fields, along the road to Moscow. The OeVP stressed its commitment to Austria, freedom and the idea of property for all as opposed to anonymous nationalisation. There was an air of optimism and prosperity in the country, and feelings of relief and jubilation accompanied the end of the occupation. The Socialists conducted a negative and mostly uninspiring campaign. Seemingly unaware of a desire among the population, especially the young, for a new start and a concern with the future, the SPOe raised spectres of the 1930s. Raab was branded for his *Heimwehr* past, and the OeVP was attacked as the successor to clerical Fascism; but for most people Raab, after 1955, was the 'State Treaty Chancellor' and was associated with freedom and the beginnings of prosperity. Although the SPOe made slight gains, the OeVP was the main victor (see Table 6.iv). The two small parties in Parliament had lost between them nine seats, and the OeVP gained eight seats, but despite its gains the OeVP was one seat short of an absolute majority in the *Nationalrat*, and discussions began on a revision of the *Proporz* which would reflect the OeVP's improved position. The outcome of this was that the SPOe was forced to dismantle Waldbrunner's 'kingdom' and relinquish jurisdiction over the nationalised industries, including oil, to a holding company under the direction of the Federal Government. Waldbrunner remained in the cabinet as Minister of Transport and Electric Power. A newly-created Ministry of Defence came within the sphere of the OeVP, although the post of State Secretary within that Ministry was filled by a member of the SPOe.

Although the nationalised enterprises had been removed from the Socialist domain, they were not directly surrendered to the OeVP Ministry of Finance, as had been the OeVP's original intention. The new holding company was to have a board of directors composed on the basis of party parity, which enabled the SPOe to retain some influence. Similar *Proporz* arrangements, which resulted from long negotiations,[10] were made for broadcasting and for the airlines.

The election of 1959 gave the Socialists a lead of 25,892 votes but one seat less than the OeVP in the *Nationalrat*. Tough bargaining followed, and lasted eleven weeks. The elections for the Federal Presidency in 1957 had been a victory for the SPOe candidate, Adolf Schaerf, Vice-Chancellor since 1945; he received 51 per cent of the vote compared with 49 per cent for his rival, a joint candidate of the OeVP and FPOe. The OeVP showed some anxiety at a Socialist increase in power and claimed that obstructionism on the part of the SPOe had necessitated an early general election. Each of the two main parties showed a neurotic concern throughout the campaign over the possibility that its opponent would become too powerful. The electorate was clearly reluctant to return a decisive verdict, although 89 per cent of the vote went to the two main parties, which did indicate decisive support for the continuation of the coalition. One of the most vivid election posters depicted the Austrian ship of state keeling over with an OeVP majority. To avoid this disaster the caption asked voters to support the SPOe and maintain balance. In the words of Uwe Kitzinger,

The party's Austro-Marxist forbears must have turned in their graves to see their revolutionary band transformed into a Socialist party which by implication aimed at no more than equality with the OeVP and which saw itself, as one half of a vessel that would no doubt sink without its 'clerical-conservative' other half.[11]

The OeVP's campaign lacked originality; it merely promised moderation and security. The SPOe attacked Raab as a reactionary capitalist and presented itself to the electorate as a new, progressive party. Most of the excitement came when the campaign was over and the two parties were engaged in the division of the spoils. The OeVP was keen to develop a more flexible coalition system, which would allow for more topics to be decided by a free vote in Parliament.

This was adamantly opposed by the Socialists who demanded an increased voice for themselves in financial policy—a demand which was unacceptable to the OeVP. After deadlock had been reached, President Schaerf intervened and directed a special committee to agree on terms for the continuation of the coalition. An independent Ministry of Foreign Affairs was set up as a result of the discussions, and was headed by the Socialist Bruno Kreisky. The management of the nationalised industries was transferred from the holding company, which had been established in 1956, to the office of Vice-Chancellor (a Socialist). The OeVP failed to realise its plans to make the coalition less rigid, an important point for the SPOe which feared that an introduction of the principle of free voting could only lead to an OeVP-FPOe alignment in the *Nationalrat*.[12] Raab continued as Chancellor, but his authority in his own party had been severely damaged. As a new decade began, a group of 'reformers' in the OeVP gained in influence and mooted ideas for a loosening of the coalition pact.

(c) Elections to the Nationalrat 1962–1979

By the time of the next election in 1962, Raab had been replaced as Chancellor, thus depriving the Socialists of one of their favourite targets. Changes in the OeVP led to an escalation of anti-Communism, which was understood to embrace the SPOe. After the close result of 1959, it was clear that even a slight shift in votes could be decisive, and so the OeVP relied once more on *Angst* propaganda, claiming that the 'reds' were conspiring to take control of Austria. One election poster showed the map of Austria being ominously threatened by the barbed wire from the 'Eastern bloc';[13] and the electorate, suitably impressed by this prospect, gave two seats to the OeVP at the expense of the SPOe. By contrast the campaign of the SPOe had been tame, presenting idyllic pictures of happy pensioners and children. This tactic, premature in the early 1960s, was later to appeal to Austrians less susceptible to the scare of the red menace.

The result had removed temporarily the imminent Socialist threat so resented by the 'new men' in the OeVP. The election was followed by the now familiar, tiresome negotiations which dragged on for four months. A few State Secretaries were shuffled around between the parties, and the respective jurisdiction of certain ministries was finely re-allocated. It seemed to the average Austrian that the coalition was becoming stale and that elections hardly brought any changes of significance.[14] After the 1962 negotiations, the SPOe retained the Foreign Ministry but sacrificed its jurisdiction over foreign trade and questions relating to the Common Market to the 'black' Ministry of Finance. Some concession was made to the idea of releasing topics from the grip of the coalition for 'free' decisions in Parliament. This was largely cosmetic and intended to pacify the reformers in the OeVP. President Schaerf had cautioned the OeVP against sabotaging the coalition and endangering stability. Neither side was prepared to risk a radicalisation of domestic politics which could have followed the fall of the coalition. In 1963 President Schaerf was overwhelmingly confirmed in office by the electorate and gained over 55 per cent of the vote, the best performance by a candidate in any post-war presidential election. The defeat of Raab, the main challenger, caused increased discontent within the OeVP. One of the most divisive issues which the coalition partners had to tackle was the intention of Otto Habsburg, the eldest son of the last Emperor, to return to Austria. The OeVP was sympathetic to this, but the Socialists opposed his return, fearing that he would meddle in domestic politics. With no favourable decision coming from the Government, Otto took his case first to the Constitutional Court, which stated that the matter was outside its competence, and then to the Administrative Court. The latter concluded that Otto's renunciation of all claims as a member of the House of Habsburg was sufficient to allow him to return. In July 1963, the FPOe joined forces with the SPOe in the *Nationalrat* against the OeVP and voted to forbid Otto Habsburg's return. This confirmed the OeVP's suspicions that the other two parties were intriguing to form a small coalition. The life of the great coalition was prolonged by securing a concession from Otto that he would not seek to cross the border while the existing parliament was in session. Possible SPOe-FPOe collusion was abortively curtailed by the revelation that the Socialist Minister of the Interior, Franz Olah, had misappropriated trade union funds to finance the FPOe. He was expelled by the SPOe (see Chapter 2), and the 'Olah affair', by discrediting the FPOe, strained relations between it and the Socialists. While causing problems for the FPOe, the Olah case crippled the Socialists as they were about to embark on the crucial election of 1966.

The campaign of 1966 was one of the most acrimonious in the history of the Second Republic. The irritation of some members of the OeVP with the shackles of the coalition was clear, and they asked for a clear mandate. The Communist Party suggested that its supporters should turn out for the SPOe, and the 'red scare' that the OeVP was in the habit of discovering before every election assumed some substance. The SPOe, under Pittermann, obliged the OeVP by not repudiating the Communists' dubious assistance. Olah contested the election with his own party, which further weakened the morale of the SPOe. The OeVP must have been grateful for these difficulties, which temporarily diverted attention from its own internal problems. It concentrated on appealing to the electorate to consider the future of Austria's children and forestall a 'red' take-over. The SPOe was portrayed on OeVP posters with the hammer and sickle hovering in the background. Such propaganda, although crude, was effective; after a frenzied whipping-up of fears of Communism, the OeVP offered voters peace, order and security. The campaign degenerated into personal attacks on leading politicians. Socialists were branded in anonymous leaflets as Titoists, and Kreisky was disparagingly asked if he would emigrate again in the event of a popular front government. It was clearly implied that his contacts with international Jewry would make this easy to arrange.[15]

The OeVP won an extra four seats which gave it an absolute majority of five in the *Nationalrat*, a landslide victory by Austrian standards. The FPOe and the SPOe lost two seats each and retired into opposition, contemplating the future under an OeVP government with some trepidation. The OeVP itself seemed curiously unenthusiastic about forming a single-party cabinet, and at first even consulted the SPOe on a revision of the coalition. However, the verdict of the electorate had strengthened the hand of the OeVP, and the new rules were not acceptable to the SPOe. The unthinkable had happened and Austria was without a coalition government. Few at the time would have believed that affairs would stay that way for the next fifteen years at least, or that at the next election the 'reds' themselves would form their first single-party cabinet.

Changes in the SPOe and difficulties for the OeVP government contributed to the reversal of roles which followed the 1970 election (see Chapter 2)—although a further election was necessary in 1971 before the SPOe could form a majority government. The electorate was highly volatile in 1966 and 1970. In 1966 almost 10 per cent of the electorate changed their party allegiance, which was repeated in the reverse direction in 1970. In 1971, 161,000 voters (3.5 per cent of the valid votes) changed party allegiance. This decreased slightly in 1975, and at the 1979 election 3.8 per cent of voters switched parties. The dramatic shifts between the *Lager* in 1966 and 1970 were a significant departure from previous voting patterns. In 1966 the Socialists lost 104,000 votes directly to the OeVP, and won 158,000 votes from the OeVP in 1970. These gains have been secured in the Socialist camp in subsequent elections and a drift back to the conservative *Lager* has been avoided.[16] The results of the 1966 and 1970 elections lead to the conclusion that formerly predictable voting behaviour is changing and that voters are more inclined to be persuaded by a party from the opposite *Lager*.[17] These potential 'fluctuating voters' seem since 1971 to have found a stable home in the SPOe camp.

The style of campaigning has changed to emphasise personalities more than issues. Kreisky's image has made it difficult for the OeVP to raise the popular front spectre. The Chancellor has always made his opposition to Communism clear and in this has been more convincing than his predecessor, Pittermann, who was easily portrayed to alarmed voters in the guise of the 'red pig'. In the campaign of 1975 the SPOe's message was simply 'Kreisky—who else?'.[18] With this concentration on personalities, pre-election television 'duels' between party leaders have become increasingly important. In the 1979 campaign the OeVP stressed the theme of 'a new spring', and its election posters showed colourful flowers. Although this campaign was generally judged to have been a disaster, it was nevertheless a refreshing change from the pre-1970 days, when the destruction of Austria by the 'reds' was so great a preoccupation. It may take some time for the OeVP to devise a suitable substitute for its old propaganda. Personalities do not constitute a strong card because since Raab the party has lacked an authoritative personality as its leader. Taus, its leading candidate in 1979, was considered bright but lacking the sort of magnetic personality that could have drawn voters away from the comfortable security of Kreisky's party. As Chancellor of Austria for more than a decade and leader of his party since 1967, Kreisky is a formidable opponent. Post-war Austrian politics have evolved from coalitions to a long period of Social Democratic rule, with a short period of alternating governments in between. Much of the SPOe's success has been based on its ability to provide security, prosperity and full employment. The expectations of the average Austrian have become greater than in the precarious days of the coalition era. The fortunes of the government elected in 1979 will depend on the promotion of the existing happy state of affairs and the avoidance of the economic troubles which are so prevalent in other European countries.

(d) 'Popular Initiatives' and Plebiscites

Voters have participated in five 'popular initiatives' (*Volksbegehren*) which have received the required number of signatures, one language census and a referendum. Article 41 of the constitution states:

Every motion proposed by 200,000 voters or by half of the voters in each of three *Laender* (popular initiative) shall be submitted by the Federal Government to the *Nationalrat* for action in accordance with the rules of procedure. The popular initiative must be put forward in the form of a draft law.

The Government intends to reduce the number required for a popular initiative to 100,000, or one-sixth of the voters, in three provinces. This is in accordance with Kreisky's concept of increased democratisation of society. The *Nationalrat*, although it must discuss a popular initiative with enough support, is not obliged to comply with any demands thus put forward. The FPOe is pressing for a further reform of this system so that the *Nationalrat* can by no means simply 'kill' any popular initiative. It proposes that provision should be made for subsequently submitting these draft laws in the form of a referendum.

In 1964 a proposal to de-politicise the broadcasting network received 832,353 signatures, which was just over 17 per cent of those entitled to vote. Most signatures were collected in Vorarlberg and Tyrol. An initiative of 1969 to introduce a forty-hour week was sponsored by just under 18 per cent of voters. Most support for this came from Burgenland, Lower Austria and Styria. Altogether 889,659 signatures were collected, of which only 2.5 per cent came from Vorarlberg and 5.3 per cent from Tyrol. The initiative which raised least interest was proposed in 1969, and concerned abolition of the compulsory ninth year of secondary school. Only 339,407 signatures were collected, with most enthusiasm being shown in Styria. Most signatures were collected for the popular initiative of 1975 directed against the Socialist abortion law. Almost 18 per cent of the electorate signed the motion, with most support coming from Vorarlberg (32.7 per cent) and Tyrol (31.8 per cent). Vienna trailed the rest of the country (with only 6.1 per cent of voters signing the motion).[19] An initiative in favour of atomic energy received over 400,000 signatures.

After debate the *Nationalrat* has usually taken no immediate positive action. Some note was taken of the popular initiatives in all cases but that of 1975 in subsequent legislation. The OeVP Government in 1966 revised the law on broadcasting, which was aimed at reducing the *Proporz* influence in radio and television. This was strongly opposed by the SPOe, which believed that its supervision over what the two other parties regarded as 'red' television was being removed. The OeVP Minister of Education disagreed with the initiative on school reform and resigned when he discovered that his party was reluctant totally to ignore it. Further reforms in education were planned, and eventually the two main parties reached a compromise on the school laws which require a two-thirds majority in Parliament. The forty-hour week was introduced by the SPOe government in 1975. No action followed the initiative against liberalising abortion, which was rejected by Parliament in a free vote. Relations between the OeVP and some Church leaders deteriorated after this initiative on abortion, with accusations of faint-hearted support and bad organisation. The initiative had proposed amending the law to allow for abortion in extreme cases only, but even this was unacceptable to some Catholics; it approximated an earlier plan of the OeVP which some Catholics had also rejected. After the Socialist Government had introduced more radical legislation, pressure mounted in the Church to adopt the original idea of the OeVP. This lack of co-ordination led to confusion and damaged relations between the Church and the OeVP; the dialogue between Catholics and Socialists was not similarly impaired. Some Socialists are also critical of the law, because it has only been successfully applied in Vienna. The reluctance of Catholic doctors to co-operate and the lack of amenities in other provinces have contributed to the discrepancy between the theory and practice of the legislation.

The Government has twice initiated moves calling on the population to participate in voting procedures other than those normally required in general and local elections. On both occasions it hoped to resolve a delicate problem which did not seem to be making satisfactory progress in Parliament. The first of these was the decision by Kreisky's government to hold a language census throughout Austria in November 1976.

The language census was an attempt to settle the inveterate conflicts in Carinthia between the Slovene minority group and some pan-German nationalists. The State Treaty had included certain clauses guaranteeing the rights of minority groups. Yugoslavia became a co-signatory to the Treaty and has the role of a protecting power for the Slovene minorities inside Austrian territory. According to Article 7 of the State Treaty,

1. Austrian nationals of the Slovene and Croat minorities in Carinthia, Burgenland and Styria shall enjoy the same rights on equal terms as all other Austrian nationals, including the right to their own organisations meetings and a press in their own language.
2. They are entitled to elementary instruction in the Slovene or Croat language and to a proportional number of their own secondary schools.
3. In the administrative and judicial districts of Carinthia, Burgenland and Styria, where there are Slovene, Croat or mixed populations, the Slovene or Croat language shall be accepted as an official language in addition to German. In such districts topographical terminology and inscriptions shall be in the Slovene or Croat language as well as in German.

The Slovenes complain that these points have not been adequately enacted, while the pan-Germans argue that the Treaty is imprecise. The latter have always demanded a count of minorities before making any concessions. The Slovenes, whose numbers have been declining, have always maintained that their rights as outlined in the

State Treaty are not dependent on a count. They have disputed official census figures, which they believe are manipulated to exaggerate the decline in their numbers.

Carinthia is the province where the minority questions have caused most problems and violence. A pathological fear exists among some elements of the German-speaking population of the province being absorbed by Yugoslavia. After the disintegration of the Habsburg empire, a new South Slav kingdom of Serbs, Croats and Slovenes was formed. The Yugoslavs invaded the adjacent territory of Carinthia, but met resistance from local volunteer forces (*Abwehrkampf*). The Allies decided that a plebiscite should take place in the disputed area, and the Klagenfurt basin was divided into two zones. In the north, Zone B was predominantly German-speaking and included the capital, Klagenfurt. A southern Zone A was established, which, according to the 1910 census, had a mainly Slovene population. The results of the plebiscite in this area in 1920 showed that 59 per cent wished to remain in the Austrian republic. This, however, could not remove the *idée fixe* that the province was threatened by the Slavs across the border.

After the Second World War, Yugoslavia once again claimed areas of 'Slovene Carinthia'. Partisan troops had retaliated against the German population in Carinthia, often quite indiscriminately and with brutality. This increased feelings of bitterness and renewed fears on the Austrian side of a possible revision of the southern border. Faced with opposition from the British occupation forces and a decline in support from Stalin, the Yugoslavs reluctantly abandoned their bid for the area, but despite this a primordial fear remained that the southern part of Carinthia was not secure and was vulnerable to take-over by Communist Slavs.

A pan-German nationalist organisation, the *Kaerntner Heimatdienst* (KHD), is dedicated to the defence of 'German' interests in the area. It believes in the need for constant vigilance against the danger of 'creeping' Slovenisation. It points to the 'domination' of Klagenfurt by Slovene shops, cultural centres, newspapers and a secondary school. The KHD has strong backing from members in the police force and the Federal army, and from local politicians, mayors and school directors. The KHD supported the 'signpost war' of 1972 when dual-language signposts were dismantled. This was the result of an ill-conceived attempt by Kreisky's Government partly to enact the State Treaty. When the Chancellor visited the province, he was greeted with chants of 'traitor' and 'Jewish swine'.

In 1976 the Socialist government tried a different approach and passed an Ethnic Groups Act, which was accepted by all three parties in Parliament. According to this Act, the Federal Government was to determine 'those areas where, on account of the relatively high number [one-quarter] of ethnic group members residing there, topographical terminology shall be in two languages'. In addition, the Act envisaged substantial improvement in the position of ethnic groups and guaranteed their social, cultural and economic interests.[20] The Act stipulated that in the application of these benefits the size of the ethnic group should be considered. A language census was to be conducted as an 'aid to orientation'. The Slovenes believed this was a violation of the State Treaty which made no reference to a census and were backed by Yugoslavia. They called for a boycott of the census and were supported by the left wing in Austria. A 'solidarity committee' with centres outside Carinthia decided to help sabotage the census by declaring a false language. The results of the census were useless as an 'aid to orientation' but the government pressed on with the implementation of the Act in areas where a large ethnic group is resident.

The government is satisfied that it has fulfilled the obligations of the State Treaty. The Slovenes maintain that they are being pushed into increasingly smaller communities, but it is unlikely that the government will review its present policy. The results of the census show that there is little interest outside Carinthia in the dispute (see Table 6.v), and Kreisky's Government is likely to assign priority to other problems facing the country.

One of the most dramatic decisions made by Austrians under the Second Republic was the rejection, in a referendum, of nuclear energy. The referendum was called by Kreisky's Government for November 1978, on the assumption that the result would be favourable to it. The anti-nuclear lobby mounted an enthusiastic and well-organised campaign which contributed to a major change in public opinion, and its victory surprised even the most committed opponents of nuclear energy and was Kreisky's first serious miscalculation.

The Socialists had wanted to put on-stream the country's first nuclear plant which had been completed at Zwentendorf, only 40 km. from Vienna. The OeVP had originally sanctioned the building of the plant when it was in government in the late 1960s; seven regional electricity companies have a 50 per cent share in the plant and six of these are in the OeVP-dominated provinces (Carinthia is the other province which is involved). Business interests and industry tend to favour the nuclear programme and have urged the OeVP to sympathise with the project. When doubts over the safety of the Zwentendorf reactor, increased, the OeVP refused to support the Government in Parliament. The FPOe allied with the OeVP in the *Nationalrat*, and Socialist deputies from Vorarlberg also had

Table 6.v RESULTS OF THE LANGUAGE CENSUS 1976 (%)

	Turn-out	German	Croat	Slovene	Hungarian	Other
Burgenland	27.4	93.1	4.1	0.1	2.5	0.2
Carinthia	86.4	98.6	0.1	0.9	0.1	0.3
Lower Austria	24.3	98.9	0.2	0.3	0.2	0.4
Upper Austria	20.5	98.8	0.3	0.4	0.2	0.5
Salzburg	18.6	98.5	0.2	0.7	0.2	0.4
Styria	25.9	98.6	0.3	0.6	0.2	0.3
Tyrol	8.8	98.2	0.2	0.5	0.3	0.8
Vorarlberg	5.1	97.2	0.2	1.1	0.6	0.9
Vienna	25.7	95.6	0.4	1.3	0.6	2.0
Austria	26.7	97.9	0.4	0.7	0.3	0.7

reservations about commissioning the plant. Demonstrations against Zwentendorf during the parliamentary debates increased, and it was becoming clear that such a decision on such a sensitive issue would need more authority than a law passed by a small SPOe majority.

The constitution allows for a referendum on all laws awaiting authentication by the Federal President. Article 45 states that 'for a referendum the absolute majority of the validly cast votes is decisive'. All parties in the *Nationalrat* accepted the decision to hold a referendum on the so-called Atom Law, passed by the SPOe. Voters were asked to judge this law authorising Parliament to commission the Zwentendorf plant. It was the first referendum to be held in the Second Republic, and the technical nature of the topic seemed to baffle many voters. Some felt that the Government was trying to avoid taking an awkward decision and was shifting responsibility on to the unfortunate 'man in the street'.

The OeVP seemed particularly confused, and at first its leader Taus opposed nuclear power. This was later modified, but finally the party decided on rejection at the eleventh hour. The SPOe was similarly divided, with strong pressure coming from the trade unions, ardent supporters of the nuclear programme, which Benya regards as a desirable means of maintaining full employment. Younger members of the SPOe were not so convinced, and the party underestimated the extent of this feeling. Some in the youth movement are suspicious that, despite the referendum's rejection of the nuclear programme, the 'social partners' will eventually find a way round the dilemma. Shortly before the referendum, the SPOe's party executive met to give an official recommendation for a 'yes' vote. The only 'rebel' on the executive was the leader of the Socialist Youth, Josef Cap, who remains opposed to nuclear energy. The SPOe in Vorarlberg was critical of proceeding with nuclear power and came out against Zwentendorf; the population of this province had once rallied stoutly to prevent the building of a reactor just across the border in Switzerland. Kreisky's son was a well-known opponent of atomic energy and his activities in the campaign received great publicity. The Chancellor himself caused some friction by branding the opponents as Fascists and Maoists: this was resented by many who were not associated with either of those political persuasions but who were beginning to think that the nuclear experiment was too dangerous.

A left-wing organisation, the 'Initiative of Opponents of Atomic Power' (IOeAG), was established in 1976 to co-ordinate the efforts of different groups. It concentrated its attack on the lack of safety precautions at Zwentendorf, although it proclaimed a general rejection of nuclear power. The proximity of the plant to Vienna was of concern to the inhabitants in the capital, and the IOeAG described in ghoulish detail the consequences of a possible catastrophe. Sensing the effectiveness of this propaganda, Kreisky intervened to link the referendum with a vote of confidence in the Government. He hinted that his resignation might follow from a vote of no-confidence, but some Socialists, opposed to nuclear energy, felt strongly enough to take this risk. This intervention by Kreisky seems to have resulted in non-Socialists, who would have otherwise voted for Zwentendorf, abstaining or voting against (see Table 6.vi). They wished to avoid any implicit support for the Government that could be deduced from a positive vote. The outcome was a narrow victory for the anti-nuclearists, who staged a jubilant procession throughout Vienna. The feeling was that, against all odds, dedication and organisation had mobilised public opinion to stop a crucial piece of legislation.

The Government had lost the referendum by only 30,068 votes, but it stated its intention to abide by the verdict. The turn-out was relatively low and was highest in Vorarlberg where the most 'No' votes were recorded. Kreisky's personal intervention seems to have been decisive in staunch socialist areas such as Vienna, Burgenland and Carinthia, which voted for the Government. The western provinces voted 'No' to Zwentendorf and, by implication, to the 'reds'. The result was most marginal in Lower Austria, the province in which Zwentendorf lies. By 11,508 votes the province decided in favour of commissioning its native reactor; in the village of Zwentendorf itself, 1,023 voted 'yes' and 821 'no' to the local reactor. It was assumed that the prospect of extra jobs in the area convinced the inhabitants that possible hazards were worth risking. A high proportion of women and the youth voted 'no' in the referendum, which was particularly disturbing for the SPOe, normally

Table 6.vi RESULTS OF THE NUCLEAR REFERENDUM 1978 (%)

	Turn-out	*'Yes' Votes*	*'No' Votes*
Burgenland	68.1	59.8	40.2
Carinthia	63.0	54.1	45.9
Lower Austria	71.9	50.9	49.1
Upper Austria	68.0	47.3	52.7
Salzburg	61.0	43.2	56.8
Styria	58.1	52.8	47.2
Tyrol	44.8	34.2	65.8
Vorarlberg	75.6	15.6	84.4
Vienna	63.8	55.4	44.6
Austria	64.1	49.5	50.5

Source: Ministry of the Interior, Vienna, 10 November 1978.

popular with these sections of the electorate.

Obituaries on the 'Kreisky era' proved to be premature, and appeals from his own party and the country dissuaded the Chancellor from resigning. The SPOe soon consoled itself with the idea that the result was better than a similarly narrow endorsement of nuclear energy would have been. Had that occurred, the Government would still have been reluctant to proceed, and nothing would have been settled. A general election followed six months later and there was no doubt then about the Government's popularity. During the general election campaign nuclear energy was discussed, especially in view of the 'Harrisburg incident' which had taken place after the referendum. The opposition parties could not make much political capital from atomic energy in Austria. It will now require a second referendum or a two-thirds majority in Parliament for the plant to be commissioned. Within his own party, Kreisky's authority was greater than ever. The maestro had shown that even apparent setbacks could neatly be turned to advantage.

The success of the anti-nuclear lobby prompted speculation about the future of similar protest groups and citizens' initiatives. The 'greens' have not, up till the present, made much impact in Austria compared with West Germany. 'Green' lists which contested the *Land* elections in Vienna in 1978 and Lower Austria in 1979 gained less than 1 per cent of the vote. All three parliamentary parties have to some extent responded to the feeling of uneasiness about unrestricted economic growth, dangers to the environment and the growth of bureaucracy. The SPOe in Vienna likes to think of itself as one large citizens' initiative, and has recognised the need for an increase in consultation. The youth in the city periodically complain of restrictions on freedom and a lack of cultural amenities. This is one source of discontent which the established parties will need to watch. The main parties are trying to integrate frustrated elements. If they succeed, it is unlikely that diverse groups which joined forces against nuclear energy will be able to proceed and consolidate their achievement.[21] The established *Lager* have survived severe upheavals in the past. They show no intention of abandoning the political stage in the future.

REFERENCES

1.   See T. Burkett, *Parties and Elections in West Germany*, C. Hurst, London, 1975, p.132.
2.   Details of the 1979 election, unless otherwise stated, are from *Die Nationalratswahl vom 6. Mai 1979*, Oesterreichisches Statistisches Zentralamt, Wien, 1979.

3. For a discussion of the system in operation before 1970 see U. Kitzinger, 'The Austrian Electoral System', *Parliamentary Affairs*, parts 3 and 4, 1959, pp.392–404.

4. A. Pelinka, 'Parteifinanzierung im Parteienstaat', in A. Khol and A. Stirnemann(ed.), *Oesterreichisches Jarhbuch fuer Politik 1977*, Verlag fuer Geschichte und Politik, Wien, 1978, p.225. This chapter provides a detailed analysis of the implications of the Party Law. See also A. Kofler, *Parteienfinanzierung und deren Auswirkung auf innerparteiliche Strukturen*, Diplomarbeit, University of Innsbruck, 1979, pp.82–3.

5. B. Wicha, 'Naemen und schaemen', *Oesterreichische Monatshefte*, 9, 1980, p.24.

6. See M.E. Riedlsperger, *The Lingering Shadow of Nazism: the Austrian Independent Movement since 1945*, Columbia University Press, New York, 1978, p.64.

7. Election posters and party slogans can be found in N. Hoelzl, *Propagandaschlachten, Die oesterreichischen Wahlkaempfe 1945 bis 1971*, Verlag für Geschichte und Politik, Wien, 1974.

8. Riedlsperger, *op. cit.*, p.69.

9. N. Hoelzl, *op. cit.*, p.60.

10. Details of the redistribution of power after 1956 are described in H.P. Secher, 'Coalition Government: the Case of the Second Austrian Republic', *American Political Science Review*, part 3, 1958, pp.791–808.

11. U. Kitzinger, 'The Austrian Election of 1959', *Political Studies*, Vol. IX, no.2, 1961, p.125.

12. For a full discussion of the negotiations see F.C. Engelmann, 'Haggling for the Equilibrium: the Renegotiation of the Austrian Coalition, 1959', *American Political Science Review*, 1962, pp.651–62.

13. N. Hoelzl, *op. cit.*, p.104.

14. H. Andics, *Die Insel der Seligen*, Molden-Taschenbuch-Verlag, Wien, 1976, p.283.

15. N. Hoelzl, *op. cit.*, p.138.

16. For details of voting behaviour see K. Blecha, *Die Nationalratswahl 1979*, Dr. Karl Renner Institut, Wien, 1979.

17. See K. Steiner, *Politics in Austria*, Little, Brown and Co., Boston, 1972, p.179.

18. For the 1975 election see M.A. Sully, 'The Austrian Parliamentary Election of 1975', *Parliamentary Affairs*, Summer 1976, pp.293–309.

19. Information supplied by courtesy of the Ministry of the Interior.

20. See M.A. Sully, 'Minority Groups in Austria: conflict or integration?', *Journal of Area Studies* (Portsmouth Polytechnic), no. 1, Spring 1980, pp.33–36.

21. See H. Wimmer, 'Institutionelle und soziale Bedingungen der Entstehung von Basisinitiativen am Beispiel der Anti-KKW-Gruppen', *Oesterreichische Zeitschrift fuer Politikwissenschaft*, nr.1, 1980, pp.57–69.

APPENDIXES

A. FEDERAL PRESIDENTIAL ELECTIONS

	Votes	%
I.*6 and 27 May 1951*		
First Ballot		
Breitner (VdU)	662,501	15.41
Fiala (KPOe)	219,969	5.12
Gleissner (OeVP)	1,725,451	40.14
Hainisch (Independent)	2,132	0.05
Koerner (SPOe)	1,682,881	39.15
Ude (Independent)	5,413	0.13
Second Ballot		
Gleissner (OeVP)	2,006,322	47.94
Koerner (SPOe)	2,178,631	52.06
II.*5 May 1957*		
Denk (OeVP and FPOe)	2,159,604	48.88
Schaerf (SPOe)	2,258,255	51.12
III.*28 April 1963*		
Kimmel (European Federalist)	176,646	4.0
Raab (OeVP)	1,814,125	40.6
Schaerf (SPOe)	2,473,349	55.4
IV.*23 May 1965*		
Gorbach (OeVP)	2,260,888	49.3
Jonas (SPOe)	2,324,436	50.7
V.*25 April 1971*		
Jonas (SPOe)	2,487,239	52.8
Waldheim (OeVP)	2,224,809	47.2
VI.*23 June 1974*		
Kirchschlaeger (SPOe nominee)	2,392,151	51.7
Lugger (OeVP)	2,238,680	48.3
VII.*18 May 1980*		
Kirchschlaeger (SPOe nominee)	3,538,748	79.9
Gredler (FPOe)	751,399	17.0
Burger (NDP)	140,741	3.2

B. POST-WAR CABINETS

The Cabinet December 1945-November 1949
Chancellor: Leopold Figl (OeVP).
Vice-Chancellor: Adolf Shaerf (SPOe).
7 OeVP Ministers, 5 SPOe Ministers (from 1947,6), 1 KPOe Minister (until 1947).
1 OeVP State Secretary, 1 SPOe State Secretary.

The Cabinet November 1949-April 1953
Chancellor: Leopold Figl (OeVP).
Vice-Chancellor: Adolf Schaerf (SPOe).
5 OeVP Ministers, 4 SPOe Ministers.
2 OeVP State Secretaries, 2 SPOe State Secretaries.

The Cabinet April 1953-June 1956
Chancellor: Julius Raab (OeVP).
Vice-Chancellor: Adolf Schaerf (SPOe).
5 OeVP Ministers, 4 SPOe Ministers.
2 OeVP State Secretaries, 2 SPOe State Secretaries.

The Cabinet June 1956-July 1959
Chancellor: Julius Raab (OeVP).
Vice-Chancellor: Adolf Schaerf; from May 1957, after Schaerf's election as Federal President, Bruno Pittermann (SPOe).
6 OeVP Ministers, 4 SPOe Ministers.
3 OeVP State Secretaries, 3 SPOe State Secretaries.

The Cabinet July 1959-April 1961
Chancellor: Julius Raab (OeVP).
Vice-Chancellor: Bruno Pittermann (SPOe).
5 OeVP Ministers, 5 SPOe Ministers.
2 OeVP State Secretaries, 2 SPOe State Secretaries.

The Cabinet April 1961-March 1963
Chancellor: Alfons Gorbach (OeVP).
Vice-Chancellor: Bruno Pittermann (SPOe).
5 OeVP Ministers, 5 SPOe Ministers.
2 OeVP State Secretaries, 2 SPOe State Secretaries.

The Cabinet March 1963-April 1964
Chancellor: Alfons Gorbach (OeVP).

Vice-Chancellor: Bruno Pittermann (SPOe).
5 OeVP Ministers, 5 SPOe Ministers.
4 OeVP State Secretaries, 2 SPOe State Secretaries.

The Cabinet April 1964-April 1966
Chancellor: Josef Klaus (OeVP).
Vice-Chancellor: Bruno Pittermann (SPOe).
5 OeVP Ministers, 5 SPOe Ministers.
4 OeVP State Secretaries, 2 SPOe State Secretaries.

The Cabinet April 1966-April 1970 (OeVP)
Chancellor: Josef Klaus, *Vice-Chancellor*: Fritz Bock (from 1968, Hermann Withalm) with all Ministers and State Secretaries OeVP nominees.

The Cabinet since April 1970 (SPOe)
Chancellor: Bruno Kreisky.
Vice-Chancellor: Rudolf Haeuser (from 1976, Hannes Androsch) with all Ministers and State Secretaries SPOe nominees.

C. THE AUSTRIAN CABINET (SPOe), 1980

Chancellor	Dr. Bruno Kreisky	Lower Austria*
Minister of Finance and Vice-Chancellor	Dr. Hannes Androsch	Vienna
Minister for Foreign Affairs	Dr. Willibald Pahr	
Minister of Construction	Karl Sekanina	Vienna
Minister for Health and Environment	Dr. Herbert Salcher	
Minister for Trade and Industry	Dr. Josef Staribacher	Vienna
Minister of the Interior	Erwin Lanc	Vienna
Minister of Justice	Dr. Christian Broad	Vienna
Minister of Defence	Otto Roesch	Lower Austria
Minister of Agriculture	Guenther Haiden	Styria
Minister for Social Affairs	Alfred Dallinger	Vienna
Minister of Education	Dr. Fred Sinowatz	Burgenland
Minister of Transport	Karl Lausecker	Vienna
Minister for Science and Research	Dr. Hertha Firnberg	Vienna
State Secretary in the Ministry for Social Affairs	Franziska Fast	
State Secretary in the Ministry of Trade	Anneliese Albrecht	Vienna
State Secretary in the Chancellory	Johanna Dohnal	
State Secretary in the Ministry of Construction	Dr. Beatrix Eypeltauer	Upper Austria
State Secretary in the Ministry of Finance	Elfriede Karl	Salzburg
State Secretary	Dr. Franz Loeschnak	
State Secretary	Prof. Dr. Adolf Nussbaumer	
State Secretary	Albin Schober	

*According to Article 70 of the Constitution, 'members of the Federal Government need not belong to the *Nationalrat*.' The regional base of cabinet members is indicated where applicable.

D. ELECTIONS TO THE *LANDTAGE* SINCE 1945

Results here are for the four main parties. Only two other parties have managed to win seats in a *Landtag* election. In 1945 a Democratic Party gained one seat in Carinthia, and in 1969 Olah's DFP won three seats in Vienna.

Burgenland

	OeVP %	OeVP Seats	SPOe %	SPOe Seats	KPOe %	KPOe Seats	WdU/FPOe %	WdU/FPOe Seats
1945	51.8	17	44.9	14	3.3	1	–	–
1949	52.6	18	40.4	13	2.9	–	3.9	1
1953	48.4	16	44.8	14	3.2	–	3.6	1
1956	49.2	16	46.0	15	1.9	–	2.9	1
1960	48.1	16	46.2	15	1.1	–	4.6	1
1964	47.3	15	48.2	16	0.9	–	3.6	1
1968	46.6	15	50.3	17	0.4	–	2.2	–
1972	45.9	15	50.5	16	0.4	–	3.1	1
1977	45.1	16	51.9	20	0.3	–	2.2	–

Carinthia

	OeVP %	OeVP Seats	SPOe %	SPOe Seats	KPOe %	KPOe Seats	WdU/FPOe %	WdU/FPOe Seats
1945	39.8	14	48.8	18	8.1	3	–	–
1949	31.9	12	40.8	15	4.0	1	20.5	8
1953	28.5	11	48.2	18	4.1	1	16.9	6
1956	32.7	12	48.1	18	3.1	1	15.7	5
1960	33.3	12	48.5	18	3.0	1	14.9	5
1965	32.9	12	49.3	18	2.8	1	13.4	5
1970	32.5	12	53.1	20	2.3	–	12.1	4
1975	32.4	12	51.4	20	2.0	–	11.8	4
1979	31.8	12	54.0	20	1.0	–	11.7	4

Lower Austria

	OeVP %	OeVP Seats	SPOe %	SPOe Seats	KPOe %	KPOe Seats	WdU/FPOe %	WdU/FPOe Seats
1945	54.5	32	40.4	22	5.1	2	–	–
1949	52.5	31	37.3	22	5.5	3	4.4	–
1954	50.7	30	40.9	23	5.8	3	2.6	–
1959	50.9	31	42.3	25	2.9	–	3.9	–
1964	51.6	31	42.8	25	2.4	–	3.0	–
1969	50.4	30	44.6	26	1.0	–	3.2	–
1974	52.1	31	43.9	25	1.0	–	3.0	–
1979	49.6	29	45.4	27	0.8	–	3.2	–

Upper Austria

	OeVP		SPOe		KPOe		WdU/FPOe	
	%	Seats	%	Seats	%	Seats	%	Seats
1945	59.1	30	38.3	18	2.6	–	–	–
1949	45.0	23	30.8	15	3.1	–	20.8	10
1955	48.1	25	39.4	19	2.9	–	9.6	4
1961	48.8	25	39.6	19	1.9	–	9.7	4
1967	45.2	23	46.0	23	0.8	–	7.5	2
1973	47.7	28	43.4	24	0.9	–	7.7	4
1979	51.6	29	41.4	23	0.6	–	6.4	4

Salzburg

	OeVP		SPOe		KPOe		WdU/FPOe	
	%	Seats	%	Seats	%	Seats	%	Seats
1945	56.7	15	39.5	10	3.8	1	–	–
1949	43.6	12	33.6	9	3.4	–	18.5	5
1954	45.9	15	38.2	13	2.3	–	13.2	4
1959	43.3	14	38.6	13	1.8	–	16.1	5
1964	44.9	15	40.9	13	1.2	–	11.8	4
1969	40.7	13	40.4	13	0.7	–	18.0	6
1974	47.1	18	36.2	13	1.2	–	15.5	5
1979	45.4	17	39.1	14	0.4	–	13.3	5

Styria

	OeVP		SPOe		KPOe		WdU/FPOe	
	%	Seats	%	Seats	%	Seats	%	Seats
1945	53.0	26	41.6	20	5.4	2	–	–
1949	42.9	22	37.4	18	4.5	1	14.6	7
1953	40.7	21	41.1	20	4.4	1	13.6	6
1957	46.4	24	43.4	21	2.6	–	6.8	3
1961	47.1	24	41.7	20	3.8	1	7.3	3
1965	48.4	29	42.2	24	3.2	1	5.8	2
1970	48.6	28	44.7	26	1.3	–	5.3	2
1974	53.2	31	41.2	23	1.3	–	4.2	2
1978	51.9	30	40.3	23	1.3	–	6.4	3

Tyrol

	OeVP		SPOe		KPOe		WdU/FPOe	
	%	Seats	%	Seats	%	Seats	%	Seats
1945	69.8	26	28.0	10	2.2	–	–	–
1949	56.4	24	24.0	8	1.6	–	17.4	4
1953	57.7	23	27.4	9	1.6	–	9.9	4
1957	59.2	23	31.0	11	0.8	–	8.5	2
1961	59.6	23	30.1	11	1.1	–	9.1	2

1965	63.6	25	30.4	10	–	–	6.0	1
1970	60.4	23	33.5	12	0.2	–	5.7	1
1975	61.1	24	32.4	11	0.6	–	5.9	1
1979	63.1	25	29.3	10	0.4	–	6.6	1

Vorarlberg

| | OeVP | | SPOe | | KPOe | | WdU/FPOe | |
	%	Seats	%	Seats	%	Seats	%	Seats
1945	70.2	19	27.3	7	2.5	–	–	–
1949	56.4	16	19.1	4	2.4	–	22.1	6
1954	58.0	16	26.0	7	2.3	–	13.7	3
1959	54.7	21	29.3	10	1.1	–	14.9	5
1964	53.5	20	29.5	10	1.2	–	15.8	6
1969	50.0	20	27.7	9	–	–	21.0	7
1974	56.9	22	27.6	10	0.9	–	13.9	4
1979	57.4	22	29.1	10	1.0	–	12.5	4

Vienna

| | OeVP | | SPOe | | KPOe | | WdU/FPOe | |
	%	Seats	%	Seats	%	Seats	%	Seats
1945	34.5	36	57.5	58	8.0	6	–	–
1949	34.9	35	49.9	52	7.9	7	6.8	6
1954	33.2	35	52.7	59	8.2	6	5.9	–
1959	32.4	33	54.4	60	5.2	3	8.0	4
1964	33.9	35	54.7	60	5.0	2	5.7	3
1969	27.8	30	56.9	63	2.9	–	7.2	4
1973	29.3	31	60.2	66	2.3	–	7.7	3
1978	33.8	35	57.2	62	1.8	–	6.3	3

BIBLIOGRAPHY

Austrian History before 1945

Albers, D. *et al.*(ed.), *Otto Bauer und der "Dritte Weg"*. *Die Wieder-entdeckung des Austromarxismus durch Linkssozialisten und Eurokommunisten* Frankfurt, 1979.

Bauer, O., *Die Oesterreichische Revolution*, Wien, 1923.

Botz, G.(ed.), *Bewegung und Klasse*, Wien, 1978.

————, *Die Eingliederung Oesterreichs in das Deutsche Reich. Planung und Verwirklichung des politisch-administrativen Anschlusses (1938–1940)*, Wien, 1976.

————, *Gewalt in der Politik Attentate; Zusammenstoesse, Putschversuche, Unruhen in Oesterreich 1918 bis 1934*, München, 1976.

Braunthal, J., *The Tragedy of Austria*, London, 1948.

Brook-Shepherd, G., *Dollfuss*, London, 1961.

————, *Anschluss*, London, 1963.

Carsten, F.L., *Fascist Movements in Austria*, London, 1977.

Duczynska, I., *Workers in Arms*, New York, 1978.

Fischer, E., *An Opposing Man*, London, 1974.

Fuchs, A., *Geistige Stroemungen in Oesterreich 1867–1918*, Wien, 1978.

Gedye, G.E.R., *Fallen Bastions*, London, 1939.

Gulick, C.A., *Austria from Habsburg to Hitler*, Berkeley, 1948.

Keller, F., *Gegen den Strom*, Wien, 1978.

Kitchen, M., *The Coming of Austrian Fascism*, London, 1980.

Konrad, H.(ed.), *Sozialdemokratie und 'Anschluss'*, Wien, 1978.

MacDonald, M., *The Republic of Austria 1918–1934*, Oxford, 1946.

Maimann, H., *Politik im Wartesaal. Oesterreichische Exilpolitik in Gross-britannien 1938–1945*, Wien, 1975.

Pulzer, P.G.J., *The Rise of Political Anti-Semitism in Germany and Austria*, New York, 1964.

Schausberger, N., *Der Griff nach Oesterreich. Der Anschluss*, Wien, 1978.

Schwarz, R., *'Sozialismus' der Propaganda Das Werben des 'Volkischen Beobachters' um die oesterreichische Arbeiterschaft 1938–39*, Wien, 1975.

Stadler, K.R., *Austria*, London, 1971.

————, *Opfer Verlorener Zeiten. Geschichte der Schutzbund-Emigration 1934*, Wien, 1974.

————, *The Birth of the Austrian Republic*, Leiden, 1965.

Vogl, F., *Widerstand im Waffenrock. Oesterreichische Freiheitskaempfer in der Deutschen Wehrmacht 1938–1945*, Wien, 1977.

West, F., *Die Linke im Staendestaat Oesterreich. Revolutionaere Sozialisten und Kommunisten 1934–1938*, Wien, 1978.

Whiteside, A., *The Socialism of Fools*, Berkeley, 1975.

Zeman, Z.A., *The Break-up of the Habsburg Empire*, London, 1961.

Post-War Austrian Politics

Altenstetter, C., *Der Foederalismus in Oesterreich*, Heidelberg, 1969.

Andics, H., *Die Insel der Seligen*, Wien, 1976.

Bader, W.B., *Austria between East and West*, Stanford, 1966.

Barker, E., *Austria 1918–1972*, London, 1972.

Benedikt, H.(ed.), *Geschichte der Republik Oesterreich*, Wien, 1977.

Bluhm, W.T., *Building an Austrian Nation*, New Haven, 1973.

Bodzenta, E.(ed.), *Die Oesterreichische Gesellschaft. Entwicklung-Strukturen-Probleme*, New York, 1972.

Brook-Shepherd, G., *The Austrian Odyssey*, London, 1957.

Ermacora, E., *Oesterreichischer Foederalismus. Vom patrimonialen zum kooperativen Bundesstaat*, Wien, 1976.

_____, *20 Jahre oesterreichische Neutralitaet*, Frankfurt, 1976.

Fischer, H.(ed.), *Das Politische System Oesterreichs*, Wien, 1977.

Hiscocks, R., *The Rebirth of Austria*, London, 1953.

Khol,A.(ed.), *Oesterreichisches Jahrbuch fuer Politik '77*, Wien, 1978.

_____, *Oesterreichisches Jahrbuch fuer Politik '78*, Wien, 1979.

_____, *Parlament und Partei*, Wien, 1976.

Klecatsky, H.R.(ed.), *Die Republik Oesterreich. Gestalt und Funktion ihrer Verfassung*, Wien, 1968.

Klenner, F., *Die oesterreichischen Gewerkschaften*, Wien, 1979.

Koren, J., *Oesterreich auf einem Weg. Handelskammern und Sozialpartnerschaft im Wandel der Zeiten*, Stuttgart, 1974.

Kreisky, B., *Neutralitaet und Koexistenz*, München, 1975.

Lachs, T., *Wirtschaftspartnerschaft in Oesterreich*, Wien, 1976.

Lendvai, P., *Kreisky*, Wien, 1974.

Mommsen-Reindl, M., *Die Oesterreichische Proporzdemokratie und der Fall Habsburg*, Wien, 1976.

Nassmacher, K., *Das oesterreichische Regierungssystem. Grosse Koalition oder alternierende Regierung?*, Köln, 1968.

Nenning, G., *Anschluss an die Zukunft*, Wien, 1973.

Oberleitner, W., *Politisches Handbuch Oesterreichs 1945–1972*, Wien, 1972.

Pelinka, A., *Demokratie und Verfassung in Oesterreich*, Wien, 1971.

Prader, H., *Die Angst der Gewerkschaft vor'm Klassenkampf. Der OeGB und die Weichenstellung 1945–1950*, Wien, 1975.

Puetz, T., *Verbaende und Wirtschaftspolitik in Oesterreich*, Berlin, 1966.

Radspieler, T., *The German Ethnic Refugees in Austria*, The Hague, 1955.

Ritschel, K., *Julius Raab. Der Staatsvertragskanzler*, Salzburg, 1975.

Schlesinger, T., *Austrian Neutrality in Post-War Europe*, Wien, 1972.

Siegler, H., *Austria-Problems and Achievements since 1945*, Bonn, 1969.

Stearman, W.L., *The Soviet Union and the Occupation of Austria*, Bonn, 1961.

Steiner, K., *Politics in Austria*, Boston, 1972.

Verdross, A., *Die immerwaehrende Neutralitaet Oesterreichs*, Wien, 1977.

Waldheim, K., *The Austrian Example*, London, 1973.

Weinzierl, E., *Die Zweite Republik*, Graz, 1972.

_____, and K. Skalnik (ed.), *Das Neue Oesterreich. Geschichte der Zweiten Republik*, Graz, 1975.

Welan, M., *Der Bundeskanzler im oesterreichischen Verfassungsgefuege*, Wien, 1971.
_____, *Gewerkschaften im Parteienstaat*, Berlin, 1980.

Parties and Elections

Berchtold, K., *Oesterreichische Parteiprogramme 1868–1966*, Wien, 1967.
Blecha, K. et.al., *Der durchleuchtete Waehler*, Wien, 1964.
Bottomore, T.(ed.), *Austro-Marxism*, Oxford, 1978.
Diem, P., *Zeit zur Reform*, Wien, 1968.
Fischer, H.(ed.), *Rote Markierungen '80*, Wien, 1980.
Fischer, H., *Positionen und Perspektiven*, Wien, 1977.
Gerlich, P.(ed.), *Nationalratswahl 1966*. Wien, 1968.
Hindels, J.(ed.), *Roter Anstoss*, Wien, 1980.
Hoelzl, N., *Propagandaschlachten. Die oesterreichischen Wahlkaempfe 1945–1972*, Wien, 1974.
Kadan, A.(ed.), *Die Grundsatzprogramme der oesterreichischen Parteien*, St. Pölten, 1979.
Kohlbacher, K., *Vorwahlen in der Steiermark*, Wien, 1975.
Konecny, A., *Sozialismus-von der Utopie zur Realitaet*, Wien, 1976.
Kulemann, P., *Am Beispiel des Austro-Marxismus. Sozialdemokratische Arbeiterbewegung in Oesterreich von Hainfeld bis zur Dollfuss-Diktatur*, Hamburg, 1979.
Leser, N., *Zwischen Reformismus und Bolschewismus. Der Austromarxismus als Theorie und Praxis*, Wien, 1968.
Marcic, R., *Die Zukunft der Koalition*, Wien, 1966.
Matzner, E., *Wohlfahrtsstaat und Wirtschaftskrise. Oesterreichs Sozialisten Suchen einen Ausweg*, Hamburg, 1978.
Mock, A., *Die Zukunft der Volkspartei*, Wien, 1971.
Moser, A.B.J., *Die Stellung der Kommunistischen Partei Oesterreichs zur oesterreichischen Neutralitaetspolitik von 1955–1972*, Salzburg, 1974.
Nenning, G., *Realisten oder Verraeter?*, München, 1976.
Neugebauer, W., *Gefahr von Rechts*, Wien, 1979.
Paterson, W.(ed.), *Social Democratic Parties in Western Europe*, London, 1977.
Pelinka, A., *Sozialdemokratie in Europa. Macht ohne Grundsaetze oder Grundsaetze ohne Macht?*, Wien, 1980.
Porta, H.T., *Fall Olah*, Melk, 1965.
Prager, T., *Zwischen London und Moskau*, Wien, 1975.
Raschke, J.(ed.), *Die politischen Parteien in Westeuropa*, Hamburg, 1978.
Reichhold, L., *Die Chance der OeVP*, Graz, 1972.
_____, *Geschichte der OeVP*, Graz, 1975.
Riedlsperger, M., *The Lingering Shadow of Nazism: the Austrian Independent Movement since 1945*, New York, 1978.
Schilcher, B., *Zwischen Pragmatismus und Ideologie*, Graz, 1972.
Shell, K.L., *The Transformation of Austrian Socialism*, New York, 1962.
Spira, L., *Ein gescheiterter Versuch*, Wien, 1979.
Staeuber, R., *Der Verband der Unabhaengigen (VdU) und die Freiheitliche Partei Oesterreichs (FPOe)*, St. Gallen, 1974.

Steiner, H., *Die Kommunistische Partei Oesterreichs von 1918–1933. Bibliographische Bemerkungen*, Wien, 1968.
Stiefbold, R., *Wahlen und Parteien in Oesterreich*, Wien, 1966.
Stueber, F., *Ich war Abgeordneter*, Graz, 1974.
Veiter, T., *Parteien, Proporz und Staat*, Bregenz, 1959.
Vodopivec, A., *Wer regiert in Oesterreich?*, Wien, 1960.
_____, *Die Balkanisierung Oesterreichs*, Wien, 1966.
_____, *Der Verspielte Ballhausplatz*, Wien, 1970.
_____, *Die Quadratur des Kreisky-Oesterreich zwischen parlamentarischer Demokratie und Gewerkschaftsstaat*, Wien, 1973.

INDEX

freedom, concept of 111–13
Freedom Group of Austria (FSOe) ix, 102
Freedom Party of Austria (FPOe) ix, 98–119; in *Bundesrat* 9; in Chambers and unions 27; and EEC 33–5; electoral support for 46, 84, 105–8, 147–55; historical background 98–100; ideology of 110–16; and minorities 35; and nationalism 31; in *Nationalrat* 8, 104, 156–64, 168; and OeVP 22, 82, 91–2, 100, 106–7, 109, 115; organisation of 108–10; and provinces 86, 98, 101, 103, 105–6, 128, 147–9; and regionalism 15, 17–19; in Second Republic 100–5; and SPOe 22, 100, 102, 107; *see also* Right
Freie Argumente 110
FSG *see* Fraction of Socialist Trade Unionists
FSOe *see* Freedom Group of Austria
Fuernberg, Friedl 134

Gassner, Johann 85, 88
GE *see* Trade Union Unity
German Nationalists 98–100, 103, 108–19, 166–7; *see also* minorities
Germany 1–2, 4, 31, 34, 66
Goetz, Dr Alexander 103–4, 106
Gorbach, Alfons 13, 71–3, 79, 90, 96, 105, 174–5
government: and industry 29–30, 61, 111, 131–2, 159–61; and politics 1–36
Gratz, Leopold 18
'Graz model' 103
Great Britian 31–3
Gredler, Willfried 107–8, 174
Group of Revolutionary Marxists (GRM) ix, 143

Haas, Dr Bruno 117
Habsburgs 1, 13, 107, 162
Haeuser, Rudolf 176
Haiden, Guenther 177

Hainisch, L. 174
Haider, Hertha 78
Hartmann, G 96
Hautmann, H. 67
Helmer, O. 126
Hindels, Josef 62, 184
historical background: of Communist Party 122–4; of government 1–36; of Freedom Party 98–100; of People's Party 69–70; of Socialist Party 38–41
Hoelzl, N. 173, 184
Horak, K. 120
Hungary 33, 128, 132–3

IAEA *see* International Atomic Energy Agency
identity crisis 1–5
ideology: of Communist Party 131–5; of Freedom Party 110–16; of People's Party 88–96; of Socialist Party 60–7
IFES *see* Institute for Empirical Social Research
imperial legacy 1–5
independence 30–2
industry 15–18, 32, 93; nationalised 29–30, 61, 131–2, 159–61
inflation 24, 30
Initiative of Austrian Opponents of Atomic Power (IOeAG) ix, 170–1
Innsbruck Programme 88–9
Institute for Empirical Social Research (IFES) xi, 43, 45
International Atomic Energy Agency (IAEA) xi, 5
internationalism 5, 33, 131, 135; *see also* Europe
IOeAG *see* Initiative of Austrian Opponents of Atomic Power
Italy 34, 142

JES *see* Young European Students
Jews *see* anti-semitism
JG *see* Young Generation
Jocha, Alfred 143
Jonas, Franz 12, 174